LITERARY PIONEERS

LONDON : HUMPHREY MILFORD

OXFORD UNIVERSITY PRESS

LITERARY PIONEERS

EARLY AMERICAN EXPLORERS
OF EUROPEAN CULTURE

By

ORIE WILLIAM LONG

Cambridge, Massachusetts

HARVARD UNIVERSITY PRESS

1935

PREFACE

ONE of the most important contributions to American intellectual life in the nineteenth century resulted from the romantic impulse which impelled a group of aspiring young scholars to pursue their studies in foreign countries. George Ticknor and Edward Everett, as students at the University of Göttingen, were the earliest of the pioneers in this movement. In the course of years they were followed by Joseph Green Cogswell, George Bancroft, Henry Wadsworth Longfellow, John Motley, and others of distinction. Their return to pursuits in various fields of knowledge in this country lent a powerful impetus to the progress of learning and to the enrichment of our cultural development. The purpose of this volume is to record the many interesting relationships which these internationally minded men experienced in Europe, especially in Germany, and to show the part which they played afterwards in the advancement of American life. The revelation is found principally in their journals and correspondence, which furnish many parallels of impressions.

The materials were gathered from manuscripts and other available sources in the Harvard University Library, the Massachusetts Historical Society, the Boston Public Library, the New York Public Library, the Library of Congress, the William A. Speck Collection of Goetheana in the Yale Library, the Library of the University of Göttingen, and the British Museum. To these institutions I wish to express my gratitude for their unfailing courtesy and kindness. I am also especially indebted to Mr. Philip Dexter and to Miss Rose Dexter for the privilege of using valuable materials in their possession, particularly the manuscript journals of Ticknor's European travels, and to Mrs. Joseph G. Thorp and to Mr. Henry Wadsworth Longfellow Dana, who generously placed at my disposal all the manuscripts and other treasures in Craigie House. To Mrs. Charles P. Parker, Mrs. James O. Watson, Mrs. David G. Haskins, and Mrs. Edward Cogswell I am under obligations for various materials relating to Cogswell; and to Lady Wavertree, of Sussex Lodge, Regent's Park, London, and to Dr. J. Franklin Jameson for valuable data pertaining to Motley. Further acknowledgment is made to Mr. Bliss Perry, Mr. Worthington C. Ford, Mr. Victor H. Paltsits, Mr. MacGregor Jenkins, Dr. Tyler Dennett, and especially to Mary Dee Long, for friendly assistance and personal interest.

O. W. L.

WILLIAMS COLLEGE
September 2, 1935.

Contents

LITERARY PIONEERS

George Ticknor

OF THE many eminent scholars who contributed to the development of early American learning, none presents a more distinguished and appealing career or more cosmopolitan interest than George Ticknor. As an originator of the liberal reforms which led to the advancement of knowledge in our universities, as the pioneer in the introduction and promotion of the study of modern languages and modern literatures in this country, as the chief founder of our earliest public library, and as, perhaps, the most marked type of the man of letters and society throughout his long, scholarly career of eighty years, he, with his remarkable achievements, deserves no small claim on the imagination and memory of the present generation. He knew everyone of importance not only in his own country but abroad, where, in the course of three periods of residence, it was his good fortune to meet almost every foreigner of distinction and often to be on intimate terms with them. In practically every land in which he traveled he was welcomed at court, in the presence of the nobility and of statesmen, and in all the prominent circles of polite society. His *Life, Letters, and Journals*,[1] published more than fifty years ago, and widely read and reviewed, are almost as entertaining as the *Diary and Reminiscences of Henry Crabb Robinson*, and furnish a valuable record of the historical, social, and literary aspects of more than half of the nineteenth century. They are, as Charles Eliot Norton once wrote to Carlyle in urging him to secure a copy from the London library,

unique in the picture they give of good society in Europe and America. No other American has had such an entrée into the close circles of the Old World. Mr. Ticknor deserved all his success; he was a "scholar and a gentleman" and had an attractive, if not very deep, nature. His very defects — the worst of which were the lack of imagination and of humour — served him in conventional society. He could take it all as much in earnest as if he had been born with a title and an entail.[2]

George Ticknor was born in Boston on the first day of August, 1791, of educated parents who had been engaged in the profes-

sion of teaching. His father, Elisha Ticknor, had graduated
from Dartmouth College in 1783 and had given instruction for a
few years in preparatory schools before drifting later into business in Boston, where he finally retired with an income sufficient
for gratifying the scholarly ambitions of his son. Ticknor's early
education was directed chiefly by his parents, with whom he frequently visited during the summer months, his grandfather at
Lebanon, New Hampshire, and the president of Dartmouth at
Hanover. On one of his visits to Boston President Wheelock
gave the boy of ten an oral examination in Cicero's Orations and
New Testament Greek, and admitted him to college. Meanwhile
he continued private instruction at home, studying Greek,
French, and Spanish.[3] After two examinations for advanced
standing, he entered the junior class at Dartmouth and was graduated in 1807, at the age of sixteen.

Ticknor states that the instruction in college was inferior to
that which his father had given him, and that he was idle and
learned little, though he "led a happy life and ran into no wild-
ness or excesses." There is evidence, however, that he was not
wholly idle. He was especially fond of reading Horace and was
interested in astronomy and art.[4] The following letter from
Elisha Ticknor to President Wheelock, while young Ticknor was
at home for a time in his senior year because of a slight illness, reveals the father's interest in the educational progress of his son:

The time is now come, in which I expected the pleasure of placing
again my son under your kind, indulgent, parental care. I have been
greatly obliged on this account, and have had all my expectations and
wishes answered. If he conducted as a student, while under your direction with as much propriety and attention to his collegiate duties as
he has since his return I can't but hope his conduct met your approbation both as a scholar and as a youth of his standing. He is but a
boy. But little can be expected of him. I am, however, not fishing
for encomiums to be put upon him. I barely wish to know, if it be
consistent with your feelings and judgment, your opinion of the
strength of his mind as a scholar, his disposition to study and whether
he has any talents, which ought to induce me to qualify or attempt to
qualify him to transact business as a physician, lawyer, or divine? I
have been at great expense on his account and am willing to be at
more. But, I have no disposition to throw my money into the ocean,
never to rise again. If I can learn therefore from you that he has been,
while under your direction, judicious, studious, manly in his deport-

ment, and persevering in whatever he undertakes; and, at the same
time, sensible of the necessity of a religious moral principle being im-
planted in the heart before he can be happy or really useful to himself
and the public, I shall be strongly inclined to give him advantages
considerably beyond those of common professional men. Of these
facts, however, it appears to me, I ought to be pretty well acquainted,
before I proceed much farther in educating him. I am of opinion he is
a lad of some genius and of some merit. It may all be imaginary. He
is my only son, and it would not be strange, if I were to deceive myself,
on this score. I, therefore, take the liberty to apply to you as a friend
to give me that kind of information, which I need, on this subject.

George Woodward, Esq. will communicate to you all new occurrences
from abroad, which are many and interesting. I am extremely sorry my
son is not able to accompany him to Hanover. He has been quite out of
health for several days past and has had a Physician several times. He
is, however, better. And, I hope he will so far recover, in a few days,
from his present indisposition as to have the honor of meeting you at
your house before the term commences. Should he be delinquent, however, by ill health, badness of weather or travelling, I beg your good-
ness will please excuse him as I am sure he has no disposition to be
absent a day in term time. Mrs. Ticknor's best respects await you,
your good Lady and best of daughters, as do mine also.[5]

During the three years following his graduation Ticknor continued his studies under private instruction, principally in the
classics, and later devoted himself to the reading and practice of
law, which he soon abandoned to prepare for the career of teacher
and scholar. Having read the American edition of Madame de
Staël's famous De l'Allemagne, a pamphlet by Charles de Villers
containing a sketch of the University of Göttingen, and an account of the library of that institution, he was inspired to go
abroad, first to Germany, to complete his education. But pre-
liminary instruction in elementary German presented a real
difficulty. The total ignorance of the subject in the vicinity of
Boston in the year 1814 is strikingly illustrated by Ticknor's
well-known account of his personal experience. He received
some elementary instruction from an Alsatian, then teaching
mathematics in Jamaica Plain, borrowed a German grammar in
French from his friend Edward Everett, and sent to New Hampshire for a dictionary. With this equipment, he was courageous
enough to write a translation of Goethe's Werther, a copy of
which had been deposited by John Quincy Adams, on going to
Europe, in the Boston Athenaeum.[6] However, before venturing

on his journey to Europe he felt it necessary to see something of his own country and to establish contacts with persons from whom he might acquire further information concerning foreign countries. Armed with letters of introduction, principally from John Adams, he spent three months during the winter of 1814–15 in visiting the most important cities as far south as Richmond and meeting various officials prominent in the affairs of the nation. He met by chance John Randolph in Philadelphia, dined with President Madison in Washington, visited Chief Justice Marshall in Richmond, and, accompanied by his friend Francis Calley Gray, spent three days early in February as the guest of Thomas Jefferson at Monticello. In his letter of introduction John Adams wrote to Jefferson:

> Mr. George Ticknor, Esquire, who will have the honor to present this to you, has a reputation here, equal to the character given him in the enclosed letter from my nephew, an Athenaeum man, whom you know.
> As you are all Heluones Librorum I think you ought to have a sympathy for each other.[7]

The visit to Monticello is important as the beginning of an intimate friendship between the young Boston Federalist and the aged Virginia statesman which continued until the close of Jefferson's career. To his elderly friend Ticknor turned repeatedly for wisdom and counsel concerning his studies abroad and his subsequent educational work, while it seems clear that for no young American of that period did Jefferson manifest so much personal interest. He provided his young friend with letters of introduction to eminent men in Europe, accepted his kindly offer to assist him in purchasing books for his private library, and exchanged numerous letters with him on various subjects, particularly those relating to education. Moreover, it is significant that in the founding and organization of the University of Virginia Jefferson not only showed profound admiration for Ticknor's ideas, but made more than one effort to secure his services as a member of the first faculty of that institution. In a long letter to his father, Ticknor describes Jefferson's home, his personality and mode of living, his collection of pictures, and above all his splendid library of about seven thousand volumes arranged "according to the divisions and sub-divisions of human

learning by Lord Bacon" — though little did the young stranger know that Jefferson was then preparing to sell his library to Congress. Jefferson discoursed on various subjects, including his experiences in Europe, and kindly offered to furnish Ticknor with letters to his remaining friends and acquaintances abroad.[8]

The deep impression which the young Bostonian made upon the Virginian is seen not only in their correspondence throughout the years but in a series of letters which Jefferson wrote shortly afterward to his friends. Writing to John Vaughan, he said:

I have received, with great pleasure, the visit of Mr. Ticknor, and find him highly distinguished by sciences and good sense. He was accompanied by Mr. Gray, son of the late Lieut. Gov. of Mass., of great information and promise also. It gives me ineffable comfort to see such subjects coming forward to take charge of the political and civil rights, the establishment of which has cost us such sacrifices.[9]

Some months later he replied to John Adams:

I thank you for making known to me Mr. Ticknor and Mr. Gray. They are fine young men, indeed, and if Mass. can raise a few more such, it is probable she would be better counseled as to social rights and social duties. Mr. Ticknor is, particularly, the best bibliograph I have met with, and very kindly and opportunely offered me the means of reprocuring some part of the literary treasures which I have ceded to Congress, to replace the devastations of British vandalism at Washington. I cannot live without books. But fewer will suffice, where amusement, and not use, is the only object. I am about sending him a catalogue to which less than his critical knolege of books, would hardly be adequate.[10]

Similar praise is noted in several letters from Jefferson commending Ticknor to some of the eminent European and American diplomats. To Lafayette he wrote:

This will be handed to you by Mr. Ticknor, a young gentleman of Boston, of great erudition, indefatigable industry, and preparation for a life of distinction in his own country. He passed a few days with me here, brought high recommendations from Mr. Adams and others, and appeared in every respect to merit them. He is well worthy of those attentions which you so kindly bestow on our countrymen, and for those he may receive I shall join him in acknoleging personal obligations.[11]

Further letters to William H. Crawford, American minister to France, Dupont de Nemours, and Jean Batiste Say, the political

economist, present Ticknor as a young man of great promise,
erudition, and merit.[12] "He has been excellently well educated,"
wrote Jefferson to Albert Gallatin,[13]

is learned, industrious, eager after knolege, and as far as his stay with
us could enable us to judge, he is amiable, modest, and correct in his
deportment. He had prepared himself for the bar, but before engaging
in business he proposes to pass two or three years in Europe to see and
to learn what can be seen and learnt there. Should he on his return
enter the political line, he will go far in that career.[14]

On his homeward journey from Monticello, Ticknor had addressed a letter to Jefferson informing him of his plans for em-
barking at an early date for Europe and requesting that letters of
introduction, which Jefferson had anticipated, be forwarded to
his address in Boston, together with "any commands in relation
to collecting a library or any other business which it may suit
your convenience to entrust to me." He added: "I cannot suffer
the opportunity to pass without repeating my acknowledge-
ments for the advice and instruction I received from you in relation to my projected voyage and visit to Europe; and all the
various kindness and hospitality which I found under your roof
and amidst your family." [15] The offer of his young friend to
assist him in purchasing books for his library made an immediate
appeal to Jefferson. On March 19 he wrote expressing his best
wishes for a pleasant voyage and profitable residence abroad and
stating that it would be some time before he would be able to
complete his "list and its accompaniments," though for purposes
of future reference he was forwarding a catalogue from Koenig,
the Strassburg bookseller. It was there that, during his years
in Paris, he had discovered "the greatest collections of classics
and of the finest editions" in Europe; and from Koenig he had
formerly bought many volumes.[16] A further letter from Ticknor
informed him of his decision to go first to England and later to
the Continent, and stated:

As occasions or subjects may offer, I shall not fail to take advantage
of the permission you have given me of keeping for myself a place in
your memory by addressing a few lines to you from amidst the literary
society of Europe, and shall consider myself singularly fortunate if,
by giving you early notice of the advance of science there, I may be
able in any imperfect degree to express my gratitude for all the kindness you have shown me.[17]

Having completed his preparations for his journey to Europe, Ticknor, in company with some friends,[18] including Edward Everett and two sons of John Quincy Adams, sailed on April 16, 1815.[19] After a voyage of twenty-six days they reached Liverpool, and were amazed to learn that Napoleon had made his escape from Elba and was again in Paris. They spent several weeks in London, where young Ticknor, in his twenty-fourth year, exhibited his social gifts in distinguished society.[20] The political turmoil of Europe made travel directly to France precarious and almost impossible. Ticknor, therefore, changed his plans and concluded to proceed at once to Göttingen. "As soon as circumstances will warrant or permit," he advised Jefferson, "I shall go to Paris. This I hope and trust will be in the course of the ensuing fall, and there I hope I shall be able to serve you in collecting your library." [21]

Meanwhile, Jefferson communicated from time to time with Ticknor's father. In forwarding through him a letter to his son, together with a list of titles which he had prepared, he refers to the pleasure of Ticknor's visit at Monticello, and to his "perfect knolege" of the best editions of books which rendered his kindly offer too advantageous not to be accepted.

For presuming to propose this trouble to you [he said] I hope you will find my excuses in the friendship of your son, and I cannot pass over the occasion of congratulating you on the possession of such a son. His talents, his science, and excellent dispositions must be the comfort of his parents, as they are the hope of his friends and country; and to those especially who are retiring from the world and its business, the virtues and talents of those who are coming after them, are a subject of peculiar gratification.[22]

To the enclosed letter to Ticknor is appended Jefferson's brief list of titles, selected from the catalogue of a London publisher,[23] which he thought might be purchased more reasonably on the Continent, along with full directions for the shipment [24] and the request that the books be sent as early as possible in order to avoid the "damage of a winter passage." He wrote as follows:

Availing myself of the kind offer of your aid in replacing some of the library treasures which I furnished to Congress, I have made out a catalogue which I now inclose. It is confined principally to the books of which the edition adds sensibly to the value of the matter. This as

to translations, notes, and other accompaniments, chiefly respects the classics; but size and type respect all. I am attached to the 8ᵛᵒ because not too heavy for the hand, and yet large enough to be open on the table according to convenience. Of the Latin classics, their notes and value to particular editions; of the Greek, their notes, and especially those of the Scholiasts, their translations and types are circumstances of preference. In some instances I have selected the edition from its description in the printed catalogues without having seen it; and as the catalogues cannot exhibit the type, I may sometimes be disappointed in the choice I have hazarded, in the Greek classics particularly by the obsolete type of that which I have selected, in the Latin by the Italian letter which is disagreeable to the eye. Sometimes there may be other editions equivalent to the one I name, in size, translation and notes, and superior in type. In these cases be so good as to avail me of your better opportunity of comparing for a selection of the best. I like good bindings and handsome, without being over elegant for use.²⁵

From London, Ticknor and Everett passed through Holland on their way to Göttingen. An entry in Ticknor's journal for August 1 reveals his state of feeling as he journeyed toward his destination:

It was in vain that I shut out the country by closing the curtains of the vehicle in which we were dragged through the sand and mud — it was in vain that I read in *Werther* and endeavored to forget myself as I had often done before, in my interest for him — it was in vain that I strove and struggled with myself, — the thoughts of home — the bitter recollections of all I had forsaken and from which I was still to be separated three years in the long, *long* pilgrimage before me, which still seemed lengthening as I advanced, — crowded upon my memory and imagination, and made my birthday one of the most miserable days of my life.

The young travelers arrived in Göttingen on August 4.²⁶ Ticknor's letters and journal during his life there furnish abundant data concerning the town and the University, his pursuits, experiences, and general impressions. The day after his arrival he began an inspection of the place and concludes: "I think we have good reason to be satisfied with our choice." ²⁷ Two days later he says:

The first thing that strikes a stranger on coming here, as we do, to establish himself, would be, I think, the adaptation of everything to this great object, which seems in some form or other to be present wherever you go. The town is small, and of course, liable to be influenced by so considerable an institution as the University; and the

University having been established nearly eighty years ago has produced its full effect.[28]

Within a short time he was comfortably settled in "an apartment" [29] and was reveling in his new environment. A long letter to his father describes the town, the founding of the University, and its administration. He wrote:

One circumstance, I believe, must strike everybody who establishes himself at Göttingen: it is a place which subsists entirely upon literature, the town and the University have been by the policy of the government so completely adapted to the wants of foreigners, and the manners and habits of the citizens and faculty so entirely accommodated to this fluctuating population, that the moment a student comes here, his situation is so well understood that every request and wish is anticipated. Wherever you go, it seems to be the express business of the persons you meet, — whether they be professors, faculty, or citizens, — to see that you are in lodgings, that you know the persons whom you ought to choose for instructors, and that you are properly furnished with everything you want. In consequence of this, a student can hardly feel himself to be stranger here, after the first day or two.[30]

Meanwhile, Ticknor had made the acquaintance of some of the most prominent professors. He found Eichhorn, professor of the Old Testament, "lively, gay, full of vigour, though not young, and interested in everything," and Blumenbach, the famous naturalist, "broken with age, but possessing much vivacity." [31] With these and other members of the faculty Ticknor and Everett soon became intimate, being received frequently in their homes, especially on Sunday evenings. The two Bostonians were great favorites in the social life of the University.[32] Ticknor was generally known as the "Doctor" and Everett as the "Professor." They had not been in Göttingen many months when they were elected members of the most exclusive society of the community, the Literary Club, which consisted of a small number of carefully selected professors and students.

We were taken in as a kind of raree-show, I suppose [Ticknor informs his father], and we are considered, I doubt not, with much the same curiosity that a tame monkey or a dancing bear would be. We come from such an immense distance, that it is supposed we can hardly be civilized; and it is, I am told, a matter of astonishment to many that we are white, though I think in this point they might consider me rather a fulfilment than a contradiction of their ignorant expectations. However, whatever may be the motives from which we were taken in, there we are, and we have as good a right to be there as the best of them. The only time I have been I found it pleasant enough, but I doubt whether I shall go often.[33]

In company with Professor Benecke, Ticknor first visited on the afternoon of August 7 the large University library, "the pride of Göttingen," containing more than two hundred thousand volumes "selected solely from a regard to what is *useful*," with a carefully arranged catalogue and offering free use of books, especially to foreign students. It impressed Ticknor as a model institution [34] and was a welcome contrast to the meagre Harvard collection of less than twenty thousand volumes, to which, in comparison, he referred in later years as "a closetful of books." Contrasting the advantages of Göttingen and Harvard, Ticknor wrote in May of the next year to Stephen Higginson, then "Steward" of Harvard, with whom the young Americans at Göttingen frequently communicated:

I cannot, however, shut my eyes on the fact, that one *very* important and principal cause of the difference between our University and the one here is the different value we affix to a good library, and the different ideas we have of what a good library is. In America we look on the Library at Cambridge as a wonder, and I am sure nobody ever had a more thorough veneration for it than I had; but it was not necessary for me to be here six months to find out that it is nearly or quite half a century behind the libraries of Europe, and that it is much less remarkable that our stock of learning is so small than that it is so great, considering the means from which it is drawn are so inadequate. But what is worse than the absolute poverty of our collections of books is the relative inconsequence in which we keep them. We found new professorships and build new colleges in abundance, but we buy no books; and yet it is to me the most obvious thing in the world that it would promote the cause of learning and the reputation of the University ten times more to give six thousand dollars a year to the Library than to found three professorships, and that it would have been wiser to have spent the whole sum that the new chapel had cost on books than on a fine suite of halls. The truth is, when we build up a literary Institution in America we think too much of convenience and comfort and luxury and show; and too little of real, laborious study and the means that will promote it. We have not yet learnt that the Library is not only the first convenience of the University, but that it is the very first necessity, — that it is the life and spirit, — and that all other considerations must yield to the prevalent one of increasing and opening it on the most liberal terms to *all* who are disposed to make use of it. I cannot better explain to you the difference between our University in Cambridge and the one here than by telling you that here I hardly say too much when I say that it *consists* in the Library, and that in Cambridge the Library is one of the last things thought and talked about, — that here they have forty professors and more than two hundred thousand volumes to instruct them, and in Cambridge twenty professors and less than twenty thousand volumes. This, then, you see is the thing of which I am disposed to complain, that we give comparatively so little attention and money to the Library, which is, after all, the Alpha and Omega of the whole establishment, — that we are mortified and exasperated because we have no learned men, and yet make it *physically* impossible for our scholars to become such, and that to escape from this reproach we appoint a multitude of professors, but give them a library from which hardly one and *not* one of them can qualify himself to execute the duties of his office. You will, perhaps, say that these professors do not complain. I can only answer that you find the blind are often as gay and happy as those who are blessed with sight; but take a Cambridge professor, and let him live one year by a library as ample and as liberally administered as this is, let him know what it is to be forever sure of having the very book he wants either to read or to refer to; let him in one word *know* that he can never be discouraged from pursuing any inquiry for want of means, but on the contrary let him feel what it is to have all the excitements and assistance and encouragements which those who have gone before him in the same pursuits can give him, and then at the end of this year set him down again under the parsimonious administration of the Cambridge library, — and I will promise you that he shall be as discontented and clamorous as my argument can desire.[35]

From the time Ticknor formally matriculated in the University on August 14, he followed a busy schedule, devoting his time from five in the morning until late at night to his studies, with occasional recreation, which included a daily walk with Everett and instruction three times a week in fencing and riding. "Visiting, as it is done in our colleges," he writes to his father, "is a thing absolutely unknown here. . . . If I desired to teach anybody the value of time, I would send him to Göttingen." [36] At the close of his first semester he writes:

For me it has been the most industrious and, I hope, the most profitable period of my life, for I have sacrificed happiness enough to purchase it . . . I could not have done more than I have without endangering my health, and it is a pleasure to me, in looking back, to find that what I have done I have done thoroughly, for of all these lessons I have missed but one during the semester.[37]

Ticknor's primary interest at Göttingen was in Greek, in which subject he attended lectures by Schultze,[38] Eichhorn, Heeren, and Dissen. From Eichhorn's exposition of the Gospels he learned much, though he was not always satisfied with the mode of treating the subject, and he hoped that the time would never come when he would "listen with pleasure to such flippant witticisms as Eichhorn has been these five months making on all that I have been taught to consider solemn and important." [39] Some months later he informs his father [40] that Dissen, from whom he received informal instruction in the literary history of Greece, fulfilled more than anyone in Göttingen his idea "of what a scholar ought to be." But he did not confine himself exclusively to the classics. He heard lectures in modern European history by Saalfeld, in aesthetics by Bouterwek, in natural history by the famous Blumenbach,[41] and received private instruction in the modern languages. In order to follow the lectures, German was of course his first objective. Shortly after his arrival he had written to his father:

My first object, of course, will be German. This will be taught me by Prof. Benecke, the Professor of English literature, who speaks English quite well. . . . Besides him, however, I intend to procure some scholar who will come to my chambers and read and speak with me. In this way, by October I think I shall be able to attend the lectures profitably, and then I shall resort to those of Eichhorn on literary history, and to those of some other professors on Greek, Roman, and German literatures.[42]

His journal records that he had his first lesson in German on August 15, and that he continued the subject several hours each week during the first two semesters. By November he was able to report to his father his progress:

On Mondays, Wednesdays, and Fridays, at the striking of eight o'clock, I am at Prof. Benecke's for my lesson in German. This has become a light study. I read with him only some of the most difficult parts of their poets, and carry to him the passages I do not understand in books I read for other purposes. He is perfectly at home in all their ancient and modern claims, and is an uncommonly good English scholar, so that I find this hour's instruction very pleasant and useful.[43]

A few days later he writes of learning Greek "entirely through the German," [44] and in June of the following year: "My chief objects are still Greek and German, my subsidiary objects Italian and French, my amusement literary history, chiefly ancient and books that will fit me for my future travels." [45] His father, at all times deeply interested in his intellectual progress, wrote emphasizing the importance of oral training in the language:

It is not of so much importance for you to read aloud to a German as it is that a German should read aloud to you. Select one of the finest oratorical readers in Göttingen, whose voice is round, and full, and melodious. Place yourself twenty feet from him, if possible. Request him to select and read aloud to you a pathetic oratorical piece in German. . . . It is the tone of the voice, and the attitude of a polished German scholar, which you need, to be able to read and speak German well, like a German gentleman and scholar. [46]

Letters to his parents and to friends in America give Ticknor's impressions of German literature and German scholarship. [47] On February 29, 1816, he forwarded to his friend Charles S. Daveis, of Portland, Maine, his survey of German literature from the time of Luther to the close of the classical period. He writes:

At length, between 1760 and 1770, from causes which perhaps it is impossible accurately to trace and estimate, but the chief of which are certainly to be sought in the humble servitude under which it had long suffered, German literature underwent a sudden and violent revolution. It is equally difficult to determine precisely to whom is to be given the honor of leading the way in this emancipation. If any one author or work must be selected, it would probably be the "Literary Letters," — a periodical publication managed by Lessing; but this was so instantly succeeded and surpassed by the earliest works of Klopstock, Wieland, and Goethe, that it is evident the spirit of regeneration had long been working in the land, and that, if Lessing was the first to call it forth, it was rather from accident than extraordinary genius or boldness.

The literature of Germany now sprang at once from its tardy soil, like the miraculous harvest of Jason, and like that, too, seems in danger of perishing without leaving behind it successors to its greatness. Besides the four whom I have named, I know of no authors who have enjoyed a general and decisive popularity, and who settled down into regular classics, except Haller, Müller, the elder Voss, Schiller, and Bürger. This number is certainly small, and Goethe alone survives, to maintain the glory of the deceased generations of his friends and rivals. But, narrow as the circle is, and though the strictness of posterity will perhaps make it narrower, still I know of none in the modern languages — except our own — where one so interesting can be found as the circle of German literature. It has all the freshness and faithfulness of poetry of the early ages, when words were still the representatives of sensible objects, and simple, sensible feelings rather than of abstractions and generalities; and yet, having flourished so late, it is by no means wanting in modern refinement and regularity. In this singular state, uniting much of the force and originality of the barbarous ages to enough of the polish of those that are more civilized, it has continued just about fifty years; but in the last thirty no considerable author has appeared. Much of this barrenness is, I am persuaded, to be charged to the philosophy of Kant, which for nearly twenty years ruled unquestioned, and absorbed and perverted all the talents of the land. It was a vast "Serbonian bog, where armies whole have sunk," and from which even the proud and original genius of Schiller hardly escaped. Its empire, however, was soon gone by; but there followed the French usurpation, which overturned at pleasure the literary establishments of the land, and silenced systematically all authors who did not write as they were bidden. This, too, has gone by; but whether their literature will return with their returning independence and peace, is a problem time only can solve.[48]

In a letter some months later to Edward T. Channing, Ticknor defends German literature against unfair criticism in foreign reviews, and against Channing's accusation that German poetry was obscure and artificial. Recalling foreign comment on Schiller's *Robbers*, Ticknor states that, though the Germans are aware of the character, talent, and circumstances which produced such a tragedy, yet it has long been banished from the stage, and the people have ceased to read it "except as a curious proof of misdirected genius" which is now domesticated in the English theatres. He adds:

Perhaps you will ask what I mean by all this tirade against other people's mistakes. I mean to show you by foreign proof that the German literature is a peculiar national literature, which, like the miraculous creation of Deucalion, has sprung directly from their own soil, and is so intimately connected with their character, that it is very difficult for a stranger to understand it. A Frenchman, or indeed any one of the Roman nations, generally makes as bad work with it as Voltaire with Shakespeare, and for the same reasons; for it deals with a class of feelings and ideas which are entirely without the periphery of his conceptions. An Englishman, too, if he studies it at home only, generally succeeds about as well, — but show me the man who, like Walter Scott, has studied it as it deserves, or, like Coleridge, has been in this country, and who has gone home and laughed at it . . .

After all, however, you will come round upon me with the old question, "And what *are* your Germans, after all?" They are a people who, in forty years, have created to themselves a literature such as no other nation ever created in two centuries; and they are a people who, at this moment, have more mental activity than any other existing. I have no disposition to conceal that this literature has many faults; but if you had read Goethe's Tasso, or his Iphigenia, or his ballads, you would never have said their poetry lacks simplicity; or if you had read the tales of Musaeus, or Wieland's Oberon, — even in Sotheby,— or fifty other things, you would not have said "the Germans do not know how to tell stories." [49]

Further letters to Channing, and also to Ticknor's father, contain an account of the organization and practices of secret societies in the universities, of the political history of the country, of German philosophy, and of the freedom of German men of letters.[50]

A man of science here lives entirely isolated from the world [wrote Ticknor to Channing], and the very republic of letters, which is a more real body in Germany than it ever was in any country, has no connection with the many little governments through which it is scattered without being broken or divided. From this separation of the practical affairs from science and letters to the extraordinary degree in which it is done in Germany, comes, I think, the theoretical nature of German literature in general, and of German metaphysics in particular.[51]

The continued correspondence between Ticknor and Jefferson at this period is of special importance for the light it throws on their careers and as a contribution to early scholarship in America. Shortly after his arrival in Göttingen, Ticknor had written with enthusiasm to his father of the superior equipment and advantages of the University, all designed to meet the wants of a scholar and "absolutely incapable of improvement." Some months later Elisha Ticknor, in transmitting these facts to Jefferson, stated: "He writes, therefore, that as he is now at a place of which he has so often dreamt, that he shall probably remain in Göttingen till April. I think it more probable he will till May, as the roads will then be good and the country will show its state of cultivation and improvement." [52] In reply Jefferson said:

I am much pleased to learn that he is so well satisfied with his situation at Göttingen, but Paris and Rome will please and profit him more. He will return fraught with treasures of science which he would not have found in a country so engrossed by industrial pursuits as ours, but he will be a sample to our youth of what they ought to be, and a model for imitation in pursuits so honorable, so improving, and so friendly to good morals.[53]

To none of his friends did Ticknor write with more appreciation than to Jefferson, who had requested that he keep him informed as to his progress and general conditions in Europe, and who was especially interested in the subject of classical training. In a long letter Ticknor writes of the literature and scholarship of the countries thus far visited, particularly of Germany, and the reasons which induced him to prolong his residence at Göttingen:

You were kind enough, I recollect, in one of the letters I had the honour to receive from you in America to ask me to write to you. If I have not as yet fully availed myself of this privilege it is not because I did not feel it to be such but because I knew not what to send that would interest you. I saw England, indeed, at the heighth of her power and pride — I saw Holland, too, a fallen and ruined nation — but, even at so great a distance, I was sure that you would estimate the probable consequence of the ominous ripeness of the one and the dotage and decrepitude of the other much better than I could, present as I was to the circumstances of both. Of their literature, I could of course say nothing, for England's is our own and in Holland, though I saw a collection of nearly four hundred volumes of their poets and as much more of other belle-lettre writing, yet I believe we are sufficiently familiar in America, but its literature is a kind of *terra incognita* to us. Its language is so strangely different from all the foreign dialects we have been accustomed to learn and their classical authors are all so recent, that it does not enter into the system of our education nor, until Mad. de Stael's book came among us, was its history or condition talked about or thought of. Yet I find it a very interesting literature. It has all the freshness and faithfulness of poetry, of the early ages, while words are the representatives of sensible objects and simple feelings, rather than of abstractions and generalities, and yet being written so late has enough of modern refinement and regularity. Goethe, who is still alive, is their most popular and successful writer — and Werther, which we know in English only by a miserable imitation of a garbled French translation, made by some one, who understood neither of the languages, is their most popular book. Klopstock — except for his odes — is out of fashion — Wieland, too, is less respected than he was in his life-time — but Bürger, Voss, Lessing and Schiller have become classicks. The flexibility of their language, — which arises in a considerable degree from its being unsettled — enables them to make better translations than any other nation. This gives them a great advantage. The Greek tragedians and orators are rendered to them with a fidelity and purity and grace, of which in English

we have no idea even from Potter and Sir Wm. Jones. Voss's Homer in
the hexameter and line for line is an extraordinary approximation to
the solitary greatness of the original and Schlegel's Shakespeare seems
to me every time I open it to be a new miracle. From what I had
read of their literature in America I was satisfied it was very extraordinary but my expectations have been much exceeded. In ancient learning they are unrivalled. Dr. Parr, the best scholar alive in England,
and certainly quite as vain of his own reputation and quite as proud
of his country as the scholar need to be, bore to me a reluctant but
decisive testimony to the superiority of Germany, which he justly
attributed to a spirit of liberality and philosophy in their learning,
which makes but slow progress in England. Winckelmann, who has
long been the first authority in France and Italy on all subjects relating
to the arts of the ancients and Heyne and his school in ancient criticism
have placed your country at the head of classical learning in Europe.
Indeed, I found from the English scholars and bibliographers, that
there is hardly a single *editio optima* of a Greek or Roman author received among them that was not elaborated in Germany. In science,
I know nothing of them as yet but by reputation. In mineralogy,
botany and entomology, I find what the Abbé Correa told me, to be
true, that they lead the rest of Europe. Professor Gauss — still a very
young man — has recently acquired extraordinary reputation by his
astronomical calculations. In the estimation of England and Germany
he is already the rival of la Place and if the accounts I have received
of the early development and present compass of his talents are true,
must soon stand before him, if further discoveries remain to be made.
But, it is in vain to speak of particular persons or even particular
branches of learning and science, for it is not from solitary and independent example, that the spirit of a nation can be measured. . . .
But no man can go far into the body of German literature — above
all no man can come into their country and see their men of letters and
professors, without feeling that there is an enthusiasm among them,
which has brought them forward in forty years as far as other nations
have been three centuries in advancing and which will yet carry them
much farther without seeing that there is an unwearied and universal
diligence among their scholars — a general habit of labouring from
fourteen to sixteen hours a day — which will finally give their country
an extent and amount of learning of which the world has before had
no example.

The first result of this enthusiasm and learning, which immediately
broke through all the barriers that opposed it, was an universal tolera-
tion in all matters of opinion. No matter what a man thinks, he may
teach it and print it, not only without molestation from the government but also without molestation from publick opinion which is so
often more oppressive than I am of authority. I know not that any
thing like it exists in any other country. The same freedom in France
produced the revolution and the same freedom in England would

now shake the deep foundations of the British throne — but here it passes as a matter of course and produces no effect but that of stimulating the talents of their thinking men. Every day books appear on government and religion which in the rest of Europe would be suppressed by the state and in America would be put into the great *catalogus expurgatorius* of public opinion but which here are read as any other books and judged according to their literary and philosophical merit. They get, perhaps, a severe review or a severe answer, but there are weapons which both parties can use and unfairness is very uncommon. Indeed every thing in Germany seems to me to be measured by the genius or acuteness or learning it discovers without reference to previous opinion or future consequences to an astonishing and sometimes to an alarming degree. Some of the examples of this are quite remarkable. This university, for instance, where there are now above nine hundred and fifty students to be instructed for Germany and Europe, is under the immediate protection and influence of the British crown. Its professors — forty in number — are paid from the treasury of Hanover and appointed by its regency. Yet the principal theologian and most popular professor here (Eichhorn) has written a very learned and eloquent book and delivers to a crowded audience lectures no less learned and eloquent to prove that the New Testament was written in the latter end of the second century — and another professor of much reputation (Schultze) teaches that a miracle is a natural and a revelation a metaphysical impossibility. If truth is to be attained by freedom of inquiry, as I doubt not it is, the German professors and literati are certainly in the high road, and have the way quietly open before them. [54]

The splendid library at Göttingen to which Ticknor had access enabled him to form an acquaintance with practically all the editions of the classics. On the day of the receipt of Jefferson's catalogue he writes of editions "that will be more to your taste, so you have expressed it in your letter, even in some cases, where you have left me no alternative." He describes editions, mostly by Germans, of Herodotus, Thucydides, Diogenes Laertius, Plutarch, Dio Cassius, Tacitus, Homer, Theocritus, Juvenal, Hesiod, Aeschylus, and Reiske's *Orators*, and adds:

I mention these items to you merely as bibliographical hints. In many instances you undoubtedly have personal and peculiar reasons for preferring the older editions to the *optimes*, for an old edition or copy in which we have been accustomed to read is like an old friend, who is not to be put aside for a younger one, even though he should be of more promise. If, therefore, I receive no further directions from you, I shall fulfil your orders as expressed in your list, immediately on my arrival at Paris, which will be as soon as the roads are comfortable in the spring.[55]

The postponement in forwarding the books, owing to Ticknor's prolonged residence in Göttingen, where, as Jefferson stated, "very possibly some of my wants might be better supplied than at Paris," was attended by no inconvenience, since it afforded Jefferson opportunity to add to his list translations of Cicero's *Works*, which he enclosed with the following explanation:

You know in how defective and deformed a state his philosophical writings especially have come down to us. In every page his annotations are challenging the text with "glossema interpretum," "emblema librariorum," "a sciolis intrusa," "ab homine stolido barbaroque profectum" etc. and in truth the corruptions of the text render the sentiments often indecypherable. Translations aid us with the conjectures of those who have made it a particular business to study the subject and its text.[56]

Jefferson willingly entrusted the choice of editions to his young friend's judgment. In February he wrote expressing his appreciation and his preference for the more recent German editions of the classics which Ticknor had listed:

I am much gratified by the information you give me of the improvements in the editions of the classics which you find in Germany. My knolege of them is such only as could be acquired in Paris 30 years ago, since which I have had little opportunity of information; and even at that time and place the northern editions were but partially known to me. I must pray you therefore to avail me of your better opportunities of selecting, and to use your own judgment where you find that there is a better edition than that noted by me. And indeed many of these were not known to me, but taken on credit from their titles as stated in printed catalogues, and I have no doubt I should have been disappointed in some of them by the obsoleteness of type, its minuteness, or other circumstance, which could not be learned from the enunciation in the catalogue. Only be so good as to remember my aversion to folios and 4^{tos} and that it overweighs a good deal of merit in the edition. The nerveless hand of a more than septuagenaire wields a folio of 4to with fatigue, and a fixed position to read it on a table is equally fatiguing. I value explanatory notes; but verbal criticisms and various readings, not much. I am attracted to the Scholia of the Greek classics because they give us the language of another age; and with the Greek classics prefer translations as convenient aids to the understanding of the author. With these recollections be so good as to exercise your own judgment and knolege freely, the value of which I can estimate from the specimens of editions noted in your letter of which I prefer at least two-thirds to those I had noticed myself.[57]

Further letters to Jefferson contain discussions of the subject of books and demonstrate Ticknor's continued enthusiasm for German scholarship and learning. "The truth, however, is," he wrote in March, "that I find Göttingen so entirely suited to my purposes, the opportunities and means and inducements to pursue those studies to which I mean to devote my life are so admirable here, that I have determined to protract my stay in Europe in order to enjoy them one year longer." Having reached this decision, his visit to France was of course deferred, but he stated in his letter that he had arranged through Jefferson's friend, Mr. Warden, "an excellent bibliograph," for the purchase of some of the books in Paris, where they were to be had at less cost than in Germany, and added:

The longer I have continued here, the better I have been satisfied with my situation, and the more reasons and inducements I have found to protract my residence. The state of society is, indeed, poor; but the means and opportunities for pursuing the study of languages, particularly the ancient, are, I am persuaded, entirely unrivalled. As I have already written you in my long letter on German literature, I was told over in England and by Dr. Parr, England's best and perhaps, vainest classical scholar, that Germany was farther advanced in the study of antiquity than any other nation. This I find to be true. The men of letters here bring a philosophical spirit to the labour of exposition which is wanting in the same class in all other countries. The consequence is that the study of the classicks has taken a new and more free turn within the last forty years and Germany now leaves England at least twenty years behind in the cause while before it always stood first. This has been chiefly affected by the constitution of the universities, where the professors are kept perpetually in a grinding state of excitement and emulation, and by the constitution of their literary society generally, which admits no man to its honours, who has not written a good book. The consequence, to be sure, is that the professors are more envious and jealous of each other than can be well imagined by one who has not been actually within the atmosphere of their spleen, and that more bad or indifferent books are printed than in any country in the world, but then the converse of both is true; and they have more learned professors and authors at this moment than England and France put together.

I would gladly hope that the favour of your correspondence may be continued to me from time to time even after the commission for your books has been executed. If you feel any interest in the state of literature in Germany which has sprung forth in the last thirty years as unhidden and as perfect as the miraculous harvest of Jason, I can be able to give you occasionally pleasant information — and when I reach France, I shall be able to write you from the midst of your old friends and from a place associated in your imagination with my many interesting though, perhaps, not always pleasant recollections. If these slight inducements are sufficient with your own kindness to procure me the favour of an occasional letter, I shall feel myself under new obligations to you. I shall also feel it as a great favour, if you will give me your opinion on the prospects of learning in the U. S., and the best means of promoting it — a subject which now occupies much of my attention.[58]

Some weeks later Ticknor informed Jefferson that the German editions of the classics, excepting that of Hesiod, were to be procured as reasonably in Göttingen as elsewhere in Europe and that he would purchase them at an early date and forward them in care of his father. He wrote again at length:

Perhaps when you have received these specimens of German editions you will be induced to permit me to send you some others. The longer I remain here, the more I learn to value the German modes of study and the enlarged and liberal spirit of German scholarship. And for the same reason I think the more you see of German editions of the classicks, the more you will be disposed to admit them into your library. Within forty years the scholars of this country, I am persuaded, have done more toward the final understanding of the classicks, than all Europe had done during the century that preceded, not by imitating the minute and tedious accuracy of the Dutch commentators, but by reducing the whole study of antiquity to a philosophical system, in which one part assists to explain the other and all together form a harmonious whole. They have, in fact, done for the ancients what Blackstone did for the English law and though I cannot say that their digest, like his, is to be found in a single treatise, yet no man is now considered a scholar here, who is not master of it. The effect of this has been particularly favourable in the investigations it has occasioned into the spirit of Grecian philosophy and the different characters it assumed in different ages — in the fine histories of Grecian arts and policy it has produced — and the new and more liberal directions it has given to the study of Greek literature and manners generally. They have, in fact, already done for all the ages of Greece, what all Bartholemy's learning, for want of a philosophical spirit to direct it, has not been able to do for one. To say nothing of the numberless editions, which are offered at every Leipzig fair, of the classical authors, the practice of bringing all learning into the form of philosophical histories and treatises is gaining ground very fast and really doing wonders . . . The great difference between a German scholar and those of England and Holland is, that, with even more minute, verbal learning than they, he treats the study of antiquity as a liberal science, while they treat it as a mechanical art. This change has been affected by the schools of Heyne and Wolf, who, by turning their immense learning to its appropriate objects, have made a revolution in the study of antiquity, which is already felt in England in defiance of the differences of language and their inveterate prejudice against everything foreign and continental — and which, I am persuaded, in thirty years more will make it toto caelo a different affair to be a scholar there from what it is now.

I am exceedingly anxious to have this spirit of pursuing all literary studies philosophically — of making scholarships as little of drudgery and mechanism as possible transplanted into the U. States, in whose free and liberal soil I think it would, at once, find congenial nourishment. It is a spirit, which in Germany now goes through everything — through theology, history, modern literature, etc . . . But I suspect it is better for me to stop; and yet I know of nobody who will more readily credit my accounts than you will, or who would more rejoice at the state and spirit of learning in Germany.[59]

On receipt of the above letters, Jefferson wrote to Ticknor's father: "The account he gives me of the German literature is very interesting; and such as I had not been before apprised of. It seems well worthy of his avail and he is accordingly sowing the seed of what with his genuis and industry will yield a rich harvest." To this Elisha Ticknor replied: "Such lines and opinions, Sir, considering the source whence they came — his experience and age — his judgment and foresight, console and calm the heart of a father, who, at times, has almost regretted the enterprise he suffered his son to undertake." [60] Meanwhile, in July, Ticknor had forwarded in care of his father to Jefferson editions of Homer and Virgil by Heyne, of Aeschylus by Schultze, of Juvenal by Ruperti, and of Tacitus by Oberlin. "When you have looked through these," Ticknor stated, "I think you will like the German editions, and if you should think proper to order any more of them in the course of the winter, I can without inconvenience, send them with my own books, which I shall in the spring forward from here through Hamburg." [61] The books arrived in Boston the following November and, in accordance with Jefferson's request, were consigned at once to his correspondents in Richmond.[62] Later Jefferson expressed to Ticknor, then in Paris, his satisfaction and delight with the volumes received:

The German editions of Homer, Virgil, Juvenal, Aeschylus and Tacitus, which you were so kind as to forward to me thro' your father, came all safe, and it was a great convenience to me to be permitted to remit the amount to him at Boston, rather than to Europe. The editions of Heyne, Ruperti, Oberlin are indeed of the first order; but especially Heyne's of the Iliad. It exceeds anything I had ever conceived in editorial merit. How much it makes us wish he had done the same with the Odyssey. In this Iliad I observe he had the benefit of Villeoison's Venetian Edition. This style of editing has all the superiority your former letters have ascribed to it, and urges us to read again the authors we have formerly read to obtain a new and higher understanding of them.[63]

In the summer of 1815 Ticknor received a communication which changed his European plans and ultimately determined the course of his career. At his death the previous year, Abiel Smith, a native of Taunton, Massachusetts, a graduate of Harvard in 1764, and a wealthy Boston merchant, had bequeathed to his alma mater a sum of money, the income from which was to be used for the maintenance and support of a teacher of the French and Spanish languages.[64] On July 26, 1816, President Kirkland informed Ticknor of the vote of the Corporation two days before in which it was stated "that the Corporation entertain a great desire to have Mr. Ticknor connected with the University in some department of instruction, which may be suited to his views and tastes, and conducive to the interests of education and learning." They were disposed to appoint him professor of belles lettres with authority to give instruction and lectures in that subject, on conditions to be determined by him and the college, but without any stipulated salary, excepting fees from students who might attend, until such time as the college "may possess some endowment for this object." The Corporation further voted that they were disposed to appoint Ticknor "Smith Professor of the French and Spanish Languages and Literature," with a salary of one thousand dollars, thus combining the two professorships. Ticknor replied stating that he assumed that as a professor of belles lettres he would have the right "to lecture on any subject of ancient or modern literature that falls within the canon of taste and general criticism." He further stipulated that he should "in no event be expected to teach any languages as such," and requested the provision of a sum of money with which to purchase books, as well as permission to reside in Boston during the lifetime of his parents.[65] A later letter requested that the appointment be made as early as possible in order that he might have time for suitable preparation in Europe.[66] The position, if accepted, meant prolonging his travels abroad, including residence in Spain, and the abandonment of his visit to Greece with Everett. The father, who had conferred with President Kirkland, wrote: "To see Athens, my son, is not worth exposing your life, nor the time nor the money you must spend to see it." [67] After an exchange of several letters, the Harvard Corporation agreed to Ticknor's terms, with the understanding that his salary for the first year be expended for books for his department, and that after two more years abroad he should return to his duties. The subject of the professorship was under discussion many months, and Ticknor had arrived in Rome, before his acceptance was forwarded on November 6, 1817.[68]

As was true of all foreign students at Göttingen, Ticknor took advantage of vacation periods for the purpose of visiting various parts of Germany. At the close of the first six weeks of study in September, 1815, he and Everett had made an excursion of five days to Hanover, where they met several well-known persons, including Charlotte Kestner, the original of Goethe's Lotte in *Werther*, and were much interested in seeing the Leibnitz collection in the library. In September of the following year they left Göttingen for a tour of almost two months, visiting most of the important cities, towns, schools, and universities in Saxony and Prussia, and meeting many distinguished people in the field of learning. For this experience Ticknor's journal provides ample information, including long and carefully written descriptions of every place visited. Passing through Weimar, where, he writes, "we breakfasted with the names and poetry of Schiller, Wieland, and Goethe often on our lips, and oftener in our recollections," [69] they spent much time in Leipzig, Dresden, Berlin, Wittenberg, and Halle, and returned through Weimar and Jena to Göttingen on November 5. At the University of Leipzig he met several classical scholars, but the University, with its adherence to Latin lectures and the philosophy of Kant, impressed him as an institution of "general antiquated air and tone." Its conservatism and exclusiveness, he states, were well understood by Goethe, who, in *Faust*, makes one of his self-complacent students say, "Es ist ein klein Paris." He visits the battlefield and Leipzig Fair, and observes "where Goethe and Lessing used to see the popular Dr. Faustus acted which gave them an idea of their tragedies." [70] The journal for Dresden devotes pages to the Picture Gallery, where, Ticknor says, "I was not prepared for such a vision." Halle, he states, was the first German university to be established in conformity with the more liberal ideas of modern times and has a "more refined tone in society" than any other university. [71] There follows a detailed account of his visit to the famous schools at Meissen and Schulpforta, including their origin, history, and organization, many features of which Ticknor would like to see adopted by other schools. [72]

However, the most important feature of this journey was the visit to Weimar and the meeting on October 25 with Goethe, to whom Ticknor and Everett presented letters of introduction from Sartorius, of the Göttingen faculty, and from Wolf, the distinguished scholar in Berlin. [73] Before this time Goethe's knowledge of America had been slight. He had known but little of the American Revolution, but had interested himself in Franklin's scientific discoveries, and having read in 1807 Humboldt's *Essay* on Mexico, he began to familiarize himself with the history and scientific aspects of the American continent. Three years later, January, 1810, he received his first American visitor, Aaron Burr, and in the same year read Franklin's *Autobiography*. The visit of Ticknor and Everett is of special significance, for it marks the beginning of those pilgrimages which several American scholars subsequently made to Weimar, thus forming an interesting contact in the nineteenth century between America and Germany's greatest poet. [74] The interview, which took place in the forenoon, lasted nearly an hour, and the two young Americans recorded their impressions. Ticknor makes the following observations:

We sent our letters to Goethe this morning, and he returned for answer the message that he would be happy to see us at eleven o'clock. We went punctually, and he was ready to receive us. He is something above the middle size, large but not gross, with gray hair, a dark, ruddy complexion, and full, rich, black eyes, which, though dimmed by age, are still very expressive. His whole countenance is old; and though his features are quiet and composed they bear decided traces of the tumult of early feeling and passion. Taken together, his person is not only respectable, but imposing, and yet I saw little in it that indicated the character he ascribes to his youth — little of the lover of Margaret and Charlotte, and still less of the author of Tasso, Werther, and Faust. In his manners he is simple. He received us without ceremony, but with care and elegance, and made us German compliments. The conversation, of course, rested in his hands and was various. He spoke naturally of Wolf, as one of our letters was from him, — said, he was a very great man, had delivered thirty-six different courses of lectures on different subjects connected with the study of antiquity, possessed the most remarkable memory he had ever known, and in genius and critical skill surpassed all the scholars of his time. In alluding to his last publication he said he had written his Life of Bentley with uncommon talent, because in doing it he had exhibited and defended his own character, and in all he said showed that he had high admiration and regard for him.

Of Lord Byron, he spoke with interest and discrimination, — said that his poetry showed great knowledge of human nature and great talent in description: Lara, he thought, bordered on the kingdom of spectres; and of his later separation from his wife, that, in its circumstances and the mystery in which it is involved, it is so poetical, that if Lord Byron had invented it he could hardly have had a more fortunate subject for his genius. All this he said in a quiet, simple manner, which would have surprised me much, if I had known him only through his books; and it made me feel how bitter must have been Jean Paul's disappointment, who came to him expecting to find in his conversation the characteristics of Werther and Faust. Once his genius kindled, and in spite of himself he grew almost fervent as he deplored the want of extemporary eloquence in Germany, and said, what I never heard before, but which is eminently true, that the English is kept a much more living language by its influence. Here, he said, we have no eloquence, — our preaching is a monotonous, middling declamation, — public debate we have not at all, and if a little inspiration sometimes comes to us in our lecture-rooms, it is out of place, for eloquence does not teach. We remained with him nearly an hour, and when we came away he accompanied us as far as the parlor door with the same simplicity with which he received us, without any German congratulations.[75]

From Riemer, the librarian, and Goethe's former secretary, Ticknor and Everett received much information concerning the poet's method of writing, his relations to Schiller, Herder, and Wieland, his manner of living in his old age, and his plans for a continuation of *Faust*.[76]

While in Weimar, Ticknor had hoped to see a performance of

Schiller's *Maria Stuart*, but he found the theatre devoted mainly
to the presentation of plays by Kotzebue and Iffland. He attended a performance of Iffland's *Hans Friede*, of Goethe's *Jery
und Bately*, "a melodrama, with pretty songs, and very well
acted, but poorly sung," [77] and spent one forenoon reading the
"unnecessarily and unjustly severe Review of Goethe's life of
himself in the Edinburgh." [78] There were excursions to Tiefurt,
to Osmannstädt, and to Jena, where he visited the Natural History collection, the Ducal Library, and the University, which
impressed him as having a "freer tone in conversation and manners" than any place he had been in Germany.[79] Journeying
toward Göttingen, they passed through Erfurt, where, Ticknor
states, they saw Faust's house, "in which he might have had
much more comfortable apartments than Goethe has given
him," and Faust's Alley, a narrow passage, where "tradition
pretends the Dr. by the Devil's assistance drove a full load of hay
without hindrance — a piece of infernal adroitness." [80] In
Gotha they saw a performance of Kotzebue's *Graf Benjowsky*,
and reaching Göttingen the afternoon of November 5 were
agreeably surprised to find their fellow-countryman, Joseph
Green Cogswell, who had arrived the first of the month to begin
his studies at the University. "It was, as if the course of nature
were interrupted to make me happy," writes Ticknor, "and in
an hour Göttingen assumed another hue and character in my
eyes." [81] During the remaining months in Göttingen Ticknor
continued his heavy schedule of studies,[82] and was making preparation for his visits to other countries. His journal includes
many pages of notes on the topography of Germany, the absence
of political spirit, the prevalence of militarism, and the different
classes of people. He finds the nobility the most corrupt class
and the peasantry the most religious, though their religion "is
only a superstition mingled with much honesty and fear" which
has less of feeling in it than that of the corresponding class in
America. He concludes that the Germans are very kind and
hospitable to strangers, but "are compelled to study so incessantly that they are unfit for the world and unacquainted with
it." At the close of his work in the University he writes:

Today I have closed the last wearisome semester of my labours and
imprisonment here. During the interval I have heard every day a

course of lectures on the modern arts by Fiorillo in Italian — a course of European statistics every day from Prof. Saalfeld in French — a course of archaeology five times a week by Prof. Welcker — and four times a week I have ridden. Besides this, I read Greek with Dr. Schultze till January and then gave it up in order to be able to hear Bouterwek's course of aesthetics — and during the whole winter have averaged two hours in the week in Italian recitations with my friend Ballhorn. Thus these six months have passed away and now that all my duties are fulfilled, I look forward with an impatience I have never felt before to my emancipation, which will bring me one important step nearer to the time when I shall once more see my home.[83]

After final visits with all of his friends, Ticknor left Göttingen on Wednesday, March 26, 1817, for further travel and study in the several countries of Europe. The route to Paris carried him through a section of Germany which he had not seen and enabled him to make brief visits in each place. In Cassel, to which point Everett had accompanied him, he paused a few hours, principally to meet Volkel, the classical scholar, and then proceeded through Marburg and Giessen to Wetzlar, where he was interested in the scenes associated with *Werther*. Of this, including the village of Garbenheim, we read:

On the way I imagined that we passed the valley where the scene between Werther and Charlotte's distracted lover happened, and the chilly wind which blew as we went through it gave me a sensation of sadness such as I have seldom felt. I was still quite alone. A little farther on, I mounted the rocks, where Werther passed the dreadful night after he had left Charlotte — and in the village itself, I needed no guide to show me the red church — the lime trees — the burying ground, and the village houses which he has described with such fidelity. On returning to the city, I stopped again on the rocks — read the description of his despair and stayed until the departing sun had almost descended behind the hills. Then I hastened to Wetzlar, and as a final farewell went a few moments to the Hibbal Gardens, which Goethe had in his recollections and fancy when he described the parting scene in the last letter of the first Book. I am, on the whole, glad I went. This cold and cheerless Spring has, indeed, saddened the valley in which Charlotte and Werther lived so thoughtlessly together; but still it is impressed in my memory as it is, and, as to the rest, even in its brightest and gayest form the scenery would have disappointed the expectations with which Goethe's poetical feelings have filled my imagination.[84]

Arriving in Frankfort, Ticknor states:

The first person I went to see this afternoon was Friedrich Schlegel, and never was I more disappointed in the external appearance of any man in my life; for, instead of finding one grown spare and dry with deep and wearisome study, I found before me a short, thick, little gentleman, with the ruddy, vulgar health of a full-fed father of the Church. On sitting with him an hour, however, I became reconciled to this strange discrepancy, or rather entirely forgot it, for so fine a flow of rich talk I have rarely heard in Germany.[85]

On another occasion he found Schlegel

good humoured, animated, and witty in conversation, unaffected, even nonchalant in his manners — and making no pretension, but on the contrary receiving information and facts with singular simplicity on subjects where he is not sufficiently informed, while at the same time he is bold and decisive on those which he has studied.[86]

At Heidelberg, Ticknor was cordially received in the home of Voss, whose personal appearance, "in some points approaching to elegance," seemed to him unlike that of most German men of letters:

He described to me his present mode of life, said he rose early and went to bed early, and divided the day between his books, his wife, and his harpsichord. Thus, he says, he preserves in his old age the lightness of heart which God gave him in his youth. . . . He showed me his library, not large, but choice and neatly arranged . . . his manuscripts all in the same form. . . . Among them was his translation of Aristophanes, — written, as he himself confessed, because Wolf had undertaken the Clouds, — and six plays of Shakespeare, in which, he said, he intended to avoid Schlegel's stiffness, but will not, I think, succeed. Of his "Louise" he told me it was written in 1785, but not printed till ten years after; and, on my remarking that there was a vivacity and freshness about many parts of it that made me feel as if it were partly taken from life, he confessed that he had intended the character of the old pastor for a portrait of his wife's father, Boier.[87]

In further conversation, Voss spoke with affection of his early friends, particularly of Hölty, the Stolbergs, and Klopstock. Continuing his journey through Strassburg, where, as the journal states, "German traits still prevail," Ticknor entered Paris on April 7.

The journal and letters for Ticknor's remaining two years in Europe provide graphic sketches of his many interesting contacts and experiences in each country visited. He spent five months in Paris, and among the most interesting acquaintances which he established there were those with August Wilhelm Schlegel, Alexander von Humboldt, and Robert Southey. After sketching Schlegel's career and his mode of life, which, he says, results in his looking "like a careworn, wearied courtier, with the manners of a Frenchman of the gayest circles, and the habits of a German scholar — a confusion anything but natural or graceful," Ticknor writes:

I found him in full dress, with his snuff-box and handkerchief by his side, not sitting up to receive company, but poring over a folio Sanskrit Grammar; for he has recently left his other studies, even his Etruscan antiquities, that employed him so zealously a year ago, when he wrote his review of Niebuhr, and has thrown himself in the Eastern languages with a passion purely German. He talked very volubly in French, with an uncommonly pure accent, on all subjects that happened to come up, — but *con amore*, chiefly on England, and above everything else on his Lectures and the English translation of them, which, he said, he should be much delighted to hear was reprinted in America. In writing them in German, he said, he endeavoured to keep before himself English and French prose, which he preferred to the German, and asked me with the eagerness of a hardened liberator, whether I had observed traces of them in reading them, — a question I was luckily able to answer in the affirmative, without doing violence to my conscience. On the whole, he amused me considerably, and I will seek occasion to see him often, if I can.[88]

Humboldt, according to Ticknor, was leading an irregular life, combining strenuous labor and social duties, and was the idol of fashionable Parisian society and a man of "prodigious acquirements, extending nearly on all sides to the limits of human discovery." In addition to his scientific pursuits, his knowledge of the classics and familiarity with the modern languages was immense. He impressed Ticknor as one of the most remarkable men he had seen in Europe, "perhaps the most so." [89] Southey discussed the history and literature of America, as well as things German, for which the journal reads:

He talked with me about the Germans and their literature a good deal, and said if he were ten years younger he would gladly give a year to learn German, for he considered it now the most important language, after English, for a man of letters; and added with a kind of decision which showed he had thought of the subject, and received a good deal of information about it, that there is more intellectual activity in Germany now than in any other country in the world. In conversation such as this three hours passed very quickly away, and when we separated, I left him in the persuasion that his character is such as his books would represent it, — simple and enthusiastic, and his knowledge very various and minute.[90]

Near the close of his residence in Paris, Ticknor wrote Jefferson of his plans and gave in detail his impressions of the French educational system, tracing its development from its organization by Napoleon after the Revolution to the present time. He stated:

In the physical and exact sciences, I presume there is nothing in Europe like Paris; but in all that relates to what is commonly called learning, England and Germany vastly exceed her. Nothing, I imagine, in the world, can be brought to oppose the sixty-four members of the Academy of Sciences; but the three other Academies could ill meet the learned men of the north. The reason is, I suppose, that this has been the nature of the publick demand, which in all such matters always creates its own supply. It is not, therefore, astonishing that after an interval of thirty years of neglect, Learning does not come into the new order of things by *adhesion* like wealth and power and rank.[91]

From Paris, Ticknor journeyed in the autumn of 1817 through Switzerland to Italy, in which country, at a villa near Venice, he renewed his acquaintance with Byron. A part of the conversation was devoted to Goethe, and Ticknor gives us the following well-known report:

He told me incidentally that M. G. Lewis once translated Goethe's Faust to him extemporaneously, and this accounts for the resemblance between that poem and Manfred, which I could not before account for, as I was aware that he did not know German. . . .

When I happened to tell Lord Byron that Goethe had many personal enemies in Germany, he expressed a kind of interest to know more about it that looked like Shylock's satisfaction that "other men have ill luck too"; and when I added the story of the translation of the whole of a very unfair Edinburgh review into German, directly under Goethe's nose at Jena, Byron discovered at first a singular eagerness to hear it, and then, suddenly checking himself, said, as if half in earnest, though still laughing, "And yet I don't know what sympathy I can have with Goethe, unless it be that of an injured author." This was the truth, but it was evidently a little more than sympathy he felt.[92]

Meanwhile, Jefferson had endeavored to keep his young friend informed concerning affairs in his own country. In June of that

year he disclosed to him the program of improvement, particularly the various projects for the development of canals, roads,
and education in several states. The letter is important in that
it contains the first information which Ticknor received of Jefferson's educational scheme for the state of Virginia, including
his plans for the University:

New York is undertaking the most gigantic enterprise of uniting the
waters of L. Erie and the Hudson; Jersey those of the Delaware and
Raritan. This state proposes several such works; but most particularly has applied itself to establishments for education, by taking up
the plan I proposed to them 40 years ago, which you will see explained
in the notes on Virginia. They have provided for this special object
an ample fund, and a growing one. They propose an elementary school
in every ward or township, for reading, writing, and common arithmetic; a college in every district, suppose of 80 or 100 miles square, for
laying the foundations of the sciences in general, to wit, languages,
geography, and the higher branches of arithmetic; and a single university embracing every science deemed useful in the present states of the
world. This last may very possibly be placed near Charlottesville,
which you know is under view from Monticello.[93]

The following November Jefferson again outlined to Ticknor
his educational plan:

I am now entirely absorbed in endeavors to effect the establishment of a general system of education in my native State, on the
triple basis: 1. of elementary schools which shall give to the children
of every citizen, gratis, competent instruction in reading, writing,
common arithmetic, and general geography; 2. Collegiate institutions for ancient and modern languages, for higher instruction in arithmetic, geography, and history, placing, for these purposes, a college
within a day's ride of every inhabitant of the State, and adding a
provision for the full education, at the public expense, of select subjects
from among the children of the poor, who shall have exhibited at
the elementary schools the most prominent indications of aptness, of
judgment, and correct disposition; 3. A university, in which all the
branches of science deemed useful at this day, shall be taught in their
highest degree. This would probably require ten or twelve professors,
for most of whom we shall be obliged to apply to Europe, and most
likely to Edinburgh, because of the greater advantage the students will
receive from communications made in their native language. This last
establishment will probably be within a mile of Charlottesville, and
four from Monticello, if the system should be adopted at all by our
Legislature, who meet within a week from this time. My hopes, however, are kept in check by the ordinary character of our State legis-
latures, the members of which do not generally possess information

enough to perceive the important truths, that knolege is power, that knolege is safety, and that knolege is happiness. In the mean time, and in case of failure of the broader plan, we are establishing a college of general science at the same situation near Charlottesville, the scale of which, of necessity, will be much more moderate, as resting on private donations only. These amount at present to about 75,000 dollars; the buildings are begun, and by mid-summer we hope to have two or three professorships in operation. Would to God we could have two or three duplicates of yourself, the original being above our means or hopes. If then we fail in doing all the good we wish, we will do, at least, all we can. This is the law of duty in every society of free agents, where every one has equal right to judge for himself. God bless you, and give to the means of benefiting mankind which you will bring home with you, all the success your high qualifications ought to insure.[94]

Ticknor remained in Italy until the spring of 1818, when he proceeded through southern France [95] to Spain. In the course of these months Jefferson continued to manifest his personal interest in his young friend's progress. "I am glad of every opportunity of endeavoring to be useful to him," he stated to Elisha Ticknor,[96] through whom he forwarded further letters of introduction. Commending Ticknor to Cardinal Dugnani in Rome, he said: "His science, his talents, the worth and correctness of his character, place him among the ornaments and hopes of our country; and my particular friendship for him will add, I think, a motive the more for your notice of him." [97] In a letter to George W. Erving, American minister to Spain, he wrote:

This will be delivered to you by Mr. George Ticknor a young gentleman of high respectability and connexions from Massachusetts and among the first in our country in point of erudition. He has been in Europe several years, first at Göttingen to fill up the measure of his education, thence he has travelled thro' France, is now probably in Italy, and expects to be at Madrid, with the same constant view of adding to his stores of science, already very great. You will find in him the most perfect correctness of conduct, and virtue which will make him a valuable addition to your friendships. Be so good as to receive him as my particular friend, and to render him all the good offices which his situation may need, and consider, whatever you can do for him as done for myself and as conferring on me a debt and obligation which I shall ever thankfully acknowledge.[98]

The letter to Erving was an important aid to Ticknor, especially in Madrid, where, in addition to his Spanish studies, he formed an acquaintance with the diplomatic circle.⁹⁹ In August he wrote to Jefferson of the advantages which he had enjoyed in the countries visited, of the library which he had collected, and of his plans for the future:

When I came to Europe, I proposed to myself to acquire a good knowledge of all the literatures of ancient and modern Europe. . . . My object in all has been to get general, philosophical notions on the genius and history of each of these literatures and to send home good collections of books relating to the history of their languages and representing the whole series of their elegant literatures. . . . All this time thus spent in Europe I consider a sacrifice of the present to the future and what I most desire is, to make the sacrifice useful to my country. . . . And now the question is what I shall do with the knowledge that has cost me some of the best years of my life. For political distinction, I have no ambition — no *thought* even and never have had. If there were a department in the general Government that was devoted to Publick Instruction, I might seek a place in it, but there is none, there is none even in my State Government. All that remains for me, therefore, seems to be to go home and exert what influence I may be able to acquire in favor of the cause of good letters and perhaps, if a proper occasion offers, which is probable, give some years to instruction by courses of publick lectures at our University.

You see, Sir, that I have spoken to you with great freedom — perhaps, with too much: but the reason is, that I desire extremely to have you know my situation exactly as it is, and to ask your advice and opinion on the course of life best for me to pursue when I reach my home and begin the world as it were a second time at the age of twenty-seven, with a moderate fortune, which makes me independent; because my wants are few. . . .

Remember me, I beg of you, to Colo. Randolph and Mrs. Randolph with their family, whom I hope to see at Monticello, if you will permit me to pay you a visit there soon after my return home. Farewell, my dear Sir, and in the idiom of the country where I am, I pray heaven to preserve you many years, since all your years are years of usefulness. I had almost forgotten to say how much I am interested in the noble plan you have formed for education in your native state. I trust and believe it will succeed, and already foresee the pleasure of witnessing your happiness in its success.¹⁰⁰

The following October, when Central College had not been converted into a state university, Jefferson replied to Ticknor, expressing his desire to have him connected with his institution and suggesting a definite professorship:

I am happy, however, to learn that your peregrinations through Europe have been successful as to the object to which they were directed. You will come home fraught with great means of promoting the science, and consequently the happiness of your country; the only obstacle to which will be, that your circumstances will not compel you to sacrifice your own ease to the good of others. Many are the places which would court your choice; and none more fervently than the college I have heretofore mentioned to you, now expected to be adopted by the State and liberally endowed under the name of "the University of Virginia." . . . I pass over our professorship of Latin, Greek, and Hebrew, and that of modern languages, French, Italian, Spanish, German, and Anglo-Saxon, which, although the most lucrative, would be the most laborious, and notice that which you would splendidly fill, of Ideology, Ethics, Belles-Lettres, and Fine Arts. I have some belief, too, that our genial climate would be more friendly to your constitution than the rigors of that of Massachusetts; but all this may possibly yield to the *hoc caelum sub quo natus educatusque essem*. I have indulged in this reverie the more credulously, because you say in your letter that "if there were a department in the central government that was devoted to public instruction, I might have sought a place in it; but there is none, there is none even in my State government." Such an institution of the general government cannot be, until an amendment of the Constitution, and for that, and the necessary laws and measures of execution, long years must pass away. In the mean while we consider the institution of our University as supplying its place, and perhaps superseding its necessity.

With stronger wishes than expectations, therefore, I will wait to hear from you, as our buildings will not be ready under a year from this time; and to the affectionate recollections of our family, add assurances of my constant and sincere attachment.[101]

Following his residence in Spain and Portugal, Ticknor sailed in the autumn of 1818 for England; to that country and Scotland he devoted four months of travel before his departure for home in May of the next year. From Edinburgh he forwarded his reply to Jefferson concerning the proposed professorship. His responsibilities upon his return home, especially to his aged father, and his obligations to lecture at Harvard precluded any consideration of the position suggested. However, he stated:

At the same time I beg you to recollect that if I can in any way contribute to the progress and success of your establishment, my humble efforts shall never be wanting. I rejoice in it, not only disinterestedly, as a means of promoting knowledge and happiness, but selfishly as the means of exciting by powerful and dangerous rivalship the emulation of our College at the North, which has so long been itself first in reputation, that this excitement will not be without a good effect on its indolence. If, therefore, you would do me a favour, you will employ me in some way in which I can be useful to your plans.[102]

Some months later, while on his return voyage, Ticknor again expressed his interest in Jefferson's program for the improvement of education in Virginia and his desire to be of assistance in furthering the success of his undertaking. "As I again approach my native country," he said, "I cannot choose but recollect the kindness you have shown me during my long absence from it, and as it comes up before me, I grow doubly anxious to do something which shall show you that I am not insensible to it, though I cannot hope to return it." He repeats his reasons which prevent his residing elsewhere than in Boston, and suggests for the position of professor of modern languages the consideration of George Blaettermann, a native of northern Germany, who had been educated chiefly at Leipzig, and with whom he had formed a partial acquaintance during his residence in England.[103]

In London, and later in Edinburgh, Ticknor mingled in the society of the most prominent literary and political figures of the day. Among the many interesting entries in his journal for London appears the following:

> One evening I heard Coleridge lecture, and I knew him besides. He is growing old fast — is fat — bloated with excesses — and, in short, is a trembling, nervous worn out old man. His lecture was on Lear — partly written and partly extemporaneous — exhibiting now and then remarkable proof of rich, original thinking, but in general, confused and dull; and often extravagant and unintelligible. . . . On the whole I was disappointed in him — and sometimes disgusted.[104]

In Edinburgh Ticknor was entertained in some of the most distinguished homes, but was welcomed nowhere more cordially than by Scott, with whom he dined frequently and who regaled him with anecdotes of Edinburgh intellectuals and took him to the theatre to witness a performance of *Rob Roy*. Meanwhile, Ticknor was joined by his friend Cogswell, who had been wandering over the Continent and the British Isles, and the two Americans were the guests of Scott for three days in March at Abbotsford. Of this visit Ticknor says:

> Mr. Scott himself was more amusing here than I had found him even in town. He seemed, like Antaeus, to feel that he touched a kindred

earth, and to quicken into new life by its influences. The Border country is indeed the natural home of his talent, and it is when walking with him over his own hills and through his own valleys, . . . and in the bosom and affections of his own family, that he is all you can imagine or desire him to be. His house itself is a kind of collection of fragments of history; architectural ornaments, — copies from Melrose in one part, the old identical gate of the Tolbooth, or rather the stone part of it, through which the Porteous mob forced its way, in another, — an old fountain before the house, and odd inscriptions and statues everywhere, make such a kind of irregular, poetical habitation as ought to belong to him. Then for every big stone on his estate, as well as for all the great points of the country about, he has a tradition or a ballad, which he repeats with an enthusiasm that kindles his face to an animation that forms a singular contrast to the quiet in which it usually rests. . . .

Nobody came to Abbotsford while we stayed there, and of course we had a happy time. The breakfast-hour was nine, and after that we all walked out together and heard any number of amusing stories, for Mr. Scott has a story for everything; and so we continued walking about and visiting till nearly dinner-time, at half past four. As soon as we were seated the piper struck up a pibroch before the windows, dressed in his full Highland costume, and one of the best-looking and most vain, self-sufficient dogs I ever saw; and he continued walking about, and playing on his bagpipes until the dessert arrived, when he was called in, received his dram, and was dismissed. Mr. Scott likes to sit at table and talk, and therefore dinner, or rather the latter part of it, was long. Coffee followed, and then in a neighboring large room the piper was heard again, and we all went in and danced Scotch reels till we were tired. An hour's conversation afterwards brought us to ten o'clock and supper; and two very short and gay hours at the supper-table, or by the fire, brought us to bedtime.[105]

There were brief visits with Southey at Keswick and with Wordsworth at Rydal. Ticknor records his impressions of the former:

He is certainly an extraordinary man, one of those whose character I find it difficult to comprehend, because I hardly know how such elements can be brought together, such rapidity of mind with such patient labor and wearisome exactness, so mild a disposition with so much nervous excitability, and a poetical talent so elevated with such an immense mass of minute, dull learning.[106]

Of his visit with Wordsworth he writes:

Wordsworth knew from Southey that I was coming, and therefore met me at the door, and received me heartily. He is about fifty three or four, with a tall, ample, well-proportioned frame, a grave and tranquil manner, a Roman cast of appearance, and Roman dignity and simplicity. He presented me to his wife, a good, very plain woman, who seems to regard him with reverence and affection, and to his sister, not much younger than himself, with a good deal of spirit and, I should think, more than common talent and knowledge. I was at home with them at once, and we went out like friends together to scramble up the mountains, and enjoy the prospects and scenery. . . . We returned to dinner, which was very simple, for, though he has an office under the government and a patrimony besides, yet each is inconsiderable. . . .

His conversation surprised me by being so different from all I had anticipated. It was exceedingly simple, strictly confined to subjects he understood familiarly, and more marked by plain good-sense than by anything else. When, however, he came upon poetry and reviews, he was the Khan of Tartary again, and talked as metaphysically and extravagantly as ever Coleridge wrote; but, excepting this, it was really a consolation to hear him. It was best of all, though, to see how he is loved and respected in his family and neighborhood. . . . The peasantry treated him with marked respect, the children took off their hats to him, and a poor widow in the neighborhood sent to him to come and talk to her son, who had been behaving ill. . . .

In the evening he showed me his manuscripts, the longest a kind of poetical history of his life, which, in the course of about two octavo volumes of manuscript, he has brought to his twenty-eighth year, and of which the "Excursion" is a fragment. It is in blank-verse, and, as far as I read, what has been published is a fair specimen of what remains in manuscript. He read me "Peter Bell, the Potter," a long tale, with many beauties but much greater defects; and another similar story, "The Wagonner." . . . The whole amused me a good deal; it was a specimen of the lake life, doctrines, and manners, more perfect than I had found at Southey's, and, as such, was very curious. We sat up, therefore, late, and talked a great deal about the living poets. Of Scott he spoke with much respect as a man, and of his works with judicious and sufficient praise. For Campbell he did not seem to have so much regard; and for Lord Byron none at all, since, though he admired his talent, he seemed to have a deep-rooted abhorrence of his character, and besides, I thought, felt a little bitterness against him for having taken something of his own *lakish* manner lately, and, what is worse, borrowed some of his thoughts. On the whole, however, he seemed fairly disposed to do justice to his contemporaries and rivals. . . . [107]

Arriving in London again, Ticknor attended the theatre and the Lord Mayor's ball with Washington Irving, and later met the little coterie of Hazlitt, Godwin, Hunt, and Lamb, whom he characterizes as "these persons," in striking contrast to the more aristocratic circle which he was in the habit of meeting. All "felt themselves bound to show off and produce an effect," writes

Ticknor, "All coming into contact and conflict, and agreeing in nothing but their common hatred for everything that has been more successful than their own works." [108]

When Ticknor arrived home on June 6, 1819, to begin his duties at Harvard as Smith Professor of the French and Spanish Languages and Literature, and Professor of Belles Lettres, he was one of the most learned and accomplished men in the United States. He had enjoyed unusual contacts with the most culti-vated society of Europe, had pursued his studies under the direc-tion of some of the most renowned scholars, and had acquired a vast fund of learning, as well as a valuable library of several thousand volumes. He brought with him not only a practical command of several modern languages and a knowledge of all the important literatures, but also an acquaintance with the educational methods of European universities. It was his desire now to give to the institution with which he was to be associated and to his country the benefit of his ripe scholarship. His formal inauguration as professor on August 10 of that year marks a sig-nificant period in the history of modern languages and literature at Harvard and in this country. [109] About the time of his induc-tion Ticknor submitted to President Kirkland his conception of the professorship and an outline of the course of lectures which he proposed to give. The lectures in belles lettres were to trace the development of literature, beginning with Greece and extend-ing to the countries of modern Europe, a plan which was actu-ally never carried out, since the character of the professorship had never been clearly defined. Inasmuch as he was officially informed that, in this field, it was necessary for him to "pass over topics which are assigned to other professors, or to take them up in a manner or show them in a light specifically different," [110] the lectures in this subject and the range of his professorship be-came necessarily restricted, and Ticknor replied that he would have to make a new plan in which belles lettres would be taught "with reference only to the literatures of Rome, modern Italy, and Germany, as these are the only literatures on which lectures will be delivered immediately." [111]

However, the lectures which Ticknor delivered from year to year were devoted principally to the literatures of France and Spain, [112] while a small staff under his direction gave instruction

in the languages to volunteer classes.[113] Andrew Peabody, a
graduate of Harvard in 1826, and one of Ticknor's students,
writes of his lectures:

These lectures had all the qualities of style and method which fitted
them for an academic audience. We knew that they were of tran-
scendent worth, and we listened to them eagerly and attentively. They
were appreciated as highly, yet not as intelligently, as they would have
been a few years later. They covered, for the most part, a then unknown territory. Spanish literature was known mainly by translations
of the few world-famous authors; and, though the capacity of reading
French was not rare, there were very few French books to be had,
and those few, the works of the great writers of the seventeenth and
eighteenth centuries, not the current literature of the time. But Mr.
Ticknor did much toward awakening curiosity, and creating the condition of things in which he might have had an audience more fully con-
versant with the literatures of which he was master.[114]

There is no evidence that in his lectures Ticknor gave much
attention to German literature.[115] He is responsible, however,
for the introduction of the study of German in the Harvard
curriculum. While visiting in Washington in January, 1825, he
was asked by Lafayette to interest himself in Charles Follen, a
native of Germany, who had fled for political reasons to Switzerland and had later made his way to the United States.[116] In
Philadelphia, Ticknor formed his acquaintance, and on the latter's recommendation Follen became instructor at Harvard the
same year.[117] Referring to Follen's first class, of which he was a
member, Andrew Peabody writes:

German had never been taught in college before; and it was with no
little difficulty that a volunteer class of eight was formed, desirous, or
at least willing, to avail themselves of his services. I was of that class.
We were looked upon with very much the amazement with which a
class in some obscure tribal dialect of the remotest Orient would be now
regarded. We knew of but two or three persons in New England who
could read German; though there were probably many more, of whom
we did not know. There were no German books in the bookstore. A
friend gave me a copy of Schiller's "Wallenstein," which I read as soon
as I was able to do so, and then passed it from hand to hand among
those who could obtain nothing else to read. There was no attainable
class-book that could be used as a "Reader." A few copies of Noeh-
den's Grammar were imported, and a few copies of I forget whose
"Pocket Dictionary," fortunately too copious for an Anglo-Saxon
pocket, and suggesting the generous amplitude of the Low Dutch cos-

tume, as described in Irving's mythical "History of New York." The "German Reader for Beginners," compiled by our teacher, was furnished to the class in single sheets as it was needed, and was printed in Roman type, there being no German type within easy reach. There could not have been a happier introduction to German literature than this little volume. It contained choice extracts in prose, all from writers that still hold an unchallenged place in the hierarchy of genius, and poems from Schiller, Goethe, Herder, and several other poets of kindred, if inferior, fame. But in the entire volume, Dr. Follen rejoiced especially in several battle-pieces from Körner, the soldier and martyr of liberty, whom we then supposed to have been our teacher's fellow-soldier, though, in fact, he fell in battle when Dr. Follen was just entering the University. I never have heard recitations which impressed me so strongly as the reading of those pieces by Dr. Follen, who would put into them all of the heart and soul that had made him too much a lover of his country to be suffered to dwell in it. He appended to the other poems in the first edition of the Reader, anonymously, a death-song in memory of Körner, which we all knew to be his own, and which we read so often and so feelingly, that it sank indelibly into permanent memory; and I find that after an interval of sixty years it is as fresh in my recollection as the hymns that I learned in my childhood.

Dr. Follen was the best of teachers. Under him we learned the grammar of the language, in great part, *in situ*, — forms and constructions, except the most elementary, being explained to us as we met them in our reading-lessons, and explained with a clearness and emphasis that made it hard to forget them. At the same time he pointed out all that was specially noteworthy in our lessons, and gave us, in English much better than ours, his own translations of passages of peculiar interest or beauty. He bestowed great pains in bringing our untried organs into use in the more difficult details of pronunciation, particularly in the o, the u, the r, and the ch, on which he took us each separately in hand. His pronunciation was singularly smooth and euphonious. I have been reminded of it in Dresden more than in either Northern or Southern Germany.[118]

Follen was unquestionably an excellent teacher, and did much to promote interest in German studies in Harvard and in the community of Boston.

Our German teacher, Dr. Follen [writes Ticknor in 1826 to his friend Charles S. Daveis], was formerly Professor of Civil Law at Basel, a young man who left his country from political troubles. He is a fine fellow, an excellent scholar, and teaches German admirably. . . . He is a modest, thorough, faithful German scholar, who will do good among us, and be worth your knowing.[119]

In 1830, owing to the generosity of some friends, a professorship of the German language and literature was established at Harvard, and Follen was appointed to the position. His inaugural address on German literature, which was delivered in the autumn of 1831, attracted keen interest, particularly that of some of the learned men, John Quincy Adams, Edward Livingston, James Marsh, and others, and was afterward published and widely read.[120] However, as a result of his anti-slavery activities Follen incurred the opposition of the Harvard authorities, and his services as professor came to an unfortunate end with his resignation in March, 1835.[121]

Meanwhile, Ticknor had continued his correspondence with Jefferson. Until near the end of Jefferson's life many letters passed between him and Ticknor on the subject of education, the work at Harvard, and the progress of the University of Virginia. In December, after Ticknor's return home, Jefferson wrote congratulating him on his success and inquiring as to his plans. "How has your health been affected by your European tour? How your mind? How the view of your own country after seeing so many others? What are your present occupations and future purposes? And how do you mean to utilize the stock of knolege you have brought home?" Stating his intention to send a confidential agent abroad in search of professors for his institution, he asks for information as to the possibility of securing men of distinction, especially those trained at Edinburgh, Oxford, and Cambridge, and urges Ticknor to make an extensive visit in the more congenial climate at Monticello. He writes further:

Some chosen books, with which I have commenced another library, might have employed the hours of amusement, and excursions to our University those of daily exercise, that goes on with much activity and hope, and will form an unique and beautiful Academical Villa, in which every Professor will have a distinct house, or pavilion, to himself, consisting of a room for his lectures, with 4 others for family accomodations. These pavilions are of the best workmanship, of strict architecture, intended as regular and classical models for the lectures on that subject. To each is annexed a garden and other conveniences. We fix the professors superiority well in the hope of attaching them to the comforts of their situation, and by that means prevent their being seduced from us by other institutions. But we shall not open until the

1st day of February twelve month, and whether we shall be ready then depends on our legislature now in session, our buildings being as yet about half completed.

The recommendations of Mr. Blaettermann were received with your last letter, and were laid before the first meeting of our board of Visitors, to whom they appeared to be so satisfactory, that had we been in readiness, his offer would, I think, have been unanimously accepted. But we cannot appoint until we are sure of the time of commencement. Whenever we do appoint to the professorship of modern languages, the probability is in his favor, and would be, I believe, a certainty, should not so distant appointment be thought to endanger too much delay in his entering into function. We feel particular preference toward him from his readiness to prepare himself to teach the Anglo-Saxon, for which a qualified teacher is the more rare in proportion to the obsoleteness of the study.

The liberality with which you view our kindred institution is what I expected from you. It could not be imagined that the single University of Cambridge, and that so near the North Eastern corner of our Union, could suffice for a country so extensive as ours. We are not therefore rivals, but fellow-laborers in the same field, where the harvest is great, and the laborers few. My confidence in your candor, and in the information acquired in your late literary tour of Europe, would have rendered an interview with you peculiarly interesting. The principle on which we proceed in the selection of professors is to receive none but those of the first grade of science in their particular branch. If such can be found among our native citizens, we shall greatly prefer them. But we shall prefer a foreigner of the 1st order to a native of the 2nd. On this principle we proposed the Professorship of Mathematics to Mr. Bowditch, and should not have been difficult, nor should we now be so, in the terms which might render his change of position satisfactory. On this principle our proposition to you was made for the department including belles lettres.[122]

Ticknor heartily approved of Jefferson's plan of securing young professors from England and Scotland. In February of the following year he wrote suggesting that the confidential agent should not at once declare his purpose, owing to the "universal prevalence of patronage and the extraordinary sacrifice of principle and truth" which he himself had discovered men in Great Britain exercising in their recommendations. He further suggests that a thorough canvass be made before a final solution, and that men of promising distinction might be tempted to come for approximately the sum of £400 a year. "Perhaps you might put it at £500 a year for five years," he said, "with leave to either party to dissolve the connexion at that time and thus give yourselves a chance of trial with means of rejection." His letter includes the following:

I am exceedingly happy to hear of the progress of your University and expect much from it. It was greatly wanted in your section of the country, and so far from being an injury to our establishment at Cambridge, I think it will render us essential service both by promoting an honourable emulation and by preventing us from having the sons of the very rich men of the South, who, from the mere circumstance that they are so far from home, become independent before they are discreet and grow idle and dissipated and do themselves no good and their associates much harm — but, who, if they were educated near their friends, would be as regular students as the young men who go to any of our colleges; and come out much better fitted for the world than they do here. On all accounts, I should be most happy to do anything that would promote your success. . . .

For myself, as you are kind enough to make so minute inquiries about me, I will add, that I am now established as Professor of Belles Lettres at Cambridge, with permission to reside in Boston, where I constantly live — that my duties consist entirely in lecturing — that in a month I shall begin a course of forty lectures on French Literature and in the Autumn one of about thirty on Spanish Literature — that afterwards I shall prepare a course of sixty or eighty lectures on the Belles Lettres generally — and when all these are ready, conclude the circle of instruction by a course on Italian and a course on English Literature. All these together will make above two hundred lectures. And in each course I shall always deliver three or four a week, so as to keep up an interest in the subject — and when I have finished the whole, I shall look about for something else to do, as I have no idea that a Professor should ever be doing anything but preparing to teach. What I saw of Europe only raised my own country in my estimation and attracted me to it yet more — and as the six months since my return have been unquestionably the six happiest months of my life, I do not think but the future promises well for me, if my health should be continued.

Permit me to close this long letter by offering myself to you again in any way in which I can be useful to you or your University.[12]

In September, 1821, Ticknor addressed a long letter to Jefferson, asking for his assistance and cooperation in a plan to petition Congress for a modification or the removal of duties on foreign books.

We have, in the last twenty or thirty years [he said], made great progress in knowledge; but, we are now, I think, arrived at the point, where we must have a large increase of our means or be much embarrassed, perhaps quite stopped, in our course, for want of them. We have done nearly all we can with our present very imperfect apparatus of books and must now have more, or give up, perhaps, something of the little we have gained.[124]

His letter closed by inquiring: "How does your new University advance? When will the lecture rooms be opened? All that concerns it interests me very much." Later in the autumn he again expressed his interest:

I am very anxious to hear more about your University, and to learn something of its success. Every day persuades me anew of the truth of an opinion I have long held, that at Cambridge we shall never become what we might be very easily, unless we are led or driven to it by a rival. I see no immediate prospect of such a rival, except in your University, and therefore I long to have it a successful operation.[125]

During the first three years of his professorship Ticknor devoted much time to careful preparation of his lectures on French and Spanish literature. In June, 1823, he forwarded to Jefferson a syllabus of his course in Spanish and a full account of his lectures:

When I accepted the place of Professor on the Smith foundation at Cambridge nearly four years since, I determined to devote myself exclusively to the preparation of the two courses of Lectures its Statutes demand, one on French and the other on Spanish Literature, until they should be completed. I began with the French and, in about two years, finished between fifty and sixty Lectures, equal in print to three good sized octavo volumes, to which I have never published a Syllabus, for reasons entirely connected with the state of the Library at Cambridge. Since that time, I have been employed on the Spanish, which I have recently completed in between thirty and forty lectures — equal in amount to two printed octavos, and to this I have just published a Syllabus. They are both in the nature of works on literary History, of which I read portions to my classes without regard to any fixed division into lectures, and as such, they are the first attempt made in this country. For the French portion, my means, compared with those accessible in Europe, were not very ample, though they were by no means deficient: — but for the Spanish portion I believe my collection of books is unrivalled — certainly there is nothing so complete in Spanish belles lettres to be found in the great libraries of England, France, Germany or even Spain itself, where, indeed, the collections have been sadly injured and scattered by the revolutions of the last fifteen years, and where their libraries being hardly an hundred years old were never properly filled. My purpose has been, in each case, to make a course of

Lectures more complete and minute than has been delivered before, and to introduce, if possible, a more detailed and thorough mode of teaching, whose object shall be to communicate genuine knowledge, rather than to exhibit the subject in rhetorical declamation. I have succeeded with the students, who have given me their willing attention, in a manner particularly pleasant to me, since I have declined from the first, any attendance on my lectures, which is not voluntary; but the Professors still keep on in the beaten track, and will not probably soon be induced to change. As a specimen of the sort of labour to which I have given the whole of my time since my return from Europe, I take the liberty to send you with this the Syllabus of my Spanish courses of Lectures. Nobody in this country, within my acquaintance, has so much knowledge of this particular subject as you have — nobody has such wide and liberal views of the general principles on which an university should be established and its teaching conducted — and I am, therefore, very anxious to know how you will regard my efforts in the cause, which I know you have so much at heart.

It has given me great pleasure to learn from some of my friends in Virginia the successful progress of your University. I trust it will soon go into effective operation and serve as a model to lead all other institutions in the country, just as our imperfect establishment at Cambridge has led all others into an unfortunate imitation of its clumsy system for the last half century. As soon as I hear it is fairly opened, I promise myself the pleasure of visiting it.[126]

A month later Jefferson sent Ticknor a print of the ground-plan of his university. "It may give you some idea," he said, "of its distribution and conveniences, but not of its architecture, which being chastely classical, constitutes one of its most distinguishing characters." [127] He welcomed Ticknor's Syllabus as a model which he wished to see adopted in the various branches of instruction in his institution, and expressed the following views:

I am not fully informed of the practices at Harvard, but there is one from which we shall certainly vary. That is, the holding the students all to one prescribed course of reading, and disallowing exclusive application to those branches only which are to qualify them for the particular vocations to which they are destined. We shall, on the contrary, allow them uncontrolled choice in the lectures they shall choose to attend, and require elementary qualifications only, and sufficient age. Our institution will proceed on the principle of doing all the good it can without consulting its own pride or ambition; of letting every one come and listen to whatever he thinks may improve the condition of his mind. The rock which I most dread is the discipline of the institution, and it is that on which most of our public schools labor. The insubordination of our youth is now the greatest obstacle to their education. We may lessen the difficulty, perhaps, by avoiding too much government, by requiring no useless observances, none which shall merely multiply occasions for dissatisfaction, disobedience and revolt by referring to the more discreet of themselves the minor discipline, the graver to the civil magistrates, as in Edinburgh. On this head I am anxious for information of the practices of other places, having myself had little experience of the government of youth. I presume there are printed codes of the rules at Harvard, and if so, you would oblige me by sending me a copy, and of those of any other academy which you think can furnish anything useful. You flatter me with a visit "as soon as you learn that the University is fairly opened." A visit from you at any time will be the most welcome possible to all our family, who remember with peculiar satisfaction the pleasure they received from your one. But were I allowed to name the time, it should not be deferred beyond the autumn of the ensuing year. Our last building, and that which will be the principal ornament and keystone, giving unity to the whole, will then be nearly finished, and afford you a gratification compensating the trouble of the journey. We shall then, also, be engaged in our code of regulations preparatory to our opening which may, perhaps, take place in the beginning of 1825. There is no person from whose information of the European institutions, and especially their discipline, I should expect so much aid in that difficult work. Come, then, dear Sir, at that, or at any earlier epoch, and give to our institution the benefit of your counsel. I know that you scout, as I do, the idea of any rivalship. Our views are catholic for the improvement of our country, by science, and indeed, it is better even for your own University to have its yokemate at this distance, rather than to force a nearer one from the increasing necessity for it. And how long before we may expect others in the southern, western, and middle region of this vast country? [128]

The Harvard College with which Ticknor had been associated since his return from Europe was a small institution, with a restricted curriculum and a provincial faculty, none of whom, excepting Edward Everett, had enjoyed the advantages of study and travel abroad. The organization, discipline, and methods of instruction were antiquated, and the regulations governing the institution Ticknor refused to furnish Jefferson, since they formed, as he declared, one of the most cumbrous and awkward systems that it would be possible to apply in the present state of the country. At the same time he gave an outline of the general plan of reform and innovations, for which he had been laboring, in the face of bitter opposition, since the summer of 1821. This included revision of the laws and their administration, organization of departments, more freedom in the choice of studies, especially for students not wishing a degree, separation of students into divisions according to proficiency, improvement in the quality of instruction, and a general expansion of the scope and function of the institution. These changes he hoped would soon be carried into effect, and a copy of the laws would be forwarded to Jefferson. "It will not, probably, be all that a few of us, who are, perhaps, over-earnest in the cause, should desire," he stated. "But, I think, it will be a good deal; and probably, more than has been done in our quarter of the Union for half a century."[129] Meanwhile, he was pleased to hear of the liberality which the Virginia legislature had shown toward the University. "How long and how earnestly I have desired to see this great experiment tried, you very well know," he wrote. "Can I now do anything to further its success? If I can, either here or in Europe, you are, I trust, quite aware that I am at your command."[130] Jefferson replied:

I am sorry to hear of the schism within the walls of Harvard, yet I do not wonder at it. You have a good deal among you of ecclesiastical leaven. The spirit of that order is to fear and oppose all change stigmatizing it under the name of innovation, and not considering that all improvement is innovation, and that without innovation we should still have been inhabitants of the forest, brutes among brutes. Patience, pressure, as unremitting as gravity itself can alone urge man on to the happiness of which he is capable.[131]

For a number of years Ticknor had looked forward to a return visit to Virginia, and Jefferson had repeatedly insisted that he come to Monticello, particularly to view his prospective university.

I think you would feel a pleasure in surveying the preparations we have made for a library establishment [he wrote in August, 1824], and I am sure we should derive advantages from the reflections and counsels which a closer view of the subject and circumstances of the institution would suggest to your experience. . . . I am now engaged in preparing a catalogue, and your *aid* in this is not among the least advantages which will welcome your visit.[132]

Again, in November, when Lafayette was his guest, he urged the young New Englander to join them.[133] Finally, Mr. and Mrs. Ticknor journeyed to Washington, and, accompanied by Webster, spent two days in December with Madison at Montpelier, and five days with Jefferson at Monticello. Writing to his friend William H. Prescott, of his journey and his experiences, Ticknor says: [134]

Yesterday we formed a party, and, with Mr. Jefferson at our head, went to the University. It is a very fine establishment, consisting of ten houses for professors, four eating-houses, a rotunda on the model of the Parthenon, with a magnificent room for a library, and four fine lecture-rooms, with one hundred and eight apartments for students; the whole situated in the midst of two hundred and fifty acres of land, high, healthy, and with noble prospects all around it. It has cost two hundred and fifty thousand dollars, and the thorough finish of every part of it, and the beautiful architecture of the whole, show, I think, that it has not cost too much. Each professor receives his house, which in Charlottesville — the neighboring village — would rent for $600, a salary of $1,500, and a fee of $20 from every student who attends his instructions, which are to be lectures, three times a week. Of the details of the system I shall discourse much when I see you. It is more practical than I feared, but not so practical that I feel satisfied of its success. It is, however, an experiment worth trying, to which I earnestly desire the happiest results; and they have, to begin it, a mass of buildings more beautiful than anything architectural in New England, and more appropriate to an university than can be found, perhaps, in the world.

Mr. Jefferson is entirely absorbed in it, and its success would make a *beau finale* indeed to his life. He is now eighty-two years old, very little altered from what he was ten years ago, very active, lively, and happy, riding from ten to fifteen miles every day, and talking without the least restraint, very pleasantly, upon all subjects. In politics, his interest seems nearly gone. He takes no newspaper but the Richmond Enquirer, and reads that reluctantly; but on all matters of literature, philosophy, and general interest, he is prompt and even eager. He reads much Greek and Saxon. I saw his Greek Lexicon, printed in 1817; it was much worn with use, and contained many curious notes. . . .

Mr. Jefferson seems to enjoy life highly, and very rationally; but he said well of himself the other evening, "When I can neither read nor ride, I shall desire very much to make my bow." I think he bids fair to enjoy both, yet nine or ten years.

In the spring of 1824 Jefferson's personal representative, Francis Walker Gilmer, had sailed for England, armed with letters to the American ambassador and to Richard Rush, Samuel Parr, Dugald Stuart, and others, and empowered to engage professors for his faculty, "characters of due degree of science, and of talents for instruction, and of correct habits and morals."

The policy of looking abroad for young scholars received considerable disapproval and opposition from some Americans at that time,[135] among them John Adams, who expressed his frank opinion to Jefferson:

> Your University is a noble experiment in your old age, and your ardor for its success does you honour. But I do not approve of your sending to Europe for Tutors and Professors. I do believe there are sufficient scholars in America to fill your Professorships and Tutorships with more active ingenuity and independent minds than you can bring from Europe. The Europeans are all deeply tainted with prejudices, both Ecclesiastical and Temporal, which they can never get rid of. They are infected with Episcopal and Presbyterian creeds, and confession of faith. They all believe that great principle, which has produced this boundless Universe, Newton's Universe, and Herschell's Universe, came down to this little Ball to be spit upon by Jews; and until this awful blasphemy is got rid of, there never will be any liberal science in the world.[136]

Although Gilmer was successful in engaging five professors in Great Britain,[137] the formal opening of the University was postponed from February 1 to March 7, 1825, owing to the late arrival of three of this number.[138] Shortly afterward Jefferson received from Ticknor a copy of his *Memoir of Lafayette*, which he had recently published in the *North American Review*,[139] and "a list of the principal German works in literary History and of the best belles-lettres writers," accompanied by the following:

> The lists, I enclose, are as you desired them to be, only of the best books in each department you indicated, but if you should like to have either or both of them enlarged, I could very easily do it. I should have much pleasure in it. Or if I can, in any other way, contribute to the completeness of your catalogue, or by any means serve your University, I should be greatly gratified, if you would command me.
> I am very anxious to hear from you and know how your establishment is begun, — how far the Professors are such as you desired to find them, how the system itself goes into action, and how many students are arrived, as well as how they came prepared for such instruction as your University proposes to give them. I am the more anxious to know of your progress and success, because I think a general and well-grounded discontent is beginning to prevail in relation to the system pursued at all our colleges in New England, which, being substantially the same, that existed here a century and a half ago, can hardly be suited to our present circumstances and wants. These colleges are now very numerous, and under one pretext or another, are

constantly becoming more so. Competition therefore is growing more and more active among them, and all are endeavoring to find new and better modes of instruction with which to contend against their rivals. This, however, is very difficult within the limits of the ancient system, and none has yet dared to pass these limits, though Cambridge is now very near it. Of course, we are all looking anxiously towards your new University. It is a case in point for us, and we much desire that the experiment may succeed according to your wishes, since we shall certainly be able in some way or other to gain instruction from it.

Our own College at Cambridge is not in a better condition than it was when I saw you. There is a good deal of difference of opinion between the different boards that have its management in their hands, and this is likely, I fear to produce more and more bitterness. I am much afraid, that for a long time, we shall not be able to put things in the condition we desire.[140]

The catalogue of German books, Jefferson informed Ticknor, "is exactly such as I wished, a collection only of their best books." In reply to Ticknor's inquiry, he reported that the University had opened "under considerable discouragement" since the late arrival of three of his professors from England, which necessitated postponement of the opening, had caused many students who planned to enter the institution to register elsewhere. He stated, however, that they had begun "with about thirty or forty" students, which number had now increased to sixty-four, and that others continued "to come in almost daily." Of his faculty he wrote:

Our Professors from England equal my highest expectations, of a high order of science in their respective lines, eager to advance their schools, of correct habits, meeting difficulties with cheerfulness, and pleased with their accommodations and prospects. The professors of the Chemical and Mathematical schools are from Cambridge, the natural philosopher is Mr. Bonnycastle, son of the mathematician of that name well known in our schools, the Medical Professor is of the Edinburgh school, and the one of modern languages, Dr. Blaettermann, you know.[141]

On May 10 Ticknor replied:

I received duly your favour of April 12 with a copy of the Exactments for your new University. It is a matter of great congratulation that you begin your Establishment under such favourable auspices, and we can now only hope that all things will succeed according to your present prospects. I shall be very anxious for further and constant information and very grateful for any it may be in your power to afford me. In return, I hope I shall soon be able to send you good accounts of beneficial changes and arrangements in our college at Cambridge.[142]

No further correspondence seems to have passed between Jefferson and Ticknor, though the latter, inspired particularly by the visit of 1824, continued his efforts for educational reforms at Harvard. He had successfully carried into effect in his own department the changes which he proposed, and his views and innovations were adopted by the Corporation and Overseers in June, 1825.[143] But he received only persistent opposition from the provincial Harvard faculty, and in 1827 the ideas were modified and practically abandoned, excepting in his own department. Finally, when somewhat gratified with the success of his own work but discouraged with his attempts to reform Harvard and to make it a more effectual educational institution, he resigned his professorship in May, 1835, though he had planned to remain until his successor, Longfellow, returned from Europe in the summer of the following year. "I am sorry to do so before Mr. Longfellow's return," he wrote to President Quincy, "but yet the situation is such that I trust little inconvenience will be felt from it." [144] A week later he was informed of the vote of the Corporation, expressing its regret at his retirement, and its "deep sense of the numerous and highly valuable services rendered by him, both to his own department and to the University in general." [145] In June, 1835, Ticknor sailed again for a period of three years in Europe, and Longfellow held the position until 1854, when he was succeeded by James Russell Lowell. Fortunate, indeed, is the history of this professorship, which numbers among its incumbents three of the most distinguished scholars of the century.

The relations between Harvard and the University of Virginia and the influence of Jefferson, through Ticknor, on Harvard's former elective system, as adopted under President Eliot in 1883, have been pointed out.[146] In reviewing the history of a voluntary system of studies at Harvard, President Eliot, in his report for 1883-84, pays tribute to Ticknor as "a reformer fifty years in advance of his time." That Ticknor returned from Europe in 1819 with educational ideas which he hoped to see adopted in this country is not to be denied. But it is also evident that these ideas were quickened and fostered by his contact with Jefferson, who, more than any other individual of his time, held advanced theories on the subject of education. Through achievements at the University of Virginia, which was the idol of his old age, Jefferson inspired young Ticknor in his efforts for reforms at Harvard, especially in the direction of elective studies. It would be conveying the wrong impression to say that Ticknor acquired his ideas from Jefferson; but it is significant that their views were practically identical. It is here, however, not a question of origins and influence. The attractive relations that existed between Ticknor and Jefferson furnish an impressive story of affectionate friendship between youth and old age and an excellent illustration of the law of exchange between a keenly intellectual, forward-looking young scholar and a wise, experienced elderly scholar and statesman. In mutual helpfulness, they cooperated for the furtherance of human knowledge.

The three years June, 1835, to July, 1838, which Ticknor spent in Europe were, from the social point of view, even more successful than his first visit twenty years earlier.[147] Everywhere he was received as a mature scholar. The first four months were devoted to England, Wales, and Ireland, where, as later on the Continent, he saw many of his old friends and added new acquaintances to his list.[148] He then passed to the Continent, and early in November entered Germany, where he was to reside, principally in Dresden, until June of the following year. The journal for these years devotes many pages to the history, customs, and art collections of each place visited. A journey up the Rhine enabled him to call on some of his old friends at Bonn, particularly August Wilhelm Schlegel, who, with "pardonable vanity," discussed politics and his Sanscrit studies. Later, in Weimar, he visited the Goethe house and was shown the last edition of the poet's works, the original manuscript of *Götz von Berlichingen*, and of the *Roman Elegies*. But even more interesting were the large collections of science and art, of which he records the following critical impressions:

The whole, in the way it is now exhibited, seemed to me a monument of the vanity of a man who was spoiled by a life — a *very long* life — of constant, uniform success, every wish not only fulfilled but anticipated, so that he came at last to think whatever related to himself to be of great consequence to the whole world. He therefore published, or left orders to publish, everything he had ever written, much of which is mere waste-paper; and now his will further directs all the little commonplace arrangements of a very ordinary study and sleeping-room to be shown to strangers, as a matter of moment and interest. The whole German nation is, however, in some degree responsible for this, for during the last five and twenty years of his life he was humored and worshipped in a way that I think no author ever was before.[149]

Arriving in Dresden on November 20, Ticknor settled down for a residence of six months of unusual intellectual and social advantages. He pursued his studies in the Royal Library, was received at court, frequently attended the opera and theatre, and formed an acquaintance with some of the most distinguished men of letters. He was intimate with Count Baudissin, the translator of Shakespeare, with Tiedge, the author of *Urania*, with Retzsch, famous for his designs of *Faust*,[150] and with Von Raumer, the historian, and was particularly fascinated by Tieck [151] and Prince John of Saxony. Of Tieck, "the acknowledged head of German literature" since Goethe's death, Ticknor's first impressions read:

> He seems past sixty; stout and well-built, with a countenance still fine, and which must have been decidedly handsome, but a good deal broken in his person and bent with the gout. He has an air of decision about him that is not to be mistaken, and is, I dare say, somewhat whimsical and peculiar in his opinions and notions, as some of his books intimate, particularly what he has published on the English drama.
>
> But I think he is agreeable; and he has a great deal of knowledge, both in old English and Spanish literature. His collection of Spanish books surprised me. It is a great deal better than Lord Holland's, a great deal better than any one collection in England; but still, in most points, not so good as mine. He has been forty years in gathering it, and he has a very minute, curious, and critical knowledge of its contents; but his knowledge of Spanish literature goes no further than his own books will carry him, and in some parts of it I remarked quite a striking ignorance which surprised me very much until I found how it happened. I have passed two evenings with him, and, as he keeps open house very simply and kindly, after the German fashion, I think I shall go there frequently.[152]

There were numerous subsequent occasions when Ticknor was either in Tieck's home or his company in the literary circle. He inspected Tieck's splendid collection of books and manuscripts in old English literature, heard him discuss the present state of the German theatre,[153] and read "some acute remarks of his own upon Goethe, whom he treated with admiration, indeed, but with an admiration more measured and discriminating than is usual among the Germans."[154] Since Tieck enjoyed the universal reputation of being the best reader in Germany, there were many evenings when it was Ticknor's privilege to hear him read Shakespearean plays in the Schlegel version,[155] and from Prince John's translations of Dante. Some years later Ticknor called Tieck "the first man of his time in Germany," [156] and in 1849 he sent him a copy of his *History of Spanish Literature*, to which Tieck replied calling it "the first of the day." [157] Ticknor found Prince John "very agreeable and much disposed for literary conversation," a real scholar and a thorough student of Dante. "I was sorry to part from him," writes Ticknor just before leaving Dresden, "for if I were to see many more princes in Europe than I shall see, I should not find one so good a scholar, and a few so entirely respectable in their whole characters, public and private." [158]

At the court theatre, of which Tieck was director, Ticknor appreciated the opportunity of seeing some of the principal dramas presented. Besides *Hamlet* and *Macbeth*, he refers briefly to performances of *Der Oheim*, a popular comedy by Princess Amalie of Saxony, Kotzebue's *Die deutschen Kleinstädter*, and some of the German classics.[159] In December he writes:

I went, too, to see Schiller's *Robbers*. The acting was excellent and the two principal actors were twice called for and applauded. The theatre was quite full; and though the piece is so exaggerated, unnatural, and impossible, it produced a great effect. I was surprised to find how much I thought about it, after I had returned home and even during the night.[160]

The following month he finds *Egmont* extremely well performed, the role of Vansen by Pauli being "the most happy hit," though "all the popular scenes were as well done as possible, particularly the first one in the second act." [161] In April he states:

I saw this evening Schiller's *Braut von Messina*; and its beautiful poetry and exquisitely finished versification failed to produce the least, proper dramatic effect. It was throughout the tedious performance — and the attempt to introduce the chorus of the ancients, in which some-

times nine and sometimes eighteen heavy bearded men pronounced the
same words together, was almost ridiculous. Indeed it proved throughout a strange mixture of the classical and the romantic, and showed
how unhappily Schiller must have struggled against his own genius,
when he was composing it.[162]

The city of Dresden impressed Ticknor in many respects as the
finest he had seen in Europe. Writing to Longfellow, whom he
had hoped to meet there during the winter, he says:

The public institutions of the city, you know, are the first of any
city *of its size* in the world — and in some respects the first in Germany.
The society is abundant, excellent, and most freely open from the court
down, with an extraordinary proportion of intellect and scholarship.
. . . Indeed, there is rather more of society of all sorts than is quite
agreeable to persons who wish to live as quietly as we do. The whole
population, too, as you know, is true and kind, so that we feel really
well off among them, and hardly expect to be situated more to our
mind till we reach home again.[163]

On May 12 Ticknor left Dresden and proceeded to Leipzig and
Wittenburg and to Berlin, where he remained until the end of the
month enjoying the advantages similar to those which he had
experienced in Dresden.[164] He established acquaintance with
various celebrities, including Ranke, Neander, Van der Hagen,
the editor of the *Nibelungenlied*, Alexander von Humboldt,
Savigny, and Varnhagen von Ense.[165] In the home of Savigny
he met Bettina von Arnim, author of *Goethes Briefwechsel mit
einem Kinde*, "a most ridiculous book" which he had read and
found disgusting. An entry in his journal reads:

I could not get through it, though it is all the rage with multitudes
in Germany. But this evening I perceived by her conversation that she
must be the Bettina, whose other name I did not know, and I told her
so. . . . It is generally understood that Goethe had taste enough to be
very little pleased with the sentimental and indecent nonsense of this
lady's correspondence, though it was full of the most violent admiration
and adoration of himself. Few of his letters appear, and they are very
cool in their tone.[166]

The visit in Berlin was followed by a week in Prague and a
fortnight in Vienna. "The race of men has been constantly improving since we left the North," writes Ticknor in Vienna,
"growing stouter and better proportioned. In Bohemia, they

looked better than in Saxony or Prussia, and here they are better yet, and often remind me even by their features of our New England race, for the Northern German character is much effaced."[167] The visit to Vienna was principally for the purpose of inspecting the Spanish collection in the Imperial Library. He was disappointed in finding Grillparzer absent from the city, but there were interviews with the orientalist Hammer-Purgstall, Anastasius Grün, and Prince Metternich. Traveling leisurely through Austria, Ticknor reached Munich for a week's visit at the end of July. Among others he met here the philosopher Schelling,[168] who was inquisitive about the state of religion in the United States. Ticknor was deeply interested in the English Garden, in the plans of his fellow-countryman, Count Rumford, and in the Munich school of painting, which he thought gave promise of reviving the great period of art. The Glyptothek he calls "the finest single building I have yet seen in Europe," and he predicts that when the New Palace is finished the city will have a street quite equal to Unter den Linden.[169]

From Munich Ticknor journeyed to various places in Switzerland, and arrived in Rome early in December. His interest in education led him to spend a day at the famous school conducted by Fellenberg at Hofwyl, which is thus described in his journal:

The weather was delightful today, the whole day clear and cool, and we passed the greater part of it in a visit to Hofwyl, which is about an hour's drive from Berne through pleasant roads and with fine prospects. It is quite a separate establishment and the approach to it, after passing a wood, over the most beautifully cultivated fields, is a specimen of the exact and systematic finish to which everything relating to it has been brought in the course of the thirty-seven years the school has existed. The buildings belonging to it are numerous and the number of pupils is two hundred; fifty in the school for the poor; nearly a hundred in the middling school and the rest in the higher gymnasium. It seemed as if we were entering a village — so ample were all the arrangements and so full of life was everything around us. We had letters to Mr. Fellenberg, and he immediately came to us. He is about sixty-five years old, with white hair, is a fine person with dignified manners. He reminded me strongly of Prince Metternich, but had more simplicity of manner, and less elegance. While Mrs. T. was with the ladies chiefly, I walked about the grounds with him, saw the different parts of the establishment as well I could just as the holidays are closing, dined with the upper set of boys, the majority of whom are

English and American, and talked with him incessantly. He is an enthusiast and is a little disappointed, probably unreasonably disappointed, that he has not been able to accomplish all he undertook, when in 1799, he separated himself from the caste of the Patricians, to whom he belonged, and undertook a system of education for all classes of society.[170]

During the winter in Rome Ticknor mingled with many celebrities, among them Kestner, the Hanoverian minister in Rome and son of Johann Kestner and Charlotte Buff, of *Werther* fame. Kestner read extracts from one hundred letters from Goethe to his parents, which gave Ticknor, presumably for the first time, "a full explanation and history of that remarkable book." Ticknor gives a summary of the facts and adds:

Mr. Kestner came again this evening and read the rest of what I wanted to hear from his letters about Goethe, Werther, etc. It was very curious and interesting. The fact seems to be that, in the first book of Werther's letters, Werther is undoubtedly Goethe himself, Charlotte is Charlotte Buff, and Albert is Kestner, and much of what is described there really passed.

In the second book Werther is undoubtedly the young Jerusalem, who was a Secretary of Legation, and met the affronts there described, and whose death and last days are described, often word for word, in Werther, from a letter sent by Kestner to Goethe. So, too, Charlotte is undoubtedly the lady that young Jerusalem was in love with, but Albert was hardly worth changing and remains the same. Yet still through the whole of the second part there are many traits that belong essentially to Kestner and Charlotte Buff.[171]

Ticknor left Italy early in the summer of 1837 for further travel, which included brief visits in Munich and in several parts of southern Germany. In Heidelberg he examined the manuscripts in the library and visited in the University circle, principally in the houses of Creuzer, the classical scholar, Schlosser, the historian, Ulmann, the theologian, and Mittermaier, the renowned authority on criminal law. On his journey down the Rhine he called at Bonn on his friend Welcker, the classicist, and on August Wilhelm Schlegel. "It was very agreeable," says Ticknor, "but Schlegel in his old age is more of a *fat* than ever. He can talk with comfort of nothing but himself." [172] The autumn and winter were spent in Paris,[173] the spring in England and Scotland, and he arrived home the middle of July. His

journal and letters, as usual, furnish ample record of his interviews with many celebrities in the course of his wanderings, and
show that he could reside nowhere without enjoying the advantages of the best society. "Indeed," says one writer, "if Ticknor
had taken it into his head to go to Olympus, the first person he
would have sought, with a letter of introduction in his pocket,
would have been Jupiter." [174]

The first ten years after his return home were devoted chiefly to
the preparation of his *History of Spanish Literature*,[175] the publication on which Ticknor's reputation as a productive scholar
principally rests,[176] and in which he is revealed as a pioneer in
that particular subject. There is, however, another reminder of
his contribution to scholarship and learning. Greatly impressed
in Europe with the value and service of great libraries, he urged
the establishment of a similar institution in his native city. Thus
came into existence, in the spring of 1852, the first public library
in America, the Boston Public Library, of which he was the chief
founder and for which, as an official, he assumed most of the responsibility during the first fourteen years of its existence.[177] In
connection with his interest in this institution he found it necessary to go to Europe again. He sailed in June, 1856, and spent
fifteen months conferring with prominent librarians and purchasing books in the larger European centres. This visit carried him
first to London, and then to Germany in the summer and early
autumn. The winter and spring were spent in Italy, the summer
of 1857 in Paris and England, and in September he returned
home. While in Germany he renewed contacts and made new
friends in all the cities which he had visited previously. In Berlin
he was received each day by the aged Humboldt, and he dined
with King Friedrich Wilhelm IV, who discussed American politics. Everywhere Ticknor was impressed with the cordiality of
the people. From Dresden he wrote to William S. Dexter:

Changes I find on all sides; enormous, and something startling.
Many friends are gone, who used to be important to us. . . . But more
remain, I think, than could have been reasonably expected, after the
lapse of so many years, and we find them very kind. Like true Germans,
they take us up just where they left us. This I say, thinking of Dresden,
but at Berlin it was the same, and so it will be, I am sure wherever we
go in Germany, for the Germans are an eminently faithful people.[178]

Throughout the years Ticknor was one of the most influential figures in the social and intellectual life of Boston and of the country, for which his knowledge of literature and scholarship and his wide contacts had fitted him. He delivered public lectures, contributed articles to the magazines, continued until the close of his career an enormous correspondence with distinguished statesmen and men of letters, and when his death occurred in January, 1871, he had been honored by numerous societies and institutions at home and abroad.[179] German literature was not Ticknor's primary interest. Although his comments in his journal and letters on the subject are appreciative and sympathetic, they are naturally limited, for at no time did he assume the role of a real critic. He had, however, a profound admiration for German scholarship, which assisted him in making an important contribution to the intellectual life of his own country. Indeed, love of society and of learning, regardless of nationality, had full play with him throughout his long career of eighty years.

At the corner of Park and Beacon streets in Boston stands a fine, dignified old house of which Hawthorne, Charles Eliot Norton, and others [180] have written charming descriptions. A large stately library, containing one of the most exclusive collections of books that America has known, formed at one time the centre of this house, which for nearly half a century was the home of Ticknor and the social gathering place of Boston. Here lived the man of scholarly tastes, refined and genial hospitality, and intellectual attainment. "Certainly," writes Hawthorne of Ticknor in 1850, "he is a fine example of a generous-principled scholar, anxious to assist the human intellect in its efforts and researches." Our literary historians have paid their respects to the European discoveries of Franklin, Jefferson, John Quincy Adams, and Washington Irving, but full justice has not been accorded one who played his part in that distinction. Few are the lives in any country comparable to that of George Ticknor, who was not only educated but cultivated. As a student, scholar, apostle of learning, and master of the art of living, he was preeminently a man of the world, whose claims on popular memory are unquestioned.

Edward Everett

At the close of his visit to Boston in December, 1813, Francis
Jeffrey of the *Edinburgh Review* wrote to Edward Everett:
"From all I have seen or heard of you, I do not hesitate to say
that I consider you the most remarkable young man I have seen
in America." [1] Two years before this, Everett, at the age of
seventeen, had graduated with highest honors from Harvard,
and subsequently, while residing in the home of President Kirkland, had pursued graduate training in literary and theological
studies, serving at the same time one year as tutor in Latin. In
1814 he became pastor of the Brattle Street Church, the largest
and most fashionable church in Boston, and in the same year was
the author of *A Defense of Christianity*, a book which added to
his reputation as a theologian.

During his preparation at Exeter and as an undergraduate,
Everett had distinguished himself in classical subjects. Since
there was no provision at Harvard for any of the modern languages, excepting French, he received, as he tells us, [2] three
months' instruction in that language, which laid the foundation
for a reading acquaintance. His interest in general literature and
theology immediately following graduation led to the acquisition,
without the aid of an instructor, of an elementary knowledge of
German. A number of letters exchanged during this period between Moses Stuart, professor of theology in Andover Academy,
and Everett throw considerable light on the latter's early interest
in the subject. As an ardent student of German theological and
philosophical writings, Stuart acquired a large collection of German books and became a stanch advocate of the early study of
the language in this country. In the summer of 1812 he writes
to Everett urging him to translate Herder, especially the *Briefe
das Studium der Theologie betreffend*. "There is a vivacity, a
beauty," he states, "an enchanting something, *je ne sais quoi*,
which will please you, I am sure." [3] In March of the following
year he writes: "I should be happy to learn from you what
course you are pursuing in German, how much time you devote

to it, and what is the subject of Lessing's book which you are reading. As it is indispensable to me to learn the German, every communication on the subject of German literature will be very gratifying to me." [4]

Writing three months later of his own struggles with the language, Stuart adds: "It affords me much pleasure to find that you have made progress in the German language." [5] Meanwhile, he offers Everett use of any of his books which he has accumulated, and again urges his attention to Herder: "To translate one letter of Herder every day would be mere pastime for you, and this would speedily finish the work." [6]

In the autumn of 1814 Everett journeyed to the South, carrying letters of introduction to various notables. One of his letters was from John Adams, commending him to Jefferson:

I have great pleasure in giving this letter to the gentleman who requests it. The Revd. Edward Everett, the successor of Mr. Buckminster and Thacher and Cooper in the politest congregation in Boston, and probably the first literary character of his age and State, is very desirous of seeing Mr. Jefferson. I hope he will arrive before your Library is translated to Washington.

By the way I envy you that immortal honour; but I cannot enter into competition with you for my books are not half the number of yours; and moreover, I have Shaftesbury, Bolingbroke, Hume, Gibbon, and Raynal, as well as Voltaire.

Mr. Everett is respectable in every vein; in Family fortune, Station, Genius, Learning and Character. [7]

But unfortunately Everett got no farther south than Washington and, unlike Ticknor, did not have the advantage of making at this time the personal acquaintance of the eminent statesman. In the meantime, the Eliot Professorship of Greek Literature having been established at Harvard, Everett was invited to be the first incumbent, with permission to travel and study abroad two years, previous to assuming his duties. [8] He therefore resigned from his pastorate, and, following his formal inauguration as professor on April 12, 1815, sailed with his friend Ticknor for Europe. [9] Later, at his request, his leave of absence was extended, and he returned home in the autumn of 1819, after a period of almost five years, more than two of which were spent in study at the University of Göttingen. [10]

Many of Everett's experiences abroad, until the close of his

Göttingen period in the autumn of 1817, were the same as those of Ticknor.[11] In London, as we have seen, they called on Byron, from whom Everett received letters and advice concerning his proposed trip to Greece. In Göttingen the two young Americans lived in the same house, and with the exception of Everett's brief visit to Holland in 1816, to see his brother Alexander, then Secretary of Legation at The Hague, they did practically everything together, including excursions during vacation periods.[12] Their teachers and lecturers were more or less the same. Everett reserved six hours only for sleep, and according to Ticknor, "struck in his studies more widely than I did. . . . His power of labor was prodigious, unequalled in my experience." [13]

Everett's letters give his impressions of his new environment. He was amused at first by the Hanoverian pride on speaking the best German,[14] and was shocked by what seemed to him to be the universal use of profanity among the men, women, and children, and especially among the Göttingen professors.[15] At the University he spared no efforts to improve his mind and to acquire his training. His enthusiasm for German scholarship appears in the following letter, written some months after he had begun his work:

Seriously if you would read Greek or Latin with unmingled edification, you would do well to spend your leisure time for six months on the German language; which from the humblest grammar up to the highest commentary, is for its store of critical aids, as far before England, as England before America, — and I can use no stronger illustration. The idea that everything German is tediously prolix and dull, is one of the most absurd prejudices I know. There are more manuals, abridgments, popular views, and every sort of device to make learning attractive and easy than in all the other European languages together; yea, there are better accounts of English literature than are to be found in any English work. When I think with what inaccessible majesty the English Literati comport themselves over all others in the world, it is very edifying to hear them spoken of here with the same good natured contempt, that the Edinburgh Review speaks of American Literature. . . . It remains, I think, an indisputable fact, that the number and extent of their [the Germans] philosophical researches, far exceed everything, of which the English can boast. I confess I sit down very humbly and study their grammars.[16]

The subject to which Everett naturally devoted most of his attention was Greek under Dissen; but there were lectures on modern history with Heeren, on civil law with Hugo, and private instruction in Hebrew and Arabic with Eichhorn. Moreover, he gave some time to the study of modern languages, particularly to perfecting his knowledge of the German language, literature, and philosophy. Shortly after his arrival he writes that he has engaged Eichhorn to give him two hours a week of instruction in German literature, and that he is looking into the works of Winckelmann. "They are a world of novelties and beauties to me," declares Everett to his brother.[17] A few days later he writes of his difficulty with Hebrew, which is "not a little aggravated by my imperfect knowledge of German, and Eichhorn's galloping enunciation," and adds: "I am looking into Winckelmann's works and find them charming, more however from the subject than from the manner in which he treats it, which is arrogant; and the German arrogance is not so hearty as the English, nor so courtly as the French. It is the airs of an upstart gentleman." [18] At the same time he was reading with pleasure the poetry of Schiller [19] and Voss's *Luise*.[20] The following year he continued his reading of Schiller,[21] but became more interested in Klopstock. He writes his brother:

I am now working up some accounts and translations of Klopstock's Messias, which contain many poetical passages in the noblest strain. How do you think a poetical blank verse translation of the whole would go down in America? I think it would be popular among the lovers of German literature and profitable in the orthodox communities of the old country and the new. And now as a sort of a touchstone whether we mean to do anything: if you will translate ten books, I will the other ten, to be finished by next November, the best London printing month. If by my more frequent occasions with the Germans, there should be any hard passages in your books, which I could expound, it would be only to send me the book and the line. In general it is very easy. I read it like English. Please send me word.[22]

But the study of Greek consumed most of Everett's time, and further correspondence shows that he was reluctant to begin the task of translating. "If we were to finish and publish it, and it were not to prove good," he states, "I should only draw reproaches upon myself for having spent my time upon it." [23] Klopstock was therefore shelved until several weeks later, when he addresses his brother:

As for our poor Klopstock whom we left so piteously in the lurch last winter, the fit of translating him has invaded me again. Though I am less anxious to press it through. But I should like to have it ready to publish on my return to America, partly from the merits of the poetry, and the other natural motives to attempt something and partly for local reasons which you will understand. If then you still like the plan you can begin and I will too, and work on as I have chance and heart. It will be easy and pleasant, and just to avoid all difficulty in the division I will translate the odd books, 1, 3, 5, etc., and you the even and we will sooner or later finish it. It can really be done in a trifle of time.[24]

No further reference is made to the subject, and apparently the plan, to which his brother agreed, was finally abandoned.

But the story of Everett's interest in Goethe offers something more tangible and valuable to the history of the poet's relations with America. In October, 1815, Everett states that he is impressed with "a very curious play of Goethe's called *Torquato Tasso*," which he has lately read.[25] This was doubtless followed by the reading of other works of the poet, particularly *Dichtung und Wahrheit*. In June of the following year he writes to his brother: "Tudor [26] hangs a little upon my conscience, and I think of tossing up Goethe's life of himself into an article. But I have no heart to go at it, for I know I shall slouch it; and to send a slouching business 4 or 5000 miles to be printed, seems hardly the thing. But I have promised to send something." [27] A month later he adds:

I am now engaged in preparing a Review of Goethe's life of himself for Tudor. I do not know whether you have read the book. I have myself only finished the first of the three volumes. My review will consist chiefly of extracts, for who wants to hear me talk when they can hear Goethe? Some portions of the book were tedious and were omitted to great advantage. Else I should think an abridged translation would be a very popular book. I shall be very bountiful in my extracts for there are passages mightily after my heart. What do you think of this at the end of the 4th book, "For my own part, I too had a mind to bring something great to pass, but what it should be, was not so clear. But one thinks rather of the reward he is to receive, than the nature of the merit, by which he gains it; and I do not deny, that when I thought of this future unknown good, it seemed to me most attractive in the form of the Laurel, which is twined for the Poet's brow"? [28]

The review was completed within a few weeks and forwarded for publication. Later, in Weimar, in observing the criticism of

Goethe's Autobiography in the *Edinburgh Review*, Everett writes: "I pity the poor Boston wits, for the horrible embarrassment into which they will be thrown, by the comparison of this review with that which I sent Tudor of the same book. However, I do not know that I should write a line different, if I were to do it again." [29]

The well-known review which Everett contributed to the *North American Review* [30] in January, 1817, bears the distinction of being the first significant paper on Goethe in any American journal. It follows the narrative of Goethe's life to the close of the Wetzlar period and includes extracts supported by Everett's favorable comments on the poet's various works and personality. He condemns the translation by which *Werther* is known to the English public, praises *Faust*, which contains "flights and touches" not easily paralleled since Shakespeare, and is of the opinion that Goethe's life, as presented in the work before him, offers much practical philosophy in illustrating the conflict between the individual and the conventions of society. Everett concludes his discussion with a plea for greater American interest in the subject:

> In returning from these reflections to the work, which suggested them, and to the great man, who forms its subject, we shall rejoice if we have succeeded in increasing the interest our readers feel in him. Goethe is as yet but inadequately known to us, by the translation of Werther and the work of Madame de Staël; but it is an injustice to ourselves to indulge such an ignorance of the literature and the men, which are working upon the condition of the human mind with such powerful engines. One could wish that such works, as that before us, might be read in America, were it only to cross the race of English and French literature, which has been propagated so long among us, that it is in danger of running out.

As we have noted, Everett and Ticknor had been granted an interview with Goethe in Weimar during the previous autumn. It is difficult to realize that their visits occurred at the same time, so different are their impressions of the poet. Ticknor, it will be remembered, was favorably impressed, while Everett assumes a critical attitude. He described the visit thus to his brother:

> I hardly know whether to try to tell you any more of my experiences, as in the multitude of them, it is hard to choose. However, at

Weimar we saw Goethe. As I gave Ma a high-flown account of the interview, I will state to you the facts as they were. We had letters to him from particular friends of his here, Mr. and Mrs. Sartorius, and one from Wolff. There was also a letter from Mrs. S. to one Professor Riemer, author of the best Manual Greek Lexicon, who had lived nine years in Goethe's house, and who was to conduct us to him, in one of his mollissima tempora fandi. He informed us that he had used, indeed, to sacrifice much time to Mr. G., but was now obliged to live for himself and wife, and that this had produced a coldness between G. and him. This I thought was rather stumbling over the threshold. The next morning we sent our letters, and asked at what time we should wait upon him, and were told at eleven. At the appointed time we went. He was very stiff and cold, not to say gauche and awkward. His head was grey, some of his front teeth gone, and his eyes watery with age. He was oppressed at feeling that we were gazing at him, looked restlessly out of the window, at which he sat, and talked low and anxiously. He spoke of Byron, and admired "The Corsair," he ascribed the English eloquence to the influence of parliamentary speaking, and asked a few questions about America. He spoke, however, with no interest, on anything. Then we went, he did not ask us to call again, but offered us some letters to Jena. These he did not send that day, nor the two next, though the day after our call he sent his servant with his card, by way of returning it, at half-past eight. This I suppose he thought was English manners, but he is mistaken. The evening of the third day we called on him again. His servant brought us down word that the Minister was sorry he could not see us, giving no reason and not saying when he should be disengaged. At Jena we found by the merest accident in the world, that he had written to the Professor of Mineralogy a note of recommendation telling him to present us each with a diploma of membership of the Jena Mineralogical Society, of which Goethe is president. As not one word had been said in our interview with him, and as I do not know a flint from a marble, till I see it in a tinder box, I thought it a very modest way of asking us to send them a box of American minerals. I forgot to say that the day after our call on G., George sent him Byron's "Siege of Corinth," which had been mentioned in the interview, of which he did not even acknowledge the receipt. And thus ended our introduction to Goethe.[31]

Everett was glad, however, to follow up his acquaintance with the poet. In September, 1817, his young Harvard friend, Theodore Lyman, who was later to accompany him to Greece, arrived in Weimar with a letter of introduction and a copy of Byron's Lament of Tasso to Goethe from Everett, together with the request that the poet autograph "any volume of your writings" for the Harvard Library and also Everett's own copy of

Hermann und Dorothea.[32] Though Everett was the first to make this request, it was Cogswell, as we shall later see, who persuaded Goethe to present the edition of his works, in twenty volumes, to Harvard University.

Everett had made plans to remain at Göttingen long enough to take a degree and to extend his travels abroad, which would offer him an opportunity to visit France, England, and above all Greece. Cogswell wrote from Göttingen to Stephen Higginson that "the Professor" was making great advancement in knowledge and in fame. He stated:

> I hope that you and every person interested in the College are reconciled to Mr. Everett's plan of remaining longer in Europe than was first intended, as I am sure you would be, did you know the use he makes of his time, and the benefit you are all to derive from his learning. Before I came to Göttingen I used to wonder why it was that he wished to remain here so long. I now wonder he can consent to leave so soon. The truth is, you all mistake the cause of your impatience: you believe that it comes from a desire of seeing him at work for and giving celebrity to the College, but it arises from a wish to have him in your society, at your dinner-tables, at your suppers, your clubs, and your ladies, at your tea-parties (you perceive I am aiming at Boston folks); however, all who have formed such expectations must be disappointed; he will find that most of these gratifications must be sacrificed to attain the objects of a scholar's ambition. What can men think when they say that two years are sufficient to make a Greek scholar? Does not everybody know that it is the labor of half a common life to learn to read the language with tolerable facility?[33]

In the spring of 1817 Everett had forwarded to his brother his busy schedule of lectures:

> The Roman Law is from 7 to 8 every day. From 8 to 9 archaeology. This course is read in the great hall of the Library, for the convenience of the copper plate works, casts, etc. at hand. The Professor has been a couple of years at Rome and passes for a *recht gescheidter* man. He is lately come to Göttingen and this is his first time reading. Then at 3 P.M. I have a course of Lectures upon Cicero's de Oratore, principally for the benefit of the Latin style. At 4 twice a week Greek syntax, and thrice a week the meters again, which you will again repeat is my *toujours Rerdrix*. From 5 to 6 private lessons upon the Art Critical, composition in Greek and Plato's Dialogues, and besides this, 4 days in the week, an exercise in speaking Latin. French and Italian to be studied at regular hours, and riding and dancing pursued at odd intervals. You will think it absurd to undertake so much, but I hope to have 5 or 6 hours for study in my room, besides; and all the students here who

pass for diligent hear far more lecturing than I. Cogswell hears 8 courses daily. But mine require some considerable preparation before and "revision" after, to borrow a bad word from Exeter; though you will be more than ever inclined to maintain it as impossible that any bad thing should come out of Exeter, as the apostle did that any good thing should come out of Nazareth. As I have already told you, I mean to pass the winter in Oxford, with leave of Providence, but my Dissen assures me that with diligent practice, meantime in speaking Latin, I may be able to dispute for a degree here, before I quit, which I shall accordingly strive to do, though it fills me with indignation that a person may pass through all our schools, academies and colleges, without being taught to speak a Latin sentence. Everybody knows how much more Latin is studied at our schools than French is with the private masters, and yet what would be thought of a French master, who should turn out a scholar at the end of 10 years, unable to speak a word of the language? Would he not be drummed out of town as a literary swindler? But our poor schoolmasters and preceptors and tutors are not to blame, they cannot teach what they never learned.[34]

The ensuing months were doubtless spent in hard labor. Among other things, Everett prepared in German a short article for publication in the *Göttingische Gelehrte Anzeigen*.[35] On the morning of September 17 his ambition for a degree was realized, for he received from the University his diploma as Doctor of Philosophy — "the first American," he informs Stephen Higginson, "and as far as I know, Englishman, on whom it has ever been conferred." [36] Thus his Göttingen experience came to an end, one semester after his friend Ticknor had concluded his studies. "I left Germany in the fall of 1817," writes Everett years later, "strongly attached to that country; and after deriving (in my opinion) very great advantage from my intercourse with learned men in various parts of it and especially from the course of studies which I pursued at Göttingen." [37]

During the winter of 1817–18 Everett continued his studies, chiefly Greek and Italian, in Paris,[38] where he mingled in the society of Alexander von Humboldt,[39] Benjamin Constant, Madame de Staël, Lafayette, and others. He chose to travel the following spring and summer in the British Isles, meeting everywhere prominent personages, as did Ticknor. In London he knew a large group, among them Murray, Gifford, Campbell, Wilberforce, Moore, and William von Humboldt.[40] In Edinburgh he was entertained by Scott and by Dugald Stuart, and

also was Scott's guest for several days at Abbotsford. He formed
definite impressions of Cambridge and Oxford. "There is more
teaching and more learning in our American Cambridge,"
Everett informs Higginson, "than there is in both the English
universities together, though between them they have four times
our number. The misfortune for us is that our subjects are not
so hopeful." [41] The winter was spent in Rome, and he departed
in February, 1819, for Greece. Finally, on October 7 of that
year, he returned home to begin his duties as professor of Greek
at Harvard.

As was true of his colleague, Ticknor, Everett had known the
flower of European culture and society, and had come home enthusiastic over his training, bringing with him quite a collection
of books, especially from Germany. The Harvard to which he
returned was slightly larger than when he had left it some years
before, but the spirit and general atmosphere of the institution
remained unchanged. He found, as did Ticknor, a restricted
course of studies, a small library, and a provincial faculty dom-
inated by clerical control. The department over which he was
to preside had recently acquired the services of John Snelling
Popkin as "College Professor of Greek," and later various tutors
were added for the elementary instruction, among them George
Bancroft, whose residence at Göttingen Everett had suggested. [42]
In the course of time Everett prepared for classroom purposes
English translations of Greek texts in German, [43] and beginning
in the spring of 1820 delivered from year to year a course of lectures on the history of Greek literature which contained an account of the life and works of every important author. He
probably recalled Goethe's statement that eloquence was out of
place in the lecture room, "for eloquence does not teach." Therefore, the lectures were free from the usual rhetoric of the young
orator, but were a powerful inspiration to the younger Harvard
generation. The influence of Everett's genius on the young
people, according to Emerson, who was one of his enthusiastic
students, "was almost comparable to that of Pericles in Athens,"
and "had the effect of giving a new lustre to the University." [44]
A further entry in Emerson's journal reads:

Edward Everett had in my youth an immense advantage in being the
first American scholar who sat in the German universities and brought

us home in his head their whole cultured methods and results, — to us who did not so much as know the names of Heyne, Wolf, Hugo, and Ruhnken. He dealt out his treasures, too, with such admirable prudence, so temperate and abstemious that our wonder and delight were still new.[45]

Far less complimentary is Samuel A. Eliot, who sent Bancroft in March, 1821, this comparison of Ticknor and Everett:

Ticknor continues to deliver the most admirable and interesting lectures; by far the finest course we have ever had here on any literary subject; he is a very admirable writer. There is so much taste and grace and judgment and moral feeling in his lectures that they are delightful. Everett's are of a different and I am very sorry to say I think of a far inferior character. They are crowded with all sorts of useless erudition upon an infinite variety of subjects; they want finish and eloquence, and are rather calculated to set forth the amount of the professor's studies than to do any particular benefit to the students.[46]

During the years of his professorship Everett contributed to the *North American Review*, of which he was editor, 1820–23, reviews of various German publications [47] and delivered many public addresses which show the influence of his German training. He corresponded with some of his Göttingen professors, and, among others in this country, with Jefferson on educational matters.[48] In 1820, in a long article on "University Training," based upon the report of the commissioners for the University of Virginia which had appeared two years previous, Everett commends Jefferson's plan for instruction in modern languages and in Anglo-Saxon. He reviews the history of University training in Europe and pleads for a more liberal policy toward higher education in the United States.[49] On reading his Harvard Phi Beta Kappa address of August 26, 1824, on "The Circumstances Favorable to the Progress of Literature in America," a copy of which Everett had forwarded to Jefferson, the statesman in graceful acknowledgment said: "It is all excellent, much of it sublimely so, well worthy of its author and his subject." [50] When Everett observed his own name among those who had severely criticised Jefferson for having imported professors from abroad for his University, he disclaimed to him:

My views upon the subject, it is true, I never tho't worth expressing; but having myself gone (at a period, when most men regard themselves as emancipated from academic restraint) and plunged into the cells of a

German university, and used all my influence — tho ineffectually — to induce our Trustees to import a German Professor in my own department, I may claim not to be suspected of so ridiculous and arrogant a sentiment, as crept into some of our newspapers, on the arrival of your teachers from abroad.[51]

The explanation was scarcely necessary, for Jefferson was well acquainted with the scholarship of his young friend. He reassured him in his reply:

I know the range of your mind too well ever to have supposed, for a moment, you could view, but with contempt, the miserable sneers on our seeking abroad some of the Professors for our University. Had I thought them worth notice, I should have asked of these Wits and Censors, these questions: 1. The seminaries of the U. S. being all of them first served with the choice of the talents of our own country, and, the mass of science among us still further reduced by the refusal of many eminent characters to accept academical situations, were we to take the refuse, and place ourselves thus at the fag-end of the whole line? 2. Would it have been either patriotism, or even fidelity in us to have sunk the youth of our state to a half lettered grade of education, by committing them to inferior instruction, and, rejecting that of the first order, merely because offered from without the limits of our Union? 3. And is this the way to advance the American character? We thought not, and as yet believe we have reason to be satisfied with the course we have pursued. I hope the only rivalship with our elder sisters will be in honorable efforts to do the most good possible.

I am happy in the expectation, which your letter authorises, that you will think our institution worthy of a visit; and I shall even hope, from your experience and kindness, to receive suggestions for its further improvement; than which, none would be more respected by me. I beg you to be assured also that no visit will be received with more welcome than yours.[52]

Strange to say, Everett had become quite dissatisfied very soon after assuming his academic labors. As early as April, 1821, he wrote to Judge Joseph Story, a Harvard Overseer:

You have occasionally, though undesignedly, planted a thorn in my side, by remarks which you have dropped, that you thought I would have been a good lawyer; — the rather as I find I am a poor professor. From the first week of my return hither, I saw that our university — as good I doubt not as the state of society admits — would furnish me little scope for the communications of the higher parts of ancient literature, and that a good grammatical driller, which I cannot consent to be, is wanted. But I find that the whole pursuit, and the duties it brings

with it, are not respectable enough in the estimation they bring with
them, and lead one too much into contact with some little men and
many little things.[53]

In short, Everett's spirit and style, as he confessed, were
cramped, and he longed for a public career. His request that he
be permitted to reside in Boston while performing his academic
duties was refused, and he was further disappointed in not being
sent on an expedition to revolutionary Greece. Finally, as
Emerson expressed it, he was attracted by "the vulgar prize of
politics," [54] and, with his election to Congress in 1824, entered
upon his long and distinguished political career, which, excepting the presidency of Harvard University, 1846–49, remained
continuous until his retirement from public life in 1854.

The following letter addressed in 1835, when Everett was
Governor of Massachusetts, to Blumenbach of Göttingen throws
some light on his further interest in German:

> So long a time has elapsed since I had the honor of writing to you,
> that I fear you will almost have forgotten me, as I am afraid also you
> will think I have forgotten my German, by my not writing to you, as
> formerly, in that language. It is true that for want of practice, I have
> lost the facility which I once possessed of writing and speaking it; but I
> still read it, with pleasure and ease, as I still retain an affectionate re-
> membrance of my German friends.[55]

Having accepted an invitation two years later to speak at the
Williams College commencement exercises, he prepared, it is
reported, an address on the subject of "The Influence of German
Thought on the Contemporary Literature of England and
America." But he found, at the last moment, that another subject would be more appropriate for the occasion, and therefore
the above paper was not presented.[56] His inaugural address, entitled "University Education," which he delivered as president
of Harvard on April 30, 1846, shows an acquaintance with German thought, particularly the views of Herder, and the influence
of German university training. "The satisfaction of men in this
appointment is complete," wrote Emerson, who attended the inauguration. "Boston is contented, because he is so creditable,
safe and prudent, and the scholars because he is a scholar, and
understands the business." [57] But Everett's brief administration
encountered many difficulties, chiefly of a disciplinary character,

and in curriculum matters he was, contrary to expectations, a conservative, quite oblivious at times of the liberalizing tendencies of foreign universities. Longfellow, who was then a member of the Harvard faculty, records in his journal for November 5, 1846: "The whole system of college studies is now undergoing revision. Everett wants to bring things back to something like the old order of things." [58]

Until his death in 1865, Edward Everett never failed in his allegiance to scholarship and learning, for which unquestionably his studies abroad had given him the first inspiration. Following his retirement from the United States Senate, he remained in constant devotion to the improvement of his country. He took the initiative, with Ticknor, in establishing the Boston Public Library, made it a substantial gift, and served as president of its Board of Trustees for twelve years. Moreover, he gave much time to various public enterprises, was in constant demand as an orator, and continued his enormous correspondence with men of eminence on both sides of the water. Many tributes have been paid to Everett as a public man, but equally pronounced should be the tribute to him as a scholar. He placed his stamp upon the intellectual character of the nation, and was an inspiration in the pursuit of classical training in the German universities to a long line of young men who followed in his wake.[59]

Joseph Green Cogswell

"BE ASSURED I shall be with you in Göttingen at the season of the vintage," wrote Joseph Green Cogswell from Marseilles in April, 1816, to his friend Ticknor.

Cogswell, a native of Ipswich, Massachusetts, and a Harvard graduate of the class of 1806, had spent a year in the practice of law, and had served two years as tutor in Latin at Harvard, having succeeded Everett in that position. He had traveled widely, and after a year in the south of France he returned home in the summer of 1816, determined to embark soon again, with Göttingen as his destination. The following September he sailed, having under his care Augustus Thorndike, a young Harvard graduate, who was to complete his education at Göttingen and to travel two or three years in Europe. After landing in Holland the first of October, they spent the month along the Rhine, and arrived on November 1 in Göttingen, where they joined Ticknor and Everett and were immediately known as "die neuen Amerikaner." [1]

Within a few days Cogswell was comfortably settled and began a heavy schedule of lectures at the University, turning first, as he expresses it, "all my forces to German." He was then thirty years of age, and found it difficult to adjust himself to the University routine. He expressed his difficulty to his friend Charles S. Daveis:

When I saw myself, fitted out in the style of a German student, with a large portfolio under my arm, trudging off to my lesson, with the regularity and punctuality of a school boy who fears the birch, it seemed that I must have gone back several years in life. At first I knew not how to reconcile myself to the situation of another period of pupilage, but habit effects anything. I soon made my tasks, construed my German and submitted to correction, with as much docility as if I had never known what it was to be myself a teacher and a governor. [2]

Shortly after his arrival, a chance remark by Dissen to the effect that he had been spending eighteen years, at least sixteen hours a day, exclusively upon Greek and was even then unable to read a page of the tragedians without a dictionary, convinced Cogswell that the subject was not to be included among his courses. "When I went home," he says, "I struck Greek from the list of my studies." [3] At first he devoted his attention to German, history, and the arts, as well as to instruction in the library, but later concentrated more upon his favorite subjects in science. At the close of the first semester he described his full life to Stephen Higginson:

Deducting the time from the 13th of December to the 27th of January during which I was confined to my room, I have been pretty industrious; through the winter I behaved as well as one could expect. German has been my chief study; to give it a relief I have attended one hour a day to a lecture in Italian on the Modern Arts, and, to feel satisfied that I had some sober inquiry in hand, have devoted another to Professor Saalfeld's course in European Statistics, so that I have generally been able to count at night twelve hours of private study and private instruction. This has only sharpened not satisfied my appetite. I have laid out for myself a course of more diligent labors the next semester. I shall then be at least eight hours in the lecture room, beginning at six in the morning. I must contrive, besides, to devote eight hours to private study. My health is now fine and a journey which I am soon to make into Prussia will provide me with new nerve and muscle, so that I expect to come to the work almost a Hercules. My old notion of preparing myself for a traveller in our own or other unexplored regions has lately revived with great force, and directed me to pursue what I have abandoned for history and philology; of my night hours I am to give one to Hausmann in Geology, one to Blumenbach in Nat. History and the third to Schrader in Botany, so that if Presi. Munroe or any else will send me to the sources of the Missouri and Columbia River, I might hope to bring back some better account of the country than Lewis and Clark have done. . . . I am not in the least Germanized, and yet it appalls me when I think of the difference between an education here and in America.[4]

The remainder of the letter is devoted to a criticism of American schools and to the contrast between the educational systems of this country and of Germany, with special reference to the famous institutions at Schulpforta, Meissen, and Grimma. His love of scientific pursuits gained a strong hold. In March he expressed his ambition to an American friend:

I have been led to believe that nothing remains for me in life but to prepare for a traveller in some parts hitherto little explored, where Science will be more use to me than Philology, History or Politics, and therefore I lay the ground work for more thorough geological, mineralogical and botanical knowledge. I have lived long enough upon my heart, I must now begin to live upon my mind. . . . I think I hear the call and I shall prepare to obey it.⁵

The vacation period followed, and Cogswell, as was true of Ticknor and Everett the previous year, spent several weeks visiting parts of Prussia and Saxony. It was on this tour that he first met Goethe, with whom, in the course of time, his relations proved to be the most interesting part of his residence in Germany.⁶ On his way to Göttingen in October of the year before he had paused in Wetzlar long enough to visit the scenes of *Werther*, and on the first day of his arrival in Göttingen had been presented to Charlotte Buff in the library of the University. In the home of Sartorius of the Göttingen faculty he had heard anecdotes of German men of letters, particularly of Goethe, with whom the family were intimate. He was told that when Benjamin Constant once called on Goethe in Weimar, he began "in the style of a true Frenchman to load him with flattery," stating that the world was wondering at the stupendous productions of his genius, and that he had secured immortal fame. Goethe is reported to have replied: "I know it, I know all that. I know too that the world regards me as a carpenter, who has built a ship of war, of the first rate, upon a mountain, thousands of miles from the ocean — but the water will rise, my ship will float, and bear her builder in triumph where human genius never reached before." "This," Cogswell states, "is vanity which can have no parallel. Next week I shall be at Weimar and probably see this strange beast, and then perhaps I may tell you something more of him." ⁷ On March 27 Cogswell arrived in Weimar. He reports later:

I went to Weimar almost for the sole purpose of seeing Goethe, but he was absent on a visit to Jena, where I pursued him and obtained an audience. From all that I had heard of him, I was prepared to meet with the most repulsive reception, but, as I actually experienced the directly opposite, you will naturally infer that I felt not a little flattered, and therefore will not be surprised if I should give you a more favorable picture of him than you find in the "Edinburgh Review." I sent him my letters of introduction, with a note, asking when he would allow me to wait upon him. In one of the letters it was observed that I had some fondness for mineralogy, and was desirous of seeing the great cabinet, belonging to the society of which he is President at Jena.[8] In a few moments he returned me an answer, that he would meet me in the rooms of the Society at noon, and there show me all that was to be seen. I liked this, as it evinced some degree of modesty in him, inasmuch as it implied that there was something beside himself, worthy of my notice, and as it was very polite, too, in offering to take upon himself the trouble of going through the explanation of a collection, filling numerous and large apartments.

At noon, then, I went to meet this great giant of German literature, the creator and sole governor of their taste. His exterior was in every respect different from the conceptions I had formed. A grand and graceful form, worthy of a knight of the days of chivalry, with a dignity of manners that marked the court rather than the closet, such as belong to Goethe, are not often the external characteristics of a man of letters. Soon after being introduced to him, with the politeness of a real gentleman, he turned the conversation to America, and spoke of its hopes and promises, in a manner that showed it had been the subject of his inquiries, and made juster and more rational observations, upon its literary pretensions and character, than I ever heard from any man in Europe. We talked, also, of English and German literature. I told him of the interest we were now taking in the latter, and found a very convenient opportunity to introduce a few words of compliment to himself, which was the least return I could make for his civility.

That you may not think I have made too great progress in German, I first observe that this convesation, which lasted an hour, was carried on in French. I suppose I might have managed the former; but I was afraid of going wrong, sometimes, with the titles of the Herr Minister von Goethe, and therefore proposed to him to adopt French, where I had only "Votre Excellence" to handle.

After we finished our literary discussions he carried me through the whole cabinet, and explained to me all its remarkables, with a facility that could not have been exceeded by a Professor of Mineralogy. When we parted he invited me to call on him, whenever I should be in Weimar, and so managed the whole interview I had with him that I left him inclined to enter the lists to his defense, if I should ever have occasion.[9]

In his diary Cogswell notes further impressions of the poet:

Introduced to him — person large and good — about six feet — a countenance expressive, his eyes large, gray, — manners very gracious — talked of America and its hopes and its prospects, discovered a minute knowledge of its physical and moral character. Spoke of Boston and its local situation, — observed that the productions of America had a character different from those of other continents, — crystallizations different, larger, on a greater scale, etc. — showed us the whole cabinet of the mineralogical society of which he is the head — explained all with great care and apparent knowledge, and was in every respect agreeable and polite.[10]

From Weimar Cogswell proceeded to Berlin, where he met various prominent figures, among them Savigny, the statesman, and Wolf, the philologist, who "employed most of his time in abusing everybody." Berlin offered fascination. "I would prefer passing a few weeks here before any other place I have seen in Germany," writes Cogswell to Ticknor, "because I am convinced it would be politically more instructive; man is a little more of an active being here than in most other parts of this country, and has some other instruments of operation besides books." Compared with Berlin, Dresden had no interest for him. He states later, "I like pictures and statues, but they are dumb, — there, nothing is to be seen of the chemical process which is now going on, out of which some strange combinations will be formed, I think." [11] After his return to Göttingen in May Cogswell became engaged in a tremendous program of lectures. He describes his daily work to Ticknor, who was then in Paris:

I go on very regularly, rising at four, study till six, then hear Hausmann on Geognosy, who is prime, as well in the understanding as the explaining of his subject. At 7 Schrader who teaches me very little; at 8 Welcker, who is exactly what you foretold he would be, abstract and obscure, always seeking to go where no one can follow him. . . . I really like him as a man and respect him as a scholar, — indeed I almost love him, since a visit I made him one morning when he talked to me wholly of you, and talked as if he had a heart and had found out also in some degree the worth of yours. . . . From 9 to 11 I am at liberty to study — 11, hear Hausmann privatissime in Mineralogy; this is accidental. A young man from Odessa whom I know had begun the course and invited me to hear it with him. I could not refuse such an opportunity of prosecuting a favorite science. From 12 to 1, free, — 1 to 2 in Botanic Garden or Library; 2, Heeren who lectures well; 3, with Reck; 4, Saalfeld in Northern History; 5, Blumenbach; 6, Benecke. . . . At 7 comes my drill sergeant and so ends the day as to the lectures I hear. At 8 I give Augustus one in Italian, and study as much afterwards, before 12, as accident and circumstances allow. With all this I do not want for exercise. I must needs walk 10,000 steps at least 4 miles every day. Saturday I make excursions with Schrader, and Sunday with Hausmann, who makes nothing of carrying us a round of 15 or 20 miles.[12]

Of this schedule of studies, no part interested him more than the valuable library training, following Ticknor's suggestion, which he received under the instruction of Benecke. Here, he tells us in his autobiographical sketch, he found the most systematically classified and arranged, and for its size the best, library in Europe. Benecke explained to him the arrangement of books on the shelves, the divisions and classifications, and made him thoroughly acquainted with its mode of administration. From this time on, wherever he journeyed in Europe, Cogswell was especially interested in public libraries and their bibliographical methods and organization. It was knowledge which was to bear fruit in later years in the plan of the Astor Library, for which his experience at Göttingen offered the original inspiration. He continued his weekly excursions through the surrounding country with Hausmann and groups of students, "all dressed in the uniform of mineralogists," investigating the various formations and carrying the usual equipment for the collection of choice specimens. Toward the end of May he was off with Everett and young Thorndike for several days' visit to Hamburg and Bremen. A few days later he confesses that he is overworking and has been ordered out of town by his physician to get recreation. This resulted in a brief journey to Cassel, most of which distance he covered on foot. On June 28 he and Everett set out for a pedestrian tour of one week in the Harz mountains, of which region Cogswell became enamoured. "It is like being among other people," he informs Mrs. William H. Prescott, "for they spoke another language, or rather languages, from what we had been used to hear, and their customs and manners carried us back almost to the ages of primitive simplicity. . . . In fact the life we led there seemed to belong rather to fiction than reality." [13]

As a Göttingen student, Cogswell did not know what use he would make of his training. From youth he had a great love for roaming and exploring, as well as for society. The thought of expeditions to Africa, and to the then unknown regions of the United States, particularly the Southwest, where he might apply some of his knowledge of botany and mineralogy, made a strong appeal. At all events, he became discouraged with his studies. He was proud of the scholarly reputation which his fellow-countrymen Ticknor and Everett had made, but felt at his age the disadvantages under which he was laboring, and therefore planned to leave Göttingen. In July he wrote to Higginson of his discouragement:

A man as a scholar must be completely *upset*, to use a blacksmith's phrase; he must have learnt to give up his love of society and of social pleasures, his interest in the common occurrences of life, in the political and religious contentions of the country, and in everything not directly connected with his single aim. Is there anyone willing to make such a sacrifice? . . . For my own part I am sorry I came here, because I was too old to be *upset*; like a horseshoe worn thin, I shall break as soon as I begin to wear on the other side; it makes me very restless at this period of my life to find that I know nothing. I would not have wished to have made the discovery unless I could at the same time have been allowed to remain in some place where I could get rid of my ignorance; and, now that I must go from Göttingen, I have no hope of doing that. It has been my misfortune to have grasped at too much, and now when I have arrived at a period of life, in which the mind can not be brought to new habits, to find myself in a situation like that of a private under the command of an irresolute captain at sea in the midst of numerous ships, when after successively selecting one and another as the choice, they are at last all making their escape — after casting about me to find to what account I might turn so many years of misused time, and the confused notion of things I have acquired, I see nothing but that of travelling as a discoverer.[14]

On September 6, 1817, Cogswell left Göttingen to spend the winter in Italy.[15] His journey south made it possible to spend a week in Munich, where he established personal relations with Sömmering, famous for his anatomical discoveries, Schilling, and others of the Royal Academy of Science, of which he was made a corresponding member in March of the following year. From Munich he passed to Vienna and through the Tyrol to Italy, arriving in Rome on November 15. Here he was welcomed by Ticknor, who wrote to Mrs. Prescott:

This morning the pleasures of 'Rome have been doubled to me by the arrival of Cogswell and Thorndike. . . . Since either you or myself saw him last he has acquired a new passion, which is now eating up all his faculties. Botany was the one that preceded it, but this new attachment to mineralogy is much more violent, and to me really alarming since he seems now disposed to make it the business of his life, and pursue it in a manner that will necessarily separate him from his friends, and defeat the usefulness they have so long expected from him. It is a perfect fanaticism in him, but it shall be no fault of mine if he is carried away by it, though as I have never seen any passion in him so decided as this, I confess I do not begin with too sanguine hopes.[16]

Among European countries, however, Cogswell felt more at home in Germany, and soon he was longing to return to that country, whose charm, he states, lies in its expression of the Middle Ages, bridging over the gulf between antiquity and modern life. With few exceptions, Italy was uninteresting to a mineralogist.

Italy [he writes from Rome to a friend] is a tame country to one who has known the delights of Germany: yes, life to me in this supposed paradise . . . is wearisome compared with the vigor I felt and the spirits I had when leaping from cliff to cliff amid German clouds. Thus I lived

"Through that which had been death to many men,
And made me friend of mountains,"

and there I learnt to admire nature and be enchanted with the "magic of her mysteries," and this is the difficulty, when one has enjoyed a life so poetical, everything else becomes dull and prosaic.[17]

During the spring and summer of 1818 Cogswell sojourned in Switzerland, covering on foot a distance of 1700 miles. In the course of his travels he visited two famous schools, that of Fellenberg at Hofwyl and that of Pestalozzi at Yverdun. The former had been established originally by the philanthropist for the purpose of teaching agriculture, and was intended for sons of the rich as well as the poor. Rewards and punishments were discarded, and the pupil was allowed to defend his own position when censured. "There was the greatest equality and at the same time the greatest respect," wrote Cogswell to Elisha Ticknor, "a respect of the heart I mean, not of fear; instructors and pupils walked arm in arm together, played together, ate at the same table, and all without any danger to their reciprocal rights; how delightful it must be to govern, where love is the principle of obedience." [18] The establishment at Yverdun Cogswell found disappointing. A brief entry in his journal reads: "Called on Pestalozzi and spent the day in examining his institution and minerals — hatred — and envy of Fellenberg — bad order — no obedience in scholars." [19]

From Switzerland Cogswell proceeded to Paris, stayed there one week, and devoted the following autumn and winter to England and Scotland. At Keswick he called on Southey, of whom he writes to Mrs. Prescott:

I found him, as you would suppose, from what you have seen of his various learning, exceedingly rich in conversation, ready upon whatever subject was started, talking well upon all and eloquently upon many, but discovering much less fancy than I had expected to find in a man who has created so many classes and hosts of imaginary beings. In fact he surprised me more in the extent and minuteness of his knowledge than in the display of his own genius and power. He is now, evidently, too much of a party politician to be a great poet; he talked of a church establishment as indispensable to a nation's security and prosperity, of hereditary monarchy as the only government suited to the character of man, of the impracticability of English reform, and maintained all the high church, high ministerial doctrines, with an earnestness I have found in no other man in England. As to America, like everybody else in Europe, he is totally ignorant of the character and spirit of the people and the genius of its institutions, but profoundly and minutely learned in its history. I was delighted to hear him say that Cotton Mather was a genius of high order, because I always thought him so myself.[20]

In Edinburgh Cogswell was on intimate terms, among others, with Scott, who entertained him and Ticknor several days at Abbotsford. "You would be charmed with this fellow," wrote Cogswell to his friend Daveis. "There never was anybody like him for simplicity of manners, good humor, spirit in conversation, variety of learning, anecdotes, and all that constitutes a pleasant companion." [21]

In the spring of 1819 Cogswell returned to Germany with his protégé Thorndike, who wished to perfect himself in the language. For this purpose they resided several months in Dresden, where Cogswell gladly availed himself of the advantages offered in the Royal Library. Early in May, on his way from Hamburg, he had paid a brief visit in Göttingen to George Bancroft, then a student at the University,[22] and to some of his former professors. "Blumenbach, good soul, made the welkin ring when he heard my name announced," Cogswell informs Ticknor. "The Hofrath and Hofräthin Sartorius were no less cordial in their greeting; and I might add the same of Eichhorn, Heeren, Fiorillo, Stromeyer, Benecke, and above all Hausmann." [23]

On May 4 Cogswell confided his state of mind to Higginson:

I hope yet to prove to those who have done me the honor to interest themselves in my welfare, that I am not a wayward, froward child: I am resolved to be reproached no longer with forming and changing plans of life and therefore I neither suffer myself to look forward to any particular course, nor to say to anyone, that I shall make this or that disposal of myself; when I return to America, I mean to listen to the calls of reason and duty and if these take me to the Poles or set me quickly down in New England, I shall cheerfully obey their dictates and go on my way rejoicing. I shall come home as soon as I can, and when there do what I might and what that shall be, I will even allow my friends to decide. I mean those of them who are reasonable and regard my future peace of mind and reputation — and now let us leave this subject till then.[24]

In the course of these few months Cogswell made various trips from Dresden to other localities. In Weimar he was impressed with the Grand Duke's interest in science, and would have termed him a model sovereign "if he were a little more moral in some respects." In Munich he fraternized with members of the Academy of Sciences, and an interview with the King of Bavaria left the impression upon him, he says, "of as much liberality in politics and religion as I want to see in any man, sovereign or subject." [25] At Töplitz he attended a ball at which King Friedrich Wilhelm III and others of the Royalty were present. He gives the following amusing description to Mrs. Prescott:

The king was dressed exactly like one of our country lawyers in court time, and forsooth at the end of the week when the clean shirt and waistcoat begin to lose their whiteness. He had on a Berlin Bond St. blue coat with gilt buttons, two of which were eminently conspicuous between the shoulders, it being somewhat short in the back, a quondam white waistcoat as I have said before, a pair of grays . . . and Suwarrow boots with tassels as long as the green ones which the Ipswich ladies made for the cushion of Dr. Dana's pulpit, a common round hat in one hand and a dandy-sticker in the other. It went against the grain to say "Your Majesty" to Royalty thus disguised, but as I was presented to him with the rest of the crowd, I could not dispense with it.[26]

Late in August Cogswell was again in Göttingen and received from the University the degree of Doctor of Philosophy. Bancroft wrote later to Everett of Cogswell's brief visit. "The philosophical faculty, however, had time to convene and make him Doctor, and print his diploma, which really makes a noble appearance, bearing on its face the names of various learned societies with that of the American Academy at the head." [27] Cogswell found it difficult to leave Göttingen friends, particularly

Blumenbach, "a noble soul, and one of the very few Germans who have taken hold of my affections." And it was "sad parting, too, from little Bancroft," adds Cogswell. "He is a most interesting youth, and is to make one of our great men." [28] In July of the next year Bancroft wrote to President Kirkland:

I think I have often mentioned how high a degree of reputation Dr. Cogswell enjoys here as a man of science. Every day gives proof of it. Blumenbach quoted him in his last lecture before the royal society. Hausmann speaks of his zeal and learning in a late number of the Göttingen Journal, and now I see last week Heeren acknowledges a favour received from "his learned friend." These are public testimonies, such as a man may be proud of, for they come from three of the most celebrated and most refined professors of Göttingen. [29]

The most significant and profitable feature of this second residence in Germany was the renewal of Cogswell's personal contact with Goethe. As we have seen, his first interview with the poet occurred in Jena in March, 1817. During the next two years, when Goethe was familiarizing himself more and more with America, considerable correspondence passed between them, relating chiefly to Goethe's proposed gift to the Harvard Library and to matters of scientific interest, Cogswell having forwarded to the poet certain publications. [30] Goethe, mindful of Everett's request of September, 1817, for "any volume" of his writings for Harvard, wrote to Cogswell on June 27 of the next year making inquiry as to the proper address, to which Cogswell replied on September 5, requesting that the books for the "University of Cambridge" be sent through correspondents in Hamburg. More than a year passed, however, before the books were forwarded to America. In the meantime, on his way to Dresden in the spring of 1819, Cogswell spent the entire evening of May 10 as Goethe's guest in Weimar. He reports this visit to Ticknor:

He was not merely gracious, but affectionate and playful even, — but he is breaking and will never do much more to increase his fame. I spent all my time in Weimar with him, which was one evening only: at supper he was unusually gay. His only remaining friend, Meyer, was present, a Baron "chose" whom I did not know, and a pretty little lively girl. . . . We sat till midnight, and of course you will conclude he must have been in glee, as such things are not often done in Germany. I made him talk of the literature of the day, and he confirmed all I wrote from Hamburg about the low state in which it is. He was enthusiastic in his praise of Byron, pronounced him the greatest and the only living poet, which was no small gratification to me, from its coincidence with my own opinion.[31]

Writing a few days later to Bancroft of this visit, Cogswell says:

At Weimar I saw Goethe; he received me very graciously and even cordially, I spent all my time there with him, that is from six to eleven at night; he was in fine spirits and as familiar and playful with me, as if I had been the friend of his youth. About nine we sat down to a petit souper, at which I got into as wild a frolic as I did at Blumenbach's; the company consisted of five, a pretty spirituelle little girl, whose name I did not hear, Prof. Meyer, the bosom friend and confidant of Goethe, a stranger Baron, G. and myself, and a right merry time we made of it. I brought Goethe out on the parting of the way, and particularly the English; he said Lord Byron was the greatest and indeed the only great living poet and you will readily imagine how much I was pleased to have my opinion confirmed by such authority. I must have been peculiarly fortunate in finding him in such a mood, for I am convinced he has not many hours now in which it would be pleasant to be with him. His appearance indicates this very clearly and beside he told me that he had grown fastidious and morbid in his feelings, and that it must be something uncommon to excite his attention in the least degree; this he applied to me as an American and not personally, and hence you will not charge me with vanity for repeating it. America in all its relations is now his paramount study.[32]

On August 17 Cogswell returned to Weimar for his farewell visit with Goethe. As was true of his first visit in 1817, he found that the poet was in Jena, where he was cordially received. He writes enthusiastically to Mrs. Prescott:

They say in Germany that he is proud and has no heart, but it has ever been my good fortune to see him when he showed none of his pride, and to be received by him as if he had a heart, and a feeling one too. I know not when I was more touched at parting from a person to whom I was bound by no particular tie, than from him. When I reached Jena he was from home. I waited several hours to see him, and, as he did not return till nearly night, I could remain but a few moments with him. "What brings you to Jena?" said he. "To take leave of you." "And how long will you stay with me?" "Half an hour." "I thank you from my heart for this mark of your regard. It delights me to find that you take such an interest in me in my old age, as to come so far to see me. Keep me, I beg you, in friendly remembrance." "Shall I write to you when I return to America?" "Yes, but you'll not wait till then I hope. Let me hear from you often while you remain in Europe." A little further conversation and I parted from him. He embraced and kissed me affectionately according to the German custom, and the tear in his eye convinced me that he felt, not feigned, what he expressed. Do not think I mean to make out of this a case to flatter my vanity. Goethe's attention to me has been highly grateful, I confess, but it gives me no occasion to be vain, because I saw clearly it was my heart and not my mind which interested him.[33]

Cogswell writes further of this visit with Goethe to his friend Daveis:

I never thought to have found such a heart in him, and it almost broke my own to say adieu to him when I discovered it. "And will you remember me," said he, "when you are surrounded by your friends at home; and may I believe that there is a heart in the new world which cares for me?" I do not presume to call myself Goethe's friend, but he parted from me as if he were willing to allow me such a distinction, and I parted from him as if I felt the value of it. I looked back upon the house in which he lived till I was out of sight of it, as I should have done had it been the abode of the dearest of friends. This year he is just 70, his birthday was celebrated in Weimar, Aug. 28, and on that account he went away. "I am too old," said he, "to take delight in the anniversary." [34]

It is not recorded that in these interviews with Goethe any mention was made of the poet's gift to Harvard. In the course of Cogswell's wanderings over parts of Germany, however, correspondence on the subject had been resumed.[35] On July 29, 1819, Goethe had written requesting further information for the forwarding of his writings, in order that, as he expressed it, "my memory may be made secure even beyond the sea." Cogswell replied on August 8 suggesting that the books be addressed to him in Dresden and expressing the gratitude of the University. He referred to other gifts to the Harvard Library by European scholars, and added "but there is no name upon its records, which it will be more proud to point out among its benefactors, than that of your Excellency." Finally, on August 11, Goethe sent to Cogswell an edition of his works in twenty volumes, together with a list of the books and a letter in which he said: "If you can, when forwarding to your dear fellowcountrymen these results of my studies and labors, represent me kindly to them, I shall acknowledge the favor gratefully." [36] The same day he wrote a letter of presentation to Harvard which was unfortunately lost, though the following translation, supposed to have been made by Everett, reads: "The above poetical and scientific works are presented to the library of the University of Cambridge in New England, as a mark of deep Interest in its high literary Character, and in the successful Zeal it has displayed thro' so long a Course of Years for the promotion of solid and elegant education." [37]

On September 21 Cogswell wrote from Dresden to Goethe acknowledging receipt of the books and again expressing his gratitude and that of Harvard. The books were forwarded through Hamburg to America, but were not received until March 20, 1820.[38] President Kirkland, on being informed by Cogswell that the shipment had been made, had addressed the following letter of gratitude to Goethe on November 27:

> The Corporation are highly gratified that the University in Cambridge New England is an object of attention and interest to this celebrated writer, possessing so elevated a rank among the men of genius and literature in Europe. They receive with great satisfaction the donation of his works for the Library, and return him the grateful acknowledgement of the University for this valuable proof of his regard.[39]

While Everett had furnished the original suggestion of Goethe's presentation to Harvard, it was Cogswell who finally induced him to execute the idea. The relations between them form an interesting link between the poet and America, for here more than in almost any other connection does one see clearly Goethe's interest in this country. He had for Cogswell more affection than for any other American whom he knew, while America owes Cogswell a debt of gratitude for aiding in establishing friendly relations between Germany's greatest poet and our oldest seat of learning. Cogswell never ceased to admire Goethe. Writing many years later, as editor of the *New York Review*, to Longfellow of Menzel's well-known attack on the poet, he said: "Menzel is unquestionably a man of high talents, but he is a one-sided prejudiced fellow, and I cannot abide him for his abuse of Goethe." [40]

With the exception of his contacts with Goethe, it seems clear that Cogswell was disappointed in the experiences of his second period in Germany. "I am free to say that my second residence in Germany," he wrote to Ticknor in August, 1819, "has quite weaned me from that strong attachment to it which my first

gave me. Dresden is not Göttingen." [41] From Prague, two
months later, he again wrote to Ticknor:

If Germany's literary reputation is not on the wane, or rather, if the
proportion of solid learning in the country is not diminishing, I am very
much deceived in the opinion I have formed during my last residence
there. . . . Wherever I have been, in Dresden, in Leipzig, in Jena, and
even in Göttingen, the great men have appeared to me small in comparison with their stature in former days, and in comparison, too, with
the real measure of practicable literary greatness. I do not except
from this remark any one of the present giants in Germany, not even
Eichhorn or Blumenbach; in my view neither of them is half so learned
as he ought to have been with the opportunities he has had. What then
do I say of our own scholars? Comparatively they deserve a vast deal
more credit than the Germans, for when a man loses the first twenty
years of his life, it is no small praise that he advances beyond the A B C
of any science. . . . Do not say I am contradicting what I have before
written and published. My doctrine has always been, it is the defects
in our education which is the cause of all our literary inferiority. [42]

In September Cogswell left Germany for a year of further
travel in other countries. Later in the autumn, in Switzerland,
he paid another visit to Pestalozzi at Yverdun, [43] and after a
winter in France and the following summer in England and Scotland returned home at the end of October, 1820.

He is the same admirable creature [wrote Ticknor], full of zeal for
everything good, and everything that will promote the cause of learning, not exactly as other people would like to have him, but always disinterested, always scattering good knowledge about him wherever he
goes, and exciting an enthusiasm for it in those he meets, from the
excess of his own. [44]

But despite his European training, Cogswell was without definite plans for the future. In Europe, as his letters have indicated, he was unable to commit himself to any particular course
in life. His Harvard friends, especially Ticknor, had expected
that on returning home he would join the Harvard faculty. This
prospect made no great appeal to Cogswell, who had declared to
Ticknor in November, 1819, "I cannot wear a professor's gown
at Cambridge." He wrote further:

I hope to see one institution in our country in which no person shall
bear that title who is not truly a scholar, a classical one, I mean, and,
as I am not that myself, I will not be such a recreant as to aid in keeping

up the hungering, starving condition of the minds of our youth, for the sake of my daily bread. I am more sensible than ever upon this point. The character I gave last winter of the state of education among us, is commendation compared with that I should now give, and it is by the instrumentality of Cambridge alone, that I hope for a reformation. In fact my scruples would be much less strong about accepting the same place in any other of our seminaries. . . . Now, the obstacles which oppose my being made professor do not apply with so much force to my being made librarian, and I do not say that I would not accept that office if I could have it. My deficiencies there would be somewhat counterbalanced by the advantage of having one who knows so much, practically, of the bookselling trade in Europe, and who could so easily enter into correspondences abroad, and if I could see that I was useful I should be contented and happy. I cannot go to my grave in peace while I think I have lived in vain in the world, and when I get back to America, I am resolved to embrace that course of life which promises me the fairest opportunity of doing good.[45]

Undecided for some time after his return home as to what course to pursue, but tired of roving, Cogswell finally accepted, in January, 1821, an appointment as professor of mineralogy and geology and librarian at Harvard. The position offered distinct advantages. His friends Ticknor and Everett were there, and Bancroft, as it happened, joined the staff in the autumn of the next year, following his return from Europe. The professorship was largely a nominal one, there being no definite fund for its support.[46] The opportunity, however, to teach his favorite subjects in science was attractive, though the lectures were not numerous.[47] The librarianship,[48] which had been held by Andrews Norton, made a more immediate appeal, since Cogswell had received considerable training in that field when abroad, and now hoped to organize the college library on the model of Göttingen. He therefore took most seriously this phase of his duties and at once began his reforms, systematically arranging and classifying the books.[49] "Cogswell is doing much good in the library, reforming it utterly," writes Ticknor in April, 1822. Later, in October, he says: "The library is in fine order. It is arranged on the same plan with that at Göttingen," and in February of the next year he reports: "Cogswell has put the library in perfect order, and is now finishing his catalogue of it, but the Corporation neither comprehend what he has done, nor respect him enough for his disinterested labor."[50] Harvard could not adapt herself to Göttingen methods nor to the educational ideas fresh from foreign institutions, and Cogswell became impatient with Harvard's imperfect system, particularly the want of liberal views as to the principles on which a library should be conducted. Bancroft likewise was more and more discontented with his position as tutor. Cogswell had formerly given Bancroft instruction in Latin, and in Europe they had formed an intimate friendship. "There are few men on earth that I have seen as yet, who please me so well as Cogswell," writes Bancroft from Göttingen to Andrews Norton in September, 1819.[51] A few weeks later Cogswell wrote humbly from Tours to Bancroft:

Why, my dearest Bancroft, you do not mistake me so much as to think I am vain enough to suppose you are the gainer in the contract of friendship we have made with each other. I have nothing to give you for your superiority in talents, virtues, and acquirements, and that you love me at all with so many disparities against me, I can hardly attribute to anything but the disposition in the human heart to attach itself to some one of its own kind, and that in the land where you now are, away from any fresh and flourishing tree to cling to, you were willing to support your affections upon my old withered trunk, rather than let them develop like ivy running on the ground.[52]

Therefore, when they found themselves associated together in Cambridge, they were closely united by mutual sympathies. One of their desires was to improve the educational system in American secondary schools, an idea which they had discussed in the course of their visits and correspondence with each other while abroad. Bancroft had inspected German schools, especially those of Berlin and the celebrated Schulpforta, with whose plan of instruction, discipline, and organization he had been impressed. Moreover, some of the letters exchanged between him and President Kirkland and Everett contained much, as we shall see later, on the feasibility of establishing at some future time a school on the European plan, particularly the German Gymnasia. Cogswell, as we have noted, had also formed an acquaintance with prominent schools abroad, including those in Switzerland. Each had returned from Europe with definite theories of education, and being weary of Harvard, they now determined to venture together on a new enterprise. They therefore gladly retired from Cambridge in 1823 to Northampton, Massachusetts, and established the famous Round Hill School.[53]

The prospectus [54] which Cogswell and Bancroft issued in June of that year clearly defined the purposes of the school and the principles by which it was to be guided. Northampton was chosen as the location because of its "salubrity and beauty," and its salutary influence of rural retirement upon the mind. We read the following:

The institution, which we propose to establish, is designed to furnish occupation for those years, which in France are spent at a *Collége*, and in Germany at a Gymnasium. A boy, who has completed his ninth year, is old enough to commence his regular studies, and to delay them longer would be to waste precious time, and (what is of still more moment) the period, when good habits are most easily formed. For learning the modern languages these years are so valuable, that the loss of them is irreparable, because during these a purity of pronunciation (we speak with particular reference to the French) may readily be acquired, which in after life no efforts can attain.

Pupils between the ages of nine and twelve are to be admitted, though it is stated "we hold ourselves ready to receive pupils at any age, however early, at which parental anxiety may be able to part from them." Methods of government to be used are "persuasion and persevering kindness," and full control of the boys' occupations is to be undertaken. We note the following statement: "The studies, which are to be pursued, are such as deserve to be esteemed essential to a liberal education. We wish to give a practical character to our institution, and educate not for an ideal world, but for the world as it is. We would make not laborious students only, but faithful and useful citizens." The subjects to be taught are English, ancient and modern languages, history, geography, and the elements of mathematics. "We hope to find a convenient time," it is stated, "for making all our pupils acquainted with the results of astronomical researches, and with the elements of physics, and also for initiating into the various branches of Natural History such as have a predilection for those pursuits." Latin is to be required, but Greek will be an optional study. Of the four modern languages in which instruction is to be offered, first rank is assigned to French. Italian is to be learned "as a recreation." German is regarded more seriously:

The German will require more labour. Its value is now recognised, and while we cannot promise to teach it to all our pupils, those, who are distinguished for the faculties requisite for acquiring languages, must not be left without the possession of this, which will introduce them to so much good literature, accurate thought and profound erudition.

It is announced that reading, declamation, and composition are to be emphasized through all the stages of the pupil's progress, that each day is to begin and end with devotional exercises, and that provision will be made daily for healthful sports and gymnastic exercises. There are to be two vacation periods each year, of three weeks each. Furthermore, it is added:

The subject of education is not new to either of us. We have both, during a long absence from our country, had the means of observing the most celebrated seminaries of learning on the continent of Europe, and one of us is familiar with the discipline and character of the schools of England and Scotland. It may be proper to add, that even while abroad we cherished the hope of one day erecting in our own country an institution such as we now propose, and that, to fit ourselves for the task, we spent much time in visiting and comparing those places of education which are in greatest esteem.

The school opened on the first of October, with twenty-five boys, ten of whom were day pupils from the village, and with one instructor [55] in addition to the two proprietors. Within three years the number had increased to 135, and the instructors to twelve, including competent teachers from Europe in the modern languages, in which subjects no other school in this country offered such advantages. Discipline and lack of sufficient preparation on the part of pupils offered at first a problem. In a few days after the opening Cogswell reports to Ticknor:

We rise at six and meet soon after prayers, study till eight, at which hour we breakfast, then play till nine, from nine to twelve Stunden, dine at half past twelve, play till two, from two to five Stunden, sup at half past five, play till seven, and then assemble for the evening occupation, which thus far has been reading only, as there was scarce one among the number who could read English decently. A little before nine they are dismissed and go to bed. Thus far all has gone on perfectly smooth, though a more patience-exhausting task was never taken in hand.[56]

He feels encouraged, however, on observing improvement in the manners, habits of study, and interest of his pupils, but states that not one of the number bears the mark of having had even tolerable teaching or discipline. Two weeks later he writes of his system:

My principle in instruction is to send a boy back to his place for a single error, which he might have avoided by care and diligence, and there is not yet one among the whole, whom I do not send back half a dozen times in every lesson. I do not form any classes, but allow every one to get as much of any book which he is studying, as he can do, in the time assigned for that exercise, telling him that he may recite as soon as he is ready, but cautioning him at the same time, that the least failure sends him back, and obliges him to wait till the rest have been brought to trial. You see, in this way, we lose the common motive of emulation, but we substitute for a desire of relative superiority, that of absolute excellence; and you know, we derive no aid from the fear of the lash. These two circumstances increase our labor very much for the present, but I am convinced the result will be worth the pains.[57]

After two months Cogswell reports that there are "no refractory boys," none who are even difficult to govern, but adds: "In the class-room they draw upon me for my full stock of patience, and that, not because they are noisy and rebellious, but because they are unreasonably dull." [58] However, a few days later he writes of the progress that he and Bancroft have made with some of the youngsters in their subjects. These were some of his reactions to the early months of his new experiment. In the course of time, as the school prospered and drew boys of considerable ability, no further complaint on this score was registered.

One of the prominent pupils, Thomas Gold Appleton, wrote to his father in February, 1826:

This school has done a good deal of good to me as to my manners, etc.; for, as you know, it is composed of boys from all quarters of the Union, as we have some from almost every State; and, on that account, the customs, phrases, and appearance of us Yankees seem strange to them; as likewise the flat dialect and strange pronunciation of the letter *a* by the Southerners seems disagreeable to our ears. On account of these dissimilitudes we are constantly quizzing one another; but I am sensible that the poor Yankees have the worst of it, as the whole school, masters and all, are constantly mentioning our faults — for instance, the pronunciation of been, *ben*, while it ought to be pronounced *bin*, the adding the letter *r* to several words that want it, and not pronouncing the *ing* in participles, and many other Boston peculiarities. The effect these things have had on me is to mend my pronunciation, cause me to walk straighter than before, and pay greater attention to neatness, which I am deficient in.[59]

The pamphlet issued in March, 1826,[60] repeats the character and purposes of the school, whose progress, influence, and reputation are noted with satisfaction. The list of subjects offered and the staff of instructors is considerably extended.[61] It is stated:

The question respecting the relative advantage of literary and scientific pursuits has been much agitated. We favor the former, because they exercise intimate and direct influence on morals; but education would be imperfect without the latter. A very considerable proportion of time is assigned to the Mathematics. We consider the study of them in connection with the languages so essential to the best discipline of the mind. The natural sciences are pursued rather as a relaxation and to quicken the powers of observation.

Again, we note the following:

We are deeply impressed with the necessity of uniting physical with moral education, and are particularly favored in executing our plans of connecting them by the assistance of a pupil [62] and friend of Jahn, the greatest modern advocate of gymnastics. We have proceeded slowly in our attempts, for the undertaking was a new one; but now we see ourselves near the accomplishment of our views. The whole subject of the union of moral and physical education is a great deal simpler than it may at first appear. And then, too, we may say, that we were the first in the new continent to connect gymnastics with a purely literary establishment.

The combining of cultural advantages with those of physical education, in accordance with the European schools, particularly those which Cogswell had observed in Switzerland, remained throughout the primary objective of Round Hill. Great emphasis was laid on various forms of physical exercise. Instruction was given in sketching, model farming, house building,[63] skating, swimming, fencing, and riding. There were frequent pedestrian tours through the country, when they would pause for rest and Cogswell would give a geological lecture, and one of the marked features was an annual excursion in the summer of considerable distance, an idea borrowed from the Swiss schools. In all these, as in many other sports, Cogswell was the leader and companion of the boys, whom he deeply influenced and who always cherished more affection for him than for Bancroft.

Cogswell, fourteen years older than Bancroft, assumed from the beginning most of the responsibility in the management of the school. Although he gave some instruction, when time permitted, he was the organizer, the father of the community, while Bancroft, whose relations will be treated later, confined himself more to teaching. Cogswell was proud of his constituency, and was a favorite with parents and pupils. "While it owed much to the proved scholarship and genius of Mr. Bancroft, the historian, and to the large staff of officers under him," wrote Thomas Gold Appleton in recalling his experiences as a pupil, "all 'Round Hillers,' as they love to call themselves, agree in attributing to the singular combination of admirable qualities in the character of Mr. Cogswell its prosperity and success." [64] Another former pupil writes:

> Mr. Cogswell was a learned man and a man of the world, and to him was largely due the breadth and liberality of the school, and its great success. The teaching was of no meagre kind, for Germany, Italy, France, and Spain each gave us of its best. But it was the friendly and pleasant relations of Mr. Cogswell and his masters with the boys, and the gymnastic and out-of-door education, which made Round Hill peculiar.[65]

From the beginning of its existence Round Hill received the cordial support of friends and soon attracted wide attention.[66] In the course of years it drew sons of prominent families [67] over the country, among them John Lothrop Motley, who was inspired to go afterward to Göttingen to complete his studies. Ticknor, in pleading for expansion of instruction at Harvard, in 1827, commented as follows:

> It would be easy to show how much more is done elsewhere, for instance, at Round Hill, where, without reckoning Mr. Cogswell and Mr. Bancroft, eight teachers, forming, I apprehend, the ablest body of instructors in the country, receive an aggregate compensation of $6250 a year and teach on an average 52 hours a day, forty-five weeks in the year, or including Mr. Cogswell and Mr. Bancroft, 68 hours a day.[68]

Jefferson, to whom Ticknor had forwarded a copy of the Prospectus of the school, also commented with appreciation and understanding:

This will certainly prove a great blessing to the individuals who can obtain access to it. The only ground of regret is the small extent of its scale, in the few who can have its advantages it will lay a solid foundation of virtue as well as of learning. But leaving it at the age of 13, they will still have a long probation of peril to their morals and industry. Nor do I see how 7 tutors are to obtain a living on the tuition fees of 40 pupils. Should this however prove a difficulty, the parties interested will doubtless find the sufficient remedy.[69]

Scholars and many other distinguished personages came from time to time to visit the school, among them Lafayette, on June 14, 1825, and Duke Bernard of Saxe-Weimar on August 11 of that year. The duke describes his visit:

From Mr. Cogswell's institute, you have a magnificent view of the fertile and well-cultivated valley of the Connecticut river, which, in this place, winds between two lofty mountains, Holyoke and Mount-toby. On the left, the lofty mountains of New Hampshire present a beautiful prospect. In 1824 this institution had but forty pupils, and in 1825, it numbered no less than seventy-four, so that Mr. Cogswell is obliged, although he has three large houses belonging to his establishment, to erect a fourth and larger one. The gymnastic exercises, for which a place is provided in the woods, with the necessary apparatus, form a principal part of the instruction of this seminary. The boys are entirely excluded from the world; but that they may not become too much estranged, Mr. Cogswell accompanies them annually in various pedestrian tours through the surrounding country. I visited Mr. Bancroft at his room. Both these gentlemen entertain the warmest enthusiasm for Germany, and the German method of instruction, and are determined to regulate everything according to that system.[70]

In a few years, in spite of his success, Cogswell began to be dissatisfied with his undertaking. In March, 1828, he wrote to his friend Daveis: "In the various situations of life through which I have before passed, a due portion of enlivening, or improving occupations has been mixed, but I am now on my fifth year of an entire devotedness to one object, and one which affords little or no intellectual gratification, and still less comfort to the heart. There must be a change ere long or I die." [71] The responsibilities of the position of schoolmaster were unquestionably too great for one of Cogswell's mercurial temperament. Unfortunately, too, relations between him and Bancroft began to be strained. Cogswell assumed more the care of youngsters, especially those who remained at the school during vacation

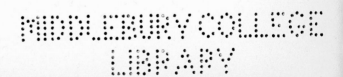

periods, while Bancroft, weary of routine and of managing im-
mature boys, spent as much time as possible in Boston literary
society. Finally, in March, 1830, Cogswell purchased Bancroft's interest in the property, but employed Bancroft one year
as an instructor. Meanwhile, the Round Hill Corporation was
organized and Cogswell, as the sole director, evidently felt renewed in spirits. "I have never felt younger, more zealous,
higher hopes or greater confidence of success than I now do in
the view of the prospects before me," he wrote to Mrs. Ticknor.
"I have had a burden upon me which bore me down to earth.
I am now free, and shall soar on my wings." [72] In the announce-
ment [73] which Cogswell issued in June, 1831, he states: "It is the
intention of the present director of the School, vigorously to
follow out all the plans of instruction and improvement, which
were concerted and matured by his former associate and himself,
and he trusts that it will be able to sustain the efforts it is making
for the cause of education." Several new subjects appear in the
list,[74] and classes, it is announced, are conducted with not more
than six pupils in each. There are nine instructors, including
Cogswell, but the names of distinguished scholars from Europe
have disappeared.[75] It is evident that the institution was de-
clining. There were fewer pupils, the financial management became more and more a burden,[76] and Cogswell soon became again
discouraged. His letters to various friends refer to his personal
disappointments and the impossibility of continuing his undertaking, especially when his health was failing and he was deriving no pecuniary benefit from his labors. "I am perfectly sure
the school was never more efficient in its instruction, or salutary
in its influence on character and morals," he wrote to the elder
Samuel Ward in July, 1832, "but various circumstances have
conspired to diminish its numbers, and therefore rendered its
receipts insufficient to defray the expenses." [77] In the spring of
the next year he made a trip south to investigate the possibil-
ities of another position. "I do not repine at ten years of lost
labor, nor at so much wasted money," he wrote later to Ticknor,
"but I am sure no attempt to provide such a place of early education as Round Hill was, will soon again be made, and I grieve
to think of its entire annihilation." [78]

Having determined to give up his struggle with Round Hill in

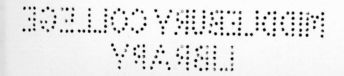

the spring of 1834, Cogswell wrote to Longfellow, endeavoring to persuade him to take over the school and offering him liberal terms. He pleaded thus:

I should be truly pleased to have you for my successor at Round Hill; I mean no flattery, but I cannot help saying that a place so beautiful ought to be in the hand of a gentleman of a mind and character like yours. I have made no disposal of the buildings as yet, and as there is no great probability that I shall be able to sell them at once, I would transfer the remainder of my lease, which runs until Jan. 1, 1836, to you on favourable terms: the property belongs to a corporation, a certain number of the shares being mine. The buildings are in fine order and as convenient for the purpose, as any could be, even if they have not originally been built for their present appropriation. . . .

Next as to prospects — in my view, they were never better . . . . Of my present pupils, you would have very few, as they are from the South and are to leave with me; but this is rather an advantage, than an objection. You will have no abuses to correct which always creep in among all communities long existing, and you can give your own stamp and character to the school. I gave notice sometime ago that I would leave, which prevented the return to the school of the pupils from New England. . . . Your own name and your own peculiar acquirements would secure you as many pupils as you would wish. There has been no difficulty which has troubled me so much as that of procuring teachers of good character for the foreign languages. Most of them are worthless fellows; this difficulty you would be entirely freed from by taking all those branches into your own hands, besides that a person to whom the English language is vernacular can always interest others who speak it, in any foreign language, which he himself knows, far better, than a foreigner.[79]

The idea appealed to Longfellow, who was then a professor at Bowdoin College and anxious to make a change. The results of his investigation, however, are included in the following letter which he wrote to his friend George W. Greene:

I heard that Mr. Cogswell of Northampton was about to relinquish the Round Hill School at that place — a school, whose renown must have reached your ears. It seemed to me a glorious opening, and I determined *instanter* to go and see for myself, what were the situation, capabilities, and prospects of this school. So off I started on the coldest day, this *mild* winter has vouchsafed to the children of the North. I stopped a day or two in Boston, to attend to some business of a friend and to get disappointed in a way, which you shall hear of anon. I reached Northampton safe and sound, and remained there two days, devoted to the business of investigating the School. The spot is lovely

indeed — lovely even beneath its mantle of snow. I have seen it in
summer — and I believe it one of the most beautiful places in New
England. But I will not pause to describe it now.

Mr. Cogswell's propositions were these: Rent of the buildings from
next June to January, *1836*, including taxes etc. $1,400. For use of
furniture during same time $350; in addition to which he required an
advance of $1,600. These terms — though they seem high — are not
unreasonable when everything is taken into consideration. The school,
however, is *run down*; and as nothing could warrant such an outlay, but
certainty of success, I found it would be necessary to pause and consider. On my return to Boston, I consulted with those whose opinions
I most valued, and they said the scheme was a bad one — that it would
be very difficult to get it upon its feet again — in short, that I ought not
to think of such an undertaking. My friends in Portland are of the
same opinion — so that I consider the whole business as blown into the
air — and I awoke as from a dream — vanished the pleasant visions of
our wandering through those romantic groves — and of the golden age
we were to leave in that still retirement.[80]

Cogswell of course regretted Longfellow's decision, though it
came as no surprise to him. "I had hoped to transfer Round
Hill to your hands," he wrote in March, "but I have not a word
to say about your decision. The times are indeed discouraging
for new enterprises. Perhaps they will change in many months
and you may be disposed to renew the negociation."[81] In the
spring of 1834 the Round Hill School was definitely closed; thus
ended an attempt to establish in this country an institution
which combined the system of the German Gymnasium with
that of Fellenberg and Pestalozzi. It was not only unsuccessful
as a financial venture, but was in some other respects a failure,
since it was impossible to adjust the methods and theories of
foreign schools to the existing educational system in this country. It was, however, the first serious effort to improve our
secondary education, and as an experiment it forms an interesting and unique chapter in the history of American schools.[82]

From Round Hill Cogswell retired, for a period of two years,
to Raleigh, North Carolina, where, in charge of an Episcopal
school for boys, he continued his efforts to put into practice
German ideals. "My cares," he wrote to a friend, "are quite as
great as they were at Round Hill, except that I have no house-
hold concerns on my hands; in all other respects I am equally a
slave, and a thousand times as much of one as any darkey I have

seen here. This is just what I cannot endure long." [83] Life here did not especially attract him. It was "a strange land," the countenances and manners of the people were strange, though they were, he states, exceedingly kind and cordial. He found the people primitive, and the youngsters at first rude and idle, but by a system of discipline "more severe," he informs us later, "than I ever thought of applying in New England, or ever supposed would be patiently borne anywhere," he succeeded in developing "refined, civil and industrious" youths.[84] Meanwhile Samuel Ward, whose three sons had been pupils at Round Hill, invited Cogswell to come into his family in the capacity of a tutor. Cogswell, therefore, gave up his position and came to New York in the spring of 1836.[85] The following October, however, he embarked with his friend Francis C. Gray to Europe for one year, spending the winter in Rome and the summer in Switzerland. During a short visit in Germany he wrote his friend Daveis from Heidelberg his impressions of Europe:

The churches, palaces, and public buildings generally seem to have dwindled, and even the public libraries, that I used to think so immeasurably great, were very well, but nothing more. In truth I do verily believe that we are much nearer to Europe, in everything desirable, both of nature and art, than I have allowed myself to think, and I rejoice very much at the new light let into the "soul's dark cottage." I shall love my country a great deal more since I have learned to respect her so much more highly, and shall no longer fear to lay claim to patriotism.[86]

On his return home Cogswell purchased, in 1838, an interest in the *New York Review*. "I am now proprietor of one half of said 'hum-drum' publication and shall do my best to impart new life and spirit to it," he informed Longfellow, in inviting him to contribute.[87] In July, 1838, Cogswell published an article on "National Education," [88] in which he expresses his admiration for the German educational system, comparing its advantages with that of England. Germany is the only country, he states, "where alone the science of education is thoroughly understood, and faithfully carried into practice." He advocates the study of ancient and of modern languages in their interdependence, and is of the opinion that, if not all the modern languages can be studied, German should receive first place in English-speaking nations. "French may be of more value for the world," he writes, "for the study, German is infinitely superior. A single shelf of German literature is of more worth to the scholar than a whole French library." Later, when Cogswell was the sole owner and editor of the *New York Review* (1839–42), he contributed an article on "University Education," [89] in which he compares the system of university training in Germany, England, and France, and pleads for the adoption in his own country of European standards of scholarship. He points to Germany as the country which has resisted all ideas of empiricism in matters of education and which exhibits "a degree of practical wisdom nowhere else to be found." He says: "It is this excellence and exactness of their system which produces this superiority; education is begun, continued, and completed upon system." Criticising the lack of an educational system in America, and the failure to emphasize thoroughness and sound learning, he writes:

In fine, the fault is owing to our wrong and crude notions on the whole subject; we have never troubled ourselves to determine in what way the precious years of youth could be most profitably employed; we are content to see it wasted, as if it were not possible that the waste could be avoided. The investment of time and treasures for learning is the only one in which we are satisfied with a small dividend, and in no other products but intellectual, will our pride allow us to put up with the mediocre.

As an editor, Cogswell accepted for publication various articles on German subjects. In 1840 Longfellow forwarded a review [90] of Menzel's *History of German Literature*, which had been translated by Felton, and received from Cogswell the following reply:

I have received the MSS of the article on Menzel and read it with care. I like it very much in every respect but one, it takes wrong ground (excuse me, I mean of course in my opinion only) on the subject of universities at least so far as the view is developed and what makes it particularly important for the present number, it is conflicting with an article of mine on university education, in which I state your principle most distinctly that adaptation to the country where an institution is, constitutes the first point of excellence. Nor do I abuse our own, I only contend for the *absolute* excellence of those in Germany on philosophic principle, and still doubt of their suitableness for lands in

which there has been no especial preparation for them. Menzel is unquestionably a man of high talents, but he is a onesided, prejudiced
fellow and I cannot abide him for his abuse of Goethe. I am sure you
will understand me rightly. I mean to keep the N. Y. Review open to
fair and free discussion, while it must preserve consistency and I assure
you our two articles clash too much to appear in the same number. If
mine were not in, I would give yours a place without a moment's hesitation. Suppose you keep it for the next number, modifying it a little, as
far as your conscience will allow.[91]

During his New York associations Cogswell had formed a
friendship with John Jacob Astor, whom he served as an adviser
in various ways, particularly in regard to collecting books, and
whom he urged to establish a public library.

Early in January Mr. Astor consulted me about an appropriation of
some three or four hundred thousand dollars, which he intended to
leave for public purposes [writes Cogswell in the summer of 1838 to
Ticknor], and I urged him to give it for a library, which I finally
brought him to agree to do, and I have been at work ever since, settling
all the points which have arisen in the progress of the affair.[92]

Astor wavered, however, in his plan of procedure, though he
commissioned Cogswell to go abroad in the autumn of 1839 to
purchase books and inspect important collections. There were
brief visits in Italy, Germany, London, and Paris. Of Berlin, to
which Cogswell devoted three weeks, he writes:

I was there in February, during the height of their season, and constantly in society, so that I made myself pretty well acquainted with
the principal people of that great metropolis, both in church and state.
It is now the first place in Germany, decidedly, for science and literature, and next after Vienna for splendor and show. It is not a little
curious for an American, accustomed to find society composed of those
who call themselves scholars, professional and business men, all having
sufficient leisure at command to be thus appropriated, to observe the
entire separation of the *savans*, in a city so full of them as Berlin, from
all the fashionable gatherings for wasting time. Humboldt was the only
individual of that class I ever met at any such places, and he is now
more of a courtier than a man of science. It is not their business, they
say, and they are perfectly satisfied to leave such things to those to
whom they properly belong. Their ambition never leads them to wish
for such a distinction. As a stranger and traveller I was desirous of
seeing as much of all classes as I could, and therefore visited the philoso-
phers in their libraries, when they would allow me, and the people of
the fashionable world in the salons when I chose.[93]

On his return in the spring of 1840 Cogswell spent most of his time with Astor, resuming his efforts in the interest of the prospective library. But having become discouraged with Astor's lack of decision, Cogswell accepted an appointment to accompany Washington Irving to Spain as secretary of legation. Irving wrote of Cogswell to the State Department:

He is a gentleman with whom I am on confidential terms of intimacy, and I know of no one who by his various acquirements, his prompt sagacity, his knowledge of the world, his habits of business and his obliging disposition is so calculated to give me that counsel, aid and companionship so important in Madrid, where a stranger is more isolated than in any other capital in Europe.[94]

Finally, when Cogswell was preparing to go to Madrid, Astor, after much persuasion, was induced in 1842 to proceed with the building and endowment of the library, and Cogswell resigned his office as secretary to accept the librarianship, which had been guaranteed him.[95] Therefore, as a result of Cogswell's suggestion and tireless efforts over a period of years, the Astor Library was established in 1848, the year of Astor's death, and Cogswell was empowered to proceed with the organization of the institution. From the time of its founding until the close of his life, the Library remained Cogswell's chief interest. He served as superintendent until December, 1861, and continued as trustee three years later. In the course of all this time he prepared a catalogue in four volumes and made four trips to Europe in the interest of the collection. Thus his early training in Germany, and his brief experience at Harvard, had paved the way for a notable achievement in the history of American scholarship.[96]

In 1864 Cogswell retired to Cambridge, Massachusetts, where he resided the remaining years of his life. His inspiring influence and lasting impression on young men were gratefully recognized by a testimonial dinner given him in Boston on December 1 of that year by Round Hill graduates. Present were twenty of his former pupils and three instructors who had been associated with him and who came to pay him tribute. No one regretted his absence more than did one of the most illustrious Round Hill pupils, John Lothrop Motley, who was then minister to Vienna, and who later wrote to Cogswell in terms of deepest affection.[97] On this occasion Cogswell spoke at length of his experiences at

Round Hill. "Of my varied occupations in life," he said, "I look upon none with so much satisfaction as that of my labors at Round Hill, endeavoring to train up ingenuous youth 'to the love of learning and the admiration of virtue.' You, my friends, are witnesses to the world that I did not labor in vain." The loyalty and affection of Cogswell's old pupils was abiding, and when his death occurred in November, 1871, they presented a marble bust of him to the Harvard Library and erected over his grave in Ipswich a simple monument, which bears, in addition to name and dates, the words: "Erected by Pupils of Round Hill, In Affectionate Remembrance."

As a teacher, editor, and librarian, Joseph Green Cogswell gave abundant evidence of his European training. While the years at the Round Hill School were unquestionably the most influential of his life, his later work, as the founder and organizer of the Astor Library, constitutes his greatest service to American scholarship. His long career is devoid of brilliant display, but he had contacts which bore fruit, and he never failed to direct his powers toward the improvement of his country. He was one of the most cultured and public-spirited men of his time, and deserves full recognition, along with Ticknor, Everett, and others, as an important mediator between Europe and America and as a distinguished figure in the intellectual progress of our country.

George Bancroft

On August 14, 1818, George Bancroft arrived in Göttingen, as a student successor to Ticknor, Everett, and Cogswell. He had prepared for college at Exeter Academy, where he distinguished himself in the classics, and in 1817 had graduated with honors from Harvard, when less than seventeen years of age. The following year he pursued graduate courses, residing in the home of Levi Hedge, whose son, Frederic Henry Hedge, was sent under his care to Germany for several years of study in various schools. During his undergraduate years, Bancroft had come under the instruction of Everett, then tutor in Latin, and of his successor, Cogswell, and had formed an intimate friendship with President Kirkland and Andrews Norton, the college librarian. Upon the recommendation of Everett, who wrote from Europe to President Kirkland, urging that someone should follow him at Göttingen, the Harvard Corporation concluded to send "little Bancroft," as Cogswell called him, to Germany on a scholarship of $1700 per annum for a period of three years,[1] to pursue theological studies and to become, as President Kirkland expressed it, "an accomplished philologian and biblical critic, able to expound and defend the Revelation of God." Therefore, contrary to the advice of John Adams, who expressed his opinion in no uncertain terms that Americans should be educated in their own country,[2] Bancroft and Hedge, the future distinguished professor of German at Harvard, sailed on June 27, 1818, for Germany. On arriving in Holland Bancroft received letters of introduction and advice from Everett, and from The Hague he wrote to Andrews Norton: "Tomorrow I depart for Göttingen. Surely a residence of three years among a new people must much change my manners and habits and character." [3]

On August 14 Bancroft arrived in Göttingen to begin his residence, and was greeted at once by town and gown riots, resulting in the interference of the Hanoverian Government for the restoration of order. He wrote immediately to President Kirkland: "Indeed, I have felt proud of home, and the good discipline that reigns there, and though there remain many things to be transplanted and naturalized among us, yet surely the foundation of your University is more solid, and the system of internal government more effective and more admirable than in the institutions of Germany." [4] Such was Bancroft's conviction on the day after his arrival. Within a short time he was comfortably established,[5] and had presented letters of introduction from Everett to members of the Göttingen faculty, particularly to Benecke, the patron of all Americans, and to Gauss, Blumenbach, Eichhorn, and Dissen.

Numerous letters to his parents and to Everett, President Kirkland, and Andrews Norton give his impressions and experiences. On September 5 he writes to Norton of the advantages of the University, the scholarship, and the men of learning. "I have come to the land of learning, of literature, of science," he says. "I have come to the pure fountains of wisdom, that I may drink of her unpolluted waters and be refreshed." A month later he writes at length to his father of the general equipment of the University, its faculty, and its advantages:

The University has no splendid buildings — economy is the rule of the day. Nothing is spent in vain, and since a plain building will answer as well as any other to hold their Library, they think the better to spend their gold in collecting new books than in ornament and display. Notwithstanding all this, everything that is necessary for the purpose of instruction, or the dignity of the Institution is procured at once, without hesitation or meanness in the use of money. They have a grand botanical garden, an anatomical Hall, an admirable observatory, superintended by one of the best astronomers in the world, several hospitals for the poor and sick, by means of which excellent Physicians are educated, a museum (though not very good), and a library of more than two hundred thousand books. This is by no means all. They have a large body of learned and powerful men collected here, men of talent, ardour and miraculous industry, and by these is this fine instrument put in motion.[6]

Although Bancroft entered upon his university life at Göttingen with an elementary knowledge of German,[7] it was his first concern, as it had been with his American predecessors, to perfect himself in the language, in order to be able to follow the lectures in his major subjects. From Leyden on August 4 he had written to Everett: "I will learn to use German with propriety and readiness in conversation." Immediately after his arrival in Göttingen he writes that the first month or two must be passed in learning the German language "for conversation," for which purpose he is spending an hour each day with his tutor, Benecke.[8] In the autumn he "went on slovenly learning" the language.[9] Meanwhile he was reading the German classics. His earliest impressions of Goethe were based, not only on direct reading of his writings, but on anecdotes that were current in Göttingen. In the home of Blumenbach he heard stories of the poet's personal habits and of his disappointment in the reception of his treatise on optics.[10] He writes to Norton:

> Goethe, they tell me, is a large stout man of some seventy years, fond of amusement and mirth, fonder of eating and drinking, and notwithstanding his love of good living and good company, is possessed of some majesty and state. Beside his works in every kind of poetry and romance, he has written on almost all the sciences. He is the author of a creditable tract on mineralogy, and what Blumenbach calls a very clever little book on botany. But not long since, being not completely satisfied with his fame, and perhaps thinking that he would demonstrate in mathematics that he was the greatest of men, he wrote a large work on optics, in three comely octavo volumes. The object of this was to annihilate Sir Isaac Newton, and gain for himself immortality at once. He secretly flattered himself that at least all the scientific world would raise a hue and cry against him for his audacity. The book was printed — and fell stillborn from the press, did not call forth even an answer. Some of the reviewers inserted in their journals the title of the book, adding merely one or two lines, in which they lamented that men would write books on subjects about which they are profoundly ignorant. Poor Goethe was mortified enough; for he had placed his greatest hopes on this unfortunate child of his brain, and the foolish mothers probably loved it more for its deformities.[11]

The journal for September 15 reads:

> I have as yet read Schiller's Abfall der Niederlande and several works of Goethe. I am only more and more astonished at the indecency and immorality of the latter. He appears to represent vice as lovely and exciting sympathy, than virtue, and would rather take for his heroine a prostitute or a profligate, than give birth to that purity of thought and loftiness of soul, which is the peculiar duty of the poet to raise, by connecting his inventions with the actions of heroes, and embodying in verse the merits of the benefactors of mankind.

He continued his study with Benecke through the autumn, was soon prepared to send his friend, the Reverend Andrews Norton, a specimen or two of "the high language of Germany, if it did not sound so flatly like blasphemy or vulgarity in English," [12] and progressed so rapidly that, in June of the following year, he records in his journal:

This morning I went out to a village in the vicinity and delivered a sermon in the German language. Many were astonished at my boldness in daring to do a thing of the kind, and feared I should fail. But I met with nothing which made me repent my having attempted to hold a sermon; on the contrary, the audience were uncommonly still and attentive, and on leaving the pulpit I received the congratulations of my friends, some of whom, though unknown to me, had been induced by curiosity or affection to become my hearers.[13]

On July 10 he reports to Norton: "What have I done since coming to Germany? I have learnt much, very much. Actually more than I had dared to hope. German, one of the most difficult of modern languages, I have learnt."

Bancroft had entered Göttingen with great ambitions. "How can I pass three years at the Georgia Augusta to the greatest advantage?" he had written in August, 1818, to Everett. "The first object should be the general improvement of the mind, and the second the acquisition of good learning." [14] Everett suggested that he concentrate at first on the classics, attaching himself particularly to Dissen, who in Everett's opinion was "the best scholar at Göttingen, and a most pure and highminded man," [15] while President Kirkland had advised him not to give his time so exclusively to critical studies as to unfit him for the ministry. On September 22, Bancroft matriculated at the University and began a course of lectures with Eichhorn in the New Testament, Köster in Hebrew, Welcker in Latin, and Dissen in Greek. The following year he added historical studies under Planck and Heeren, and made a beginning in Syriac with Eichhorn. That the hours of each day were fully occupied is seen by the schedule which he sent to Norton:

I rise at 5½, of course am ready for study at 6, from 7 to 8 with Prof. Benecke on the German language — from 8 to 9 private study, 9 to 10 with Eichhorn on the Greek of the New Testament merely critical; 10 to 11 with Dr. Köster on Hebrew grammar, and so forth; 11 to 12 the Philological Seminarium (a school where nine Germans interpret in Latin or Greek authors in the Latin language, the Professor superintending; besides these nine who interpret others called adspirantes are allowed to assist from time to time); 12 to 1 dinner and a short walk, 1 to 2 in the library to consult and read in such authors as are never lent; 2 to 3 I shall probably hear Tacitus Annals interpreted by Welcker, a famous man; 3 to 4 Aeschylus and Demosthenes de Corona by Dissen, the best scholar at Göttingen. From 4 till late at night I have several hours to prepare myself for my lectures on the coming day and to pursue my studies, which will relate I think particularly to the Greek for the present. These lectures are continued for six months. At the end of that time, I shall have become acquainted with the true nature and bounds of Philology, and can see if I will make of myself a mere scholar or a theologian.[16]

His enthusiasm for German learning and instruction appears in the following letter to Norton:

Yet I am glad that I am now in Göttingen. I would rejoice at it, were it only for the pleasure of feeling that my country is pure, in comparison with Europe. The sciences, too, are pursued here with the utmost avidity. All that industry and labour, and may I not add acuteness can effect has been performed. It is wonderful to see how a learned man can go back into antiquity, how intimately he can commune with her, how he rests upon her bosom as upon the bosom of a friend whom he has long and intimately known. If a period of history be dark, see how light it soon becomes, when reason and discretion are united with perseverance and patience. It is admirable to see the alacrity with which every author is studied, every manuscript collated, every work perused which can be useful, be it dull or interesting, or the work of genius or stupidity; to see how the coins and medals, the ruins of art, and even the decay of nature herself is made to bear upon the investigated subject. Indeed the national character of Germany is astonishing. It is refreshing to see what men can do, though labouring under the most discountenancing circumstances, and to think how nobly all good literature would thrive, if we could transport it to America, if we could engraft it on a healthy tree, if we could join it with religion, and at once enlighten and improve the understanding, and purify and elevate the heart.[17]

A further letter to Norton within a few days repeats substantially this attitude:

Yet much as I love my country, my home, I rejoice that I am now in Göttingen. I am contented, for I am treated kindly, I am happy, for I am industrious. Yet I know no man in Göttingen, whom I can honour with my whole heart and reason. I know no man, with whom I can actually interchange ideas, no man in whose vicinity I seem to breath purity. The sciences are carried on here as a trade, though an elevating and important one. All that labour, learning, and may I not add acuteness, can effect has been performed. It is wonderful to see how a learned man can look back upon antiquity, how intimately he can commune with her, how he rests upon her brow as upon the bosom of a friend. He can hear the still feeble voice, that comes from remote ages, and which is lost in the distance to common ears. The darkest portions of history become almost transparent, when reason and acuteness are united with German perseverence. It is admirable to see with what calmness and patience every author is read, every manuscript collected, every work perused, which can be useful, be it dull or interesting, the work of genius or stupidity; to see how the most trifling coins and medals, the ruins of art and even the decay of nature is made to bear upon the investigated subject. . . . If the national character of Germany be not enviable, it is at least astonishing; if her literary men are not distinguished for their piety, their example is only so much the more encouraging. It is refreshing to see what man can do, though labouring under the most unfavourable circumstances; and to think, how nobly all good literature would thrive, if we could transplant it to America, if we could engraft it on a healthy tree, if we could unite it with a high moral feeling, if learning would only go to school to religion.[18]

During the winter Bancroft enjoyed Göttingen society, the Sunday evening balls, where he learned to waltz,[19] and the homes of the professors.

Every foreigner is welcome in Göttingen [he reports to President Kirkland]. He receives honours which no native can hope for, and is allowed liberties which no German dares take. This is the case, partly because a professor feels himself flattered by seeing his house the resort of strangers, and partly because the large body of German students are wretchedly rough in their manners; and as their only object in studying is to earn their living, they have very little taste for society.[20]

A letter to his mother informs her that he has had to accustom himself to much that was new and disagreeable. "I am by this time, too, become quite accustomed to Germans and German customs," he says, "and were you to see me at present in my German costume, I am afraid you would hardly recognize me. . . . I am become quite Germanized." [21] His disapproval of German students appears in the following letter to his sister:

It is a strange world we live in, and full of more things than are dreamt of in your philosophy. My life on it, you have not formed a conception of a set of beings like the German students. I remember even now the first time that I saw a party of them collected and I believed never to have seen any of my fellow beings so rough, uncivilized and without cultivation. They are young, and therefore wild and noisy — live chiefly among themselves, without mixing in society, and are therefore careless in their deportment, awkward and slovenly. Many of them wear mustachios, a thing almost unknown in America, and all of them make themselves vile by a Beard, dirty and monstrous. Scarcely one of them uses a hat, but instead of it a cap which sometimes can scarcely be distinguished from a nightcap. This business of wearing only an apology for a hat I find so exceedingly convenient, that I have fallen into it. When the scholars are assembled for a lecture the collection of unpleasant odours is prodigious, and until the professor enters the room there is a great noise of whistling, talking and disputing, all of which however is instantly hushed on sight of the Professor though generally wound up by a short but violent hiss. This hiss is only a signal for order and tranquility. When silence is thus put in possession of the throne the professor begins.[22]

Further letters during the year 1819 describe the unrest among the students in German universities, particularly in connection with the assassination of Kotzebue on March 23,[23] and contain much information concerning the progress of Bancroft's studies. In January he was able to report to President Kirkland:

Your wish, I believe, was, that I should study with the thought ever on my mind, that I am to be for my life a student of Theology. I have now for six months laboured chiefly at the Greek and Latin Languages, making use of course of those books, which are to be connected with those studies. I have also laid a good foundation for Hebrew; and now in a short time I shall be ready, if you hold it expedient, to go upon the wide sea of oriental Literature. If my destination is to be that of a biblical critic rather than that of a Philologian, Syriac must give me work for a half year, and Arabic for a year and an half; and in case it were possible to fix my residence in the vicinity of a library rich in Arabic books and *Manuscripts* another half year would give a very good stock of knowledge of the language.

I act in all things according to your advice. In the mean time it is not to be concealed that neither money, nor, in the present state of the American public, fame is to be acquired by these pursuits. Perhaps too I shall never find one individual, who will have perseverance enough to learn of me the eastern dialects. On the other hand, it will be very fine, to be able to assist in raising among us a degraded and neglected branch of study, which in itself is so noble, and to aid in establishing a thorough school of Theological Critics. This is after all the only certain and effectual way of arriving at length at the minds of the people. Mr. Everett will bring to you all that is valuable of German philology; would it not be well, if I could assist him in his labours not so much [in his] own branch as in that sister one of biblical Criticism?

The plan of life, which I have adopted, indicates very clearly that I must become, either an instructor at the University, or a clergyman, or set up a high school. There may be no need of me at Cambridge; it may be either disagreeable or impracticable to found an honourable school; I may expect, therefore, that I am to become a preacher. Now for all these situations classical literature is good; and my attention will always be sufficiently devoted to the learned languages to qualify me for one of the two first mentioned places, if opportunity occur. Arabic and Syriac will not enable me to write better sermons, but will teach me to understand my bible more thoroughly.

I have said, I believe, enough to be intelligible. I will conform myself to your advice, and I pray that you will favour me with it by the first opportunity. I add one word about German Theology. I have nothing to do with it, except so far as it is merely *critical*. Of their infidel systems I hear not a word; and I trust I have been too long under your eye, and too long a member of the Theological Institution under your inspection to be in danger of being led away from the religion of my Fathers. I have too much love and esteem for my friends at home, and too little for those, who can trifle with the hopes of thousands, to suffer myself to be overpowered by a jest or a sophism. I say this explicitly, because before I left home I heard frequently expressed fears, lest I should join the German School.²⁴

President Kirkland was much gratified with Bancroft's progress, and replied urging him to include Oriental subjects among his studies. "But it would be very satisfactory and very useful," he said, "to have you thoroughly versed in the oriental department, provided it will not expose you to any other evil." ²⁵ In July Bancroft informed President Kirkland that he had definitely added Hebrew and Syriac to Latin and Greek. "Nothing remains now but Arabic," he stated, "and yet I entertain doubts of the expediency of undertaking it." ²⁶ To Norton he wrote with satisfaction of his progress in classical literature and in his new subjects: "I have attempted Syriac, and though I have not read much, yet I am so far advanced, that I can use a Hebrew dictionary, *i.e.* know where a Hebrew word can properly be interpreted from a Syriac one." ²⁷ In August he informed Everett that he possessed enough theology for use in America and that Göttingen was no place to study the subject. "'Tis out of the question to expect, that in any American university whatsoever the station of Professor of theology would be offered me or any one else, who had got his theology in Germany. Would it not be well, then, to add history to my studies?" ²⁸ But Everett assured him that while there was no objection to his studying history, it was a subject which could be studied at home, and that his knowledge of theology and languages would find a good market in America, where "the cause of liberality is stronger than you appear to think." [29] Cogswell showed equal approbation of Bancroft, as is seen in his letter to Higginson:

It was truly generous and noble of the corporation to send out Bancroft in the manner I understand they did; he will reward them for it. I thought very much of him, when I had him under my charge at Cambridge, and now he appears to me to promise a great deal more. I know not at whose suggestion this was done, but from the wisdom of the measure, I should conclude it must be the President's; it is applying the remedy exactly where it is most wanted, a taste once created for classical learning at the College, and the means furnished for cultivating it, and the long desired reform in education in my opinion is virtually made; knowledge of every other kind may be as well acquired among us as the purposes to which it is to be applied demand. We are not wanting in good lawyers or good physicians, and if we could but form a body of men of taste and letters our literary reputation would not long remain at the low stand which it now is.[30]

Vacation followed, and on September 4 Bancroft started with three German students on a pedestrian tour of six weeks which carried him as far east as Prague. In each city visited he was introduced to various German intellectuals.

Nothing has pleased me more in the places I have visited [he writes to President Kirkland] than to find how well remembered and how highly esteemed Messrs. Everett and Cogswell and Ticknor universally are. Wherever I go, the first question is always, do you know them? and whenever I meet a scholar who did not see them, while they were in Germany, he always thinks it necessary to give a reason for it, as that he was absent at the time of their calling on him, etc., etc.[31]

In Dresden, where he saw Cogswell, he learned, he tells us, to feel as much reverence for the painter as for the poet, and that a good picture is as overpowering and admirable as a good epic. On his return he stopped in Jena and Weimar for the purpose of meeting Goethe, of whom he had written only a few months before in his journal:

I do not love Goethe. He is too dirty, too bestial in his conceptions. There is nothing of a noble, high, enthusiastic soul in him. His genius is admirable. His knowledge of life wonderful. But the whole is spoilt by the immortality of his writings, by the vulgarity of his characters.

It may be, that all this happens in the world, but at any rate, this remains a blot on his fame, which all the waters of the ocean cannot make white and which justify in his censures a moral man, who cannot find in him a single work of genius.[32]

But now he was to meet the poet for the first time. The interview, which took place at Jena in the forenoon of October 12, is described in Bancroft's journal and letters. He reports:

I visited Goethe towards noon. He was talkative and affable, began at first with speaking of common affairs. Then the discourse came on German philosophy. Kant was mentioned with reverence. The state of America became then the subject of conversation. He seemed to think he was quite well acquainted with it. He spoke of several books on the country, of Warden's Statistical Account of America, and so on. Then too, Cogswell had given him an essay on American Literature, which appeared in Edinburgh. This essay Goethe praised much for the beauty of its style and for the liveliness and fancy with which it was written, and smiled as he mentioned the freedom with which he spoke of the different professions. Then the talk was of Cogswell, a lieber Mann — a man of great excellence.

He spoke with pleasure of the visits Cogswell had paid him, and so on. At length I, gathering courage from talking with him, took occasion to bring him upon the English poets. Byron he praised in the highest terms, declared himself one of a large party in Germany who admired him unboundedly and seized on and swallowed everything that came from him. Of Scott we had time to talk; of Wordsworth — Southey he knew nothing; of Coleridge, the name — had forgotten however his works. The author of Bertram was praised. "The tragedy," said Goethe, "has many admirable passages." Byron, however, seemed to remain the most admired of all. After this, Goethe asked after my pursuits, praised me, on my mentioning them, for coming to Germany, and spoke a word or two on Oriental matters. After this he asked what way I was to take the next day, and finding I was going to Weimar, offered me at once a letter which should make me welcome to the library. After a few more remarks I departed. In speaking of matters, I came into a strait almost as bad as poor Jennie with the Queen. Of Byron I said his last poem was reported to contain the most splendid exertions of poetical power, mixed with the lowest and most disgraceful indecencies. I did not think at the moment of Goethe's Faust. I mentioned, too, Byron's wife, forgetting that Goethe had not been happy in the married state. . . . I spoke a word, too, of Eichhorn's writing so many books, forgetting that Goethe had found no end with writing many.

As for his person, Goethe is somewhat large, tho' not very, with a marked countenance, a fine clear eye, large and very expressive features, well built, and giving at once a favourable impression. In his manners he is very dignified, or rather he has a sort of dignified stiffness, which he means should pass for genuine dignity. He walks amazingly upright. I found him quite in dishabille. He had on an Oberrock — i.e. a surtout, but no waistcoat, a ruffled shirt, not altogether clean, a cravat like the shirt, fast inclining to dark complexion. His boots were of quite an ordinary cut. No Dandi would have worn them. He received me in the garden.[33]

Some weeks later Bancroft wrote of the same interview to President Kirkland:

Goethe received me with unusual kindness, and spoke of America, as if our country was one of the objects that most interest him in his old age. I got him to talk about the present race of English poets. He spoke of Byron with quite as much admiration, as even John Randolph can ever have felt for him. Goethe is now exceedingly old, yet vigorous, dignified and active. He talks with liveliness and quickness, yet never relaxes from a high air of majesty, which is meant to inspire everyone with proper awe, though not more than half of it is genuine gravity of character, the other moiety being nothing more than the importance excited by the feeling of being prime minister to the Duke of Weimar. It was nearly twelve when I went to deliver my letter to him, and I went thus late, that I might be sure not to find him in negligé. Nevertheless I did find him clad in a most unseemly manner. He had thrown on a surtout, but without coat or even waistcoat beneath, and both his shirt and his cravat were become dark-coloured. But that is only in conformity to the German character.[34]

A further account of this visit to Goethe in Jena is included in a letter to Bancroft's sister in May of the following year:

The town has a pleasant situation, is small but neat. I was particularly gratified by seeing the first poet of the Germans — I mean Goethe. Perhaps of all popular writers alive, he is in Germany the most popular. Whatever he writes they are ready to admire, and he bends them to his taste and whims at pleasure. He is now very old yet still vigorous and firm in his walk. His features are large and expansive, and must once have been very handsome. His eye is dark and sparkling. He is well built, and dignified in his deportment and his hair is white and finer than I have ever seen on an old man's head. He received us in the garden. His dress was somewhat that of a sloven; indeed all the German professors and men of letters are horribly dirty fellows in their dress and manners. But Goethe has seen the world, and knows well what propriety demands. He wore a neckcloth of a dark complexion, and his shirt was not so light coloured as linen ought to be. He had on a surtout, but neither coat nor waistcoat beneath it, and his boots were not at all of a fashionable cut. But then he had an air of majesty about him, and his grey locks made him look so respectable that I wondered how I could mind such a trifle as his dress. Among other things which he talked about were the present living poets of England. He spoke of Byron in terms of the highest admiration. Every new work of Byron he seizes on with avidity, as he said. I was glad to hear our opinion of Byron confirmed by such high authority. On leaving him, he gave me a letter to his family at Weimar, which procured me an introduction to the library of the Grand Duke also.[35]

Bancroft promised to send Goethe a book on the early inhabitants of North America,[36] and proceeded the following day to Weimar, where he presented a letter of introduction from the poet to Kräuter, secretary of the library, and was entertained in Goethe's home. He found Ottilie "a very pretty little woman, of lively sprightly manners, witty and agreeable . . . knowing always what to say," and the son "rather a stupid and ignorant fellow." After being shown the poet's library and various collections, he left to attend a performance in the Weimar theatre.[37] Again, on July 10, 1820, Bancroft wrote to President Kirkland of the "profound state of tranquility" in the German literary world. He stated:

The veteran Goethe continues his course with industry and, one might almost add, with the vigour of youth. He publishes a journal, and besides that, he is now continuing his speculations on several subjects of natural history. A work is just commenced on "Morphology." Last autumn appeared one of the most lively and most pleasant works, which he has ever written. It was an attempt to write songs in the manner of the Eastern poets. But the best part of the whole was a dissertation, annexed to the poems, in which he gave an interesting description of the poetry of each of the most polished oriental nations, closing the volume with the praises of Herder and Eichhorn and Hammer, and so forth.[38]

During the winter months Bancroft faithfully devoted his time to work. He concluded that it was impossible to make much progress in oriental tongues, since the facilities at Göttingen for learning the subject were considerably restricted. Theology interested him less and less, and he therefore gave most of his attention to classical literature. Letters to President Kirkland and to Norton express his critical state of mind. He wrote to the former in January:

But the worse the weather is for amusement, the better it is for study, and as the society of Göttingen has no charms or rather no existence, we have no means of passing our long winter evenings but in conversing with the great through their works. It is really a very high enjoyment, that one can have at Göttingen, to hear men of profound learning and of good minds discourse from hour to hour on subjects, that most interest him, and then to compare what is taught by the living with what the dead or the distant have said on the same subjects. For in Göttingen are assembled the choicest instructors and all good books of all ages and tongues. Still the satisfaction of living at Göttingen can result solely from a feeling of gaining knowledge, for of amusements there are none here, and men of polished manners are not to be looked for. A German man of letters is very different from the idea formed of a scholar in America. Here learning is not made the companion in public life, nor the beautifier of retirement, nor the friend and comforter in affliction, but it is attended to as a trade, is cultivated merely because one can get a living by it. The men of science are distinguished from the rest of the world neither by pure morals, nor refined taste, nor love of fame. They are neither polished in their manners nor elevated in their ways of thinking, nor very agreeable, witty or interesting in their conversation. In one word, they learn Hebrew, because it is better to teach Hebrew than till the earth. They learn law or medicine, because 'tis more pleasant to heal the sick or get places under government than to make shoes or cut out coats as their fathers have done before them. To say of a man, he is a philologian is almost equivalent to saying he is of low origin, and to call one a theologian implies he is quite a vulgar fellow. And I have not seen yet an instance of a theologian whose manners were agreeable, and scarcely two whose manners were decent. In conversation they are dull, indulging in the most trite commonplaces; I have seldom been able to get any information from any of them, in company, never from a Göttingen Professor. The answer always is, I read a lecture on the subject, which you can hear next summer. . . . This degrading love of money is carried beyond bounds, and I should look upon myself as traducing the good people shamefully if I had not had too good reasons to know how true it is. How often when begging information for directing my studies, have I gained for an answer, "indeed it would cost time to tell you now, but you can hear what I have to say on the matter, in a course I am going to deliver next term." . . . The theologians form a very peculiar body. They have no idea of the sublimity or sanctity of their science. 'Tis reduced to a mere matter of learning. I never heard anything like moral or religious feeling manifested in their theological lectures. They neither begin with God nor go on with him, and there is a great deal more religion in a few lines of Xenophon, than in a whole course of Eichhorn. Nay, the only classes, in which I have heard jests so vulgar and indecent, that they would have disgraced a jail-yard or a fishmarket, have been the theological ones. The bible is treated with very little respect, and the narratives are laughed at as an old wife's tale, fit to be believed in the nursery. And yet these men who cannot believe the apostles are as children in regard to everything else. They will swallow any tale you choose to tell them.[39]

Such a communication undoubtedly made a profound impression upon the president of Harvard and the Reverend Norton, and Bancroft hastened to give them certain assurance. He stated to Norton:

I think that in these four months I have read little I need be ashamed of, except perhaps Anacreon, and yet I have not been hurt much by him. Little as I have seen of the world, I have learnt to see folly without regarding it as unnatural, and vice in a great variety of forms, without being struck by it as anything out of the way. I am afraid, however, that I may speak while I think of it, that you have taken up a too unfavourable opinion of the famous men round me from my letters. Everything I may have said of their vulgarity, their ill manners, their want of good breeding is strictly true. As to their want of fine feeling and hence of genuine religion, that is true also. But they are in general very moral, well behaved people, making faithful husbands and good citizens.[40]

The explanation to Norton was carried further a month later:

I am afraid you think me a very scandalous fellow for telling so many tales out of school and laughing at so many people, and saying so little of ye wonders and glories of Germans, who have been civil to me, or have meant to be so. You must not believe all that I say. I am very apt to make sweeping assertions, and to predicate absolutely, what is true only when qualified. Thus though I may not love the learned of the land much, I certainly wonder at them, and tho' I cannot esteem them very highly for moral feeling, they still have vigorous understandings, and though the style of most German books is tedious, and void of beauty, still the matter contained in them is wonderfully deep. A spirit of learning pervades everything. Their works teem with citations, and have at least the merit of being written for the most part by men who are masters of their subjects.[41]

And a letter to President Kirkland stated:

... When I first came to Göttingen I had expected to find in the learned something venerable and great, and it was a good while before I could learn to honour them for their erudition without despising them for their vulgarity and their meanness. But now I perceive that they make the best teachers that could be wished for; and the more circumscribed their views are, the more perfect they are in the few subjects they have attended to. There are none of them men of taste and feeling, men, who could appear in the world without running the risk of being laughed at; but the most of them carry on a trade with the labours of the soul, one selling Latin and another Greek, and a third philosophy and a fourth the art of poetry. But then they are all to be honoured sincerely; for they are capital tradesmen in their respective lines of business.[42]

This note of mixed criticism appears in some general observations on German learning and German literature which Bancroft recorded from time to time in his journal and notebook beginning in March, 1819.

German literature is truly a wilderness. The number of writers is immense, but the number of meritorious works can all be too easily counted. The German literary world is a perfect democracy. No man acknowledges the supremacy of another, and every one feels himself perfectly at liberty to follow his own inclinations in his style of writing and in his subject. A thousand new ways are every day discovered and brought to notice. They are entered, and if they lead to anything, they are followed, if not immediately deserted. No laws are acknowledged as limiting the field of investigation or experiment. No models are looked up to as exhibiting an insurpassable degree of excellence or as proscribing a model, which must always be held in eye. It is the science which is glorious in Germany and not the individual writers. On every learned subject one generation begins an enquiry, which the second pursues, and the third is scarcely able to complete. But when the work is finished, it is no longer necessary to labour through the writings of those who broached the subject, and who had only a dark inkling of the truths to which this investigation would lead. A German does not write for immortality, but for bread. . . . If he can write a better book on any subject than the last, he is content. His works supersede those that have gone before him, and are soon to be superseded by his immediate successors. In the line of poetry and polite letters there is little to praise, and scarcely nothing to admire. . . . The class of literary men in Germany is far different from that of any other land. It is composed of men of no high rank in society according to their birth. The most study because they wish to earn their bread. They must labour and become learned, but literature is merely preserved as a sort of business. Much knowledge is collected, that one may have a chance of selling himself at a higher price. Hence there is nothing of sublimity in the whole body of German literati. The literary class of Germany had little or no influence on the people. The learned write for the learned. . . . The literature of the Germans at present consists in a general measure of compendia. There is little originality, but much industry, accuracy and acuteness displayed in them. In this way they have incorporated into their own language all the discoveries of other nations, reducing them to a much less compass, and a more intelligible form. So for instance in voyage and travels the Germans have undertaken but few. 'Tis the English, who write so many. Yet the knowledge that must be hunted up in so many costly and thick quartos in England is to be found in Germany condensed in one little octavo. Of good Geographies the Germans have many, and they were written by men of science, which are far superior to anything of the kind written in any other modern language. Countless, too, is the number of translations. They are to be found everywhere.

Found elsewhere in his journal and notebook is his summary of the characteristics of German literature that we have seen expounded in the above passage and in his letters:

1. The multitude of authors in all branches.
2. The want of originality, — the multitude of translations.
3. The propensity to imitate in the lower orders of poets, etc.
4. The want of a great city where the men of letters might unite.
5. The little attention paid to style and beauty of language.
6. The division of the sciences, each forming a body distinct from the rest.
7. The little direct influence on the public.
8. The want of a moral spirit.
9. The democratic state of letters, no men acknowledged as masters.
10. The tendency to say new things.
11. German language not yet purified.
12. The Germans excel all nations in critical accuracy.
13. The sciences live and are advanced; individuals die and are forgotten.
14. The multitude of school books and compendia.
15. The cultivated state of literary history.

Also, his summary of the characteristics of German men of learning conveys succinctly his low opinion:

1. They are mostly from the lower orders of society.
2. They are at least very many of them book worms.
3. They have no taste for domestic enjoyment.
4. They have very little feeling for the beauty of devotion.
5. They have not good manners, such as to fit them for good company.
6. Hence they are not noticed in their travels except by men like themselves.
7. They have no nice feelings, either moral or of good breeding.
8. Hence no idea of beauty of style, of grace in speech.
9. They regard letters as a trade, are then on a level with mechanics.
10. They write for money, even the richer part of them.
11. They embrace a life of study from no high motives.
12. They are no more of everlasting fame than the common herd.

In the spring of 1820 Bancroft was ready for a second vacation journey. In company with four students, including a native of Livonia, a Polish nobleman, a Dutchman, and a young German from Hanover, he took a walking tour through the Harz. "I found the views often charming, very pleasant, very lovely," he informs Norton, "but I have not yet seen anything answering my notions of the sublime, nothing terribly grand or awfully bold." Another diversion added to his program during these months was a course in riding, under "the celebrated Ayner, an adept in the art of *equery* and vociferation." [43] Meanwhile, when the Fourth of July arrived, Bancroft found himself alone with one other American, James Patton of Middlebury College,[44] and the two therefore proceeded to celebrate. "I am sure of it," wrote Bancroft to Norton, "never did two Americans deliver a more patriotic oration or more exalted poem, or think toasts more full of love of country than these two forlorn pilgrims at Göttingen." [45] Patton contributed the poem, while Bancroft delivered the following fervid oration:

Countrymen, friends:

Sweet and elevating is the festival, which we have now met to celebrate. We have come together to commemorate the era of the birthday of our country, the day that raised her to a seat among the empires of the earth, the day that gave her political existence, and secured her political importance. From the remote lands, where we now are performing our pilgrimage, from regions, where the hard hand of absolute power wears down the spirit of the oppressed, we turn our eyes with the greater longing to the home of our friends, to our own home. The heart of an American may justly swell in triumph on a day like this, and the scenes, which we are here obliged to witness, complaints of tyrannic violence which we every day hear, should only serve to make us remember the more frequently and the more forcibly the land of our nativity, land of the mountain and the wood, land of the valley and the flood, the land where freedom has planted her standard.

We meet to cherish and call into action our feelings of national pride, to raise our hearts in company, and borne up by mutual ardour to rise to a height of feeling worthy of the occasion. 'Tis well for us, that on whatever part of our history we turn our attention we have good cause for national pride. If we look back to the day, on which our country started into being, we see Hancock and Adams at the head of our councils, and Washington in the front of our armies. Search the pages of history, from the day when Troy was besieged to the day when Napoleon fell, all the world during this whole course of time cannot produce another scene so grand. Never was seen a cloud of men like these, so eminent for moral rectitude, for upright habits, rigid principles of honour and of religion, bravery in the field and wisdom in the cabinett. Many a bright name has the historic Muse written in letters of light on the tablets of time, but never a name like Washington.

Well then may we be proud of the origin of our country, and rejoice in the heroes that God gave her. Like Pallas from the head of Jupiter she started into being perfectly developed, and clothed in panoply — and like Pallas she made herself first known by the rattling of her armour and the clang of her spear.

Following the course of our history we may glory in the years which succeeded. Do but think of the grandeur of the scene, when the sages of America, the deputies of the people assembled to form a system of government for the largest republic the World had ever seen, to lay the foundations of a building, whose turrets might rise to the heavens, and which might last forever. That was the moment, when the wisdom of our statesmen shone clearly. The book of time lay open before them. They could there read the fates of nations. The stream of life was flowing by them. There they could see the courses which other statesmen had steered and grow wise by the lessons time gave them. They could see the rocks, on which other nations had split, and learn to guide the American ship gaily and triumphantly over the waves. The constitution was framed, order was established. Washington still guided the state, and she rose in dignity, in glory and in opulence. We see her redeeming her credit, combatting tyranny, establishing and securing her independence. Happy land! to which Heaven granted such a birth and such an infancy, in its birth more glorious than other nations in their maturity, in its infancy signalized by deeds of wisdom and valour.

As Adams appeared at the helm of state, storms gathered and the heavens lowered. But the firmness of our ruler bore us up against foreign menaces and internal dissension. Our fathers, too, tell us of the glorious war then waged by our young navy in the waters of the Mediterranean, when the Pirates of Africa were taught to respect the American flag.

And of the years which followed, who can think, without acknowledging the genius and patriotism of Jefferson. Time may have shown, that some of the principles of his administration were unfortunate. But he gained for us the vast territory of the West, and this deed alone entitles him to the gratitude of his country and to a glorious monument in the history of the world.

My countrymen, I have descended to times which still live in your memory. Need I speak of points, which you know so well? Need I remind you of the rapid march of our country to glory, wealth and power? Need I remind you, that the voice of civilized man is heard in the wilderness, where but twelve years ago not an American had trod? That the hum of business, and the noise and bustle of cities are heard, where in the days of our childhood the snake reposed undisturbed, and the wild beast formed his lair in security? Or call to your minds, how the trees of the great forests of the West are bowing beneath the axe of the agriculturalists, how the lakes and rivers of the wilderness are already covered and crowded with the vessels of commerce and trade? Oh! my countrymen, never was a land blessed of heaven like our's. Let us rejoice in her prosperity; let us exult in her glory.

Nor is it only in continued advances towards opulence and power, that our country has shone forth gloriously. The free states of America have produced their great men, fertile in genius and rich in valour. I will not recount to you the names of those, who have adorned and dignified our country, giving honour to the nation, that delighted to honour them. They live in our memories. Never can we forget the bright line of sages, who have guided our councils, the heroes that fought for and defended our liberties, the seamen who gained honour to our navy over the earth, and made even the shores of Africa and the cities of the world tremble before American prowess.

But were I to continue till morning I could not exhaust the grand theme, on which I was discoursing. The sources of glory to our country like the stars of heaven cannot be counted — Her future greatness cannot be predicted.

As for us, we need but look around us, and see the imperfect protection afforded by arbitrary power to man in his natural rights, the relics of barbarism, and the sorrowful oppression of the lower orders bequeathed to the present age from the times of feudal tyranny; and we feel our bosoms swell with gratitude at being born in a republic.

My countrymen, we are Americans. The arts and sciences of Europe cannot make us forget it. Thank God we are Americans. Come then; let us unite in the frugal but friendly meal. We are few in number, but we have the hearts of freemen. The love of country shall bless our repast.

In keeping with the exuberant tone of the occasion, the following toasts, evidently by Bancroft, were offered:

1. The memory of Washington.
2. The President of the United States.
3. The American flag. God bless our stars.
4. Our country. Perish the heart, that can forget thee oh! our mother.
5. The literary prospects of America. May riches bow to wisdom.
6. The American eagle. A terror to the vulture, may she never wound the lamb.
7. The speedy Abolition of Slavery. May our country learn to practice at home the sublime lesson she has taught the world.
8. The sweet nymph Liberty. Europe gives her high mountains to dwell on. America consecrates to her her most extended plains.
9. Our Country. The Asylum of the oppressed. May her benevolence not prove her poison.

10. Our literary institutions. Watered by the dews of heaven and quickened by the genial warmth of freedom. May they ever be the nurseries of enlightened Patriots.
11. The heroes of the revolution.
12. The memory of the day we celebrate. The birthday of freedom, the wonder of the world.

Throughout his residence in Göttingen, Bancroft had assumed, in most of his judgments, a superior and critical attitude toward the Germans. He had, as we have seen, an aversion for what he called their bad manners and customs, their vices and want of religion, all of which made a deep impression on the young New Englander. In one of his letters to Norton he stated that he had hope of "getting through the land without being essentially altered in his ways of thinking." Therefore, when Norton questioned some of his criticisms of the University he was impelled, at the close of his two years, to forward to him his final impressions:

I have been out on a walk through our fine vale this afternoon, and have been thinking of you all the while. 'Tis now exactly two years since I entered this city of the learned, where I have passed the last days of boyhood, some gay hours and some unpleasant ones. The continued expressions and evidences of recollecting friendship have been most grateful to me, and perhaps doubly so, because there were none near me, who had any claims to my affections. Well! two years have rolled away most rapidly, and another moon sees me turn my back on the spires of Göttingen. This changing place is making one step towards returning home, and though my wanderings are to continue many a month yet, I feel that the hardest and most trying part is over. I have not however finished my life as a German student. One term yet is to be spent among the wise of Berlin, and then adieu to the northern universities. If I were to speak in general of the mode of instruction at this institution, I should say that for practical purposes it was the best that could be invented. It is not the best method to quicken talent, or cultivate taste, but for rapid advancement in knowledge, for thoroughness, and above all, for method most admirable. 'Tis a misfortune that the powers of the student are not sufficiently exercised in invention, and hence it comes, that the herd of compilers and translators is so immense. Everything is taught by lectures, from the rudiments of grammar up to the most abstruse parts of metaphysics. There is hardly an art, or a science, a language (of value) or period of history, about which lectures are not held. Some of the good consequences of this are: the students become accustomed to pursuing their studies with the utmost *method*; beginning with a course introductory to his science, and continuing then to hear a series of lectures on each separate branch of it. And then he gets a full view of the whole field. He learns what his science is, and what must be done to excel in it. This way of teaching, too, saves time and health, contributes to clearness of thought, for how much easier it is to comprehend the living voice than the dead letter? But an evil, and that to a very great and very extensive one, is: many students content themselves with the words of their master. They write down every syllable he utters, learn that by heart, and then think themselves very wise and sufficiently erudite. You might enter the room of many a student, whose library consists for the most part of his neatly written notes, bound nicely in black, and if you conversed with him, would soon perceive that he had brought the one idea from the lectureroom of Mr. Eichhorn, another from Planck, and a third from Stäudlin. You will not find much originality or much tendency to self-execution. Or ask a question, which cannot be answered out of one of the courses, and see how sensible an answer he will give you. For instance, an intelligent young Prussian from Königsberg called on me the other day, and among other things, spoke in unbecoming terms of the divine Prometheus. I dissented from him most vehemently; he answered: "To be sure I ought not judge as I have not yet heard the course on criticism." I mention these trifles to show you how sensible I am of the evils which may result from teaching by lectures. Nevertheless, I do praise the Germans' way for giving a young man exactly the notions he wants, guiding him in the newest and most direct way to a perfect knowledge of his science, keeping him on with general views, and teaching him clearness and method. Hence it comes that the land is rich in really well bred scholars, who know their trade in all its branches. . . . Now a word or two of the students. There are here many from good families, who prepare themselves at the University for life. These are in general well behaved, industrious, not at all dissipated, and by no means riotous. I assure you, I am astonished at the good order they preserve. But I have never found *one* or certainly not *three*, who were preparing themselves for elegant scholars, who had one other view than to develop and improve their faculties, and cultivate a taste for elegant letters. Alas, that it is so! But by far the larger portion of the students are men to say the least of the middling lower ranks of society. You know perhaps how strict the distinctions of rank are kept up. This has the effect of confining polished manners and in some measure quick feelings to the highest orders. 'Tis not here, as with us, where the son of an honest countryman is perhaps most likely to think freely and sublimely. Now these men come up to the University, and when they get there have no other aim than to get so much learning as is necessary in order to secure themselves the situation in life, they are longing for. The theologian gets just as much of Hebrew, Greek, the dogmas, and church history, as is necessary in order to sustain an examination before the consistory. A lawyer idles away perhaps the first months; but in his last half year works hard at the Corpus juris, that he may be sure of getting a license as advocate. Now this is by no means the case with all; (I have given over all general assertions) but it is the case with very many, certainly with the *greater number* of theologians. I should think of students of law and medicine too. Now in their manners these men are boors. My classmate Wright would make a most genteel figure among them. They dress, *all of them,* as no civilized man ought to dress; *many of them* like barbarians. I hope you observe how exactly I weigh my words. All wear coarse clothes, caps that once were clean, and change their apparel seldom; moreover their clothes are of such a fashion, that they would most certainly draw a mob after them if they appeared in Boston or Cambridge. *Some of them,* and here I have freer scope, dress I repeat like Barbarians: for to them I refer such a habit as that of wearing an apology for a shirt made of dark cotton, and worn till time's hand tears it in pieces. Now mind me: I cannot aver, that those men do not change these collarless shirts sometimes. But I know not why they are fastened as firmly behind, or why they are black or dark coloured, unless to save the trouble of washing them. At any rate, the habit came from the northern Barbarians. To barbarian practices I reckon the custom of wearing a beard on the cheeks, the upper lip, on the lower lip and the chin and under the chin. More hairy than the wild father of the Ishmaelites are many of these precious souls, that are here sucking in wisdom from the breasts of Georgia Augusta. Nay, but to see two of these two-legged animals meet one another in the street, after a vacation, and kiss each other thrice with their dirty beards faces and all, kiss each other thrice as lustily as ever Romeo kissed Juliet, this is a sight, which might melt even your savage heart to sympathy and teach you to have some respect for the soft emotions of sentimentality. I count it too a barbarous custom, to wear pantaloons, lined on the seat and down the inner part with such leather as in America is used for boots and shoes. Now the other half of these pantaloons being black velvet, they endure many a shock, and if I might judge, as of the age of a rattle snake by the number of his rattles, so of the age of such an article of dress by the layers of greasy particles of matter, which decorate their exterior, I should fall into extasies in admiring the economy of the contrivance. Now of these three marks of barbarity, it would not be difficult to show many a man, who has one of them. I do not remember to have seen many, who united them all in one and the same person. If I now went over to the kindred chapter of vulgarities, such as hawking and spitting during dinner, spitting I mean on the floor, wearing old clothes, eating with dirty, never-a-brush-seeing teeth, I should only mention a great many unpleasant things, which certainly are strongly exemplified at Göttingen, but which may be found too in other parts of the world. Now as to dissipation, there is none here, on a high scale. The vices which are common enough here, are all of a sneaking nature, and practised by the sneaking and low-lived. Chastity is a word named only to be laughed at. Religious feeling may be sought; but you would never find a bible at Paris. I will not say, that few students have religious feeling; only I may say, I never saw any signs of it. I never saw anything at Göttingen, that made me think the people cared much about God or his worship. Though they would be furious, if they knew any one said this of them. 'Tis the lower class, the poorer class of students, who have the least morals. Vice is cheap. A man of spirit, a gentleman, is in no danger of growing a profligate. Waiting maids and ugly women may be seen on the ramparts any fine night, and students follow them, but they are not the sons of good families that do this. Lastly, the class of men here for whom I have the least respect, to whom I should be most unwilling to trust my life or fortune, who to me appear to have the least high moral feeling, God forgive me if I am uncharitable, are the students of theology. After saying so much evil, I must add of the students, what I trust I have always set forth, their industry if not miraculous, is at any rate prodigious. As a body, the most prominent characteristick of the Göttingen students is their diligence.

Now before closing this letter I must say a word in defence of myself against a charge, which it seems I have brought against myself. You have taken a few words I may have written, too seriously. I have not been guilty of exaggeration. I do not remember to have described any man to you, otherwise than he may have appeared to me. Only I was afraid, that you had drawn too hard and unjust conclusions, from what I had said: and in that I should be to blame. I have said some things playfully, and have sometimes told a story, as it was told me, without vouching for its truth; but I have never made an assertion which I was doubtful about; and never expressed a judgment, which I did not feel was right. And from your letters all along it has appeared to me that you have on the whole understood me, as I should wish to be understood. I may have made some false conclusions. If I heard a man cursing and swearing, I inferred he reverenced God very little; perhaps an unjust conclusion. If they told me, this man never goes to church, I thought he cared little for religion; applicable in America but not in Germany. If I caught a man on a morning call in a night gown and slippers without breeches on, I judged him a sloven; altogether falsely; for give him a clean shirt and a new suit of clothes and he will dress very respectably for a public occasion. This is pretty much all the retraction I wished to make; for I have always taken heed to my words, and that will always do.[46]

Two weeks from the writing of this letter Bancroft passed, in the presence of eight members of the Göttingen faculty, a satisfactory examination for his degree, and after defending on September 9 nine theses, in accordance with the requirements, he was declared a Doctor of Philosophy. "Now," he informs Norton, "from one end of the town to the other, to many ears so enchanting, Dr., *Herr* Doctor, are cried out to me by friends and foes, men and women, tradesmen and mechanics and beggars." [47] He looked back upon his two years, his journal states, as having been usefully employed, but he wrote to President Kirkland:

I go from Göttingen without much regret. The people here are too cold and unsocial, too fond of writing books and too incapable of conversing, having more than enough of courtesy, and almost nothing of hospitality. I admire their industry; but they do not love labour; I consider their vast erudition with astonishment; yet it lies as a dead weight on society. The men of letters are for the most part ill bred; many of them are altogether without manners. [48]

An entry later in his journal repeats his dissatisfaction with Göttingen, for he found there, as he expressed it, "a want of religious sentiment, an absence of moral feeling." [49] Berlin, with such scholars as Boeckh, Buttmann, Wolf, Hegel, and Schleiermacher, offered, he believed, more advantages. Therefore, with two Greek companions, Maurus from Constantinople and Polyzoides from Thessalonica, he set out on foot the morning of September 19 to spend a semester in Berlin. [50] Reluctantly he bade adieu to his friends and the pleasant little city with its picturesque surroundings where he had spent two years. Renewed appreciation of its magnificent institutions filled his heart and brought forth the sentiment, "Farewell, oh! Georgia Augusta, and mayst thou long continue to bring forth offspring worthy of thy present glory."

The five months which Bancroft spent at the University of Berlin were, according to accounts in his journal and letters, most profitable and satisfactory. He pursued philological studies under Boeckh, Hirt, and Wolf, and attended lectures in philosophy by Hegel, and in the science of education by Schleiermacher. It is not surprising that his own style at this time reflected his masters'. His friend Samuel A. Eliot warned him: "I observe some few Germanisms in your style. Take care." [51] He gave some time to private lessons in French and Italian, as well as in dancing—this last, he said, "for the sake of wearing off all awkwardness and uncouthness." [52] He reveled in the society of the metropolis, being a frequent guest in the homes of the intellectuals, especially those of Savigny, Wilhelm von Humboldt, and Schleiermacher. On meeting some of his professors shortly after his arrival he heard criticisms of Wolf, whom everyone seemed to dislike cordially, "some obviously hating him, many envying him, and a few arrogant enough to speak of him contemptuously." To this Bancroft adds: "When and where shall I hear one German man of letters speak well of another?" A call on Hegel led him to conclude at once that this philosopher was "very sluggish for one of Schlegel's school. But it is not well to form hasty judgments." [53] Of Wolf, Bancroft wrote to President Kirkland:

> He is a genius of the first order; one of the few great men whom it has been my lot to meet in Germany. Hated by his countrymen, he consoles himself with the consciousness of being the most learned man on the continent. . . . But Wolf has neither dignity of character, nor purity of morals. He is stubbornly vain, childish, and licentious. . . . He is now the laziest man I have ever seen; rising after daylight, and going to bed at nine.[54]

There were discussions of literary and educational subjects with Wilhelm von Humboldt, whose genius and erudition were much admired by Bancroft. An entry in the journal reads: "Baron von Humboldt, speaking of German style, agreed with me that too little attention was paid to harmony in the construction of sentences. Goethe's style is beautiful, but a little *manierirt*. Schiller in some of his small pieces is perfect. A. W. Schlegel's prose style is good, but his poems frosty." [55] After hearing Savigny lecture, Bancroft said: "He has that plainness of manners, which become a man of letters so well." [56] But Schleiermacher made the most favorable impression, as the following entries in his journal give evidence:

> Schleiermacher delighted me extremely. He has a sharp eye, a remarkable countenance, and in general his appearance is very striking. He is small and somewhat hump-backed; but his manners are so lively and spirited, that one hardly notices his personal ugliness. He spoke with a good deal of interest of the religious affairs of America. . . . Schleiermacher's mode of preaching is very dignified and severe. Language flows from his lips most fluently and uninterruptedly. He is the best extempore speaker I have ever heard. He makes almost no use of his hands, but without gesture pronounces his discourse with rational warmth, but never with impassioned vehemence. He is a preacher for the understanding, not for the heart. His voice is clear and distinct,

his countenance intelligent and expressive, his eye black and clear, and in the pulpit his whole appearance is full of dignity.[57]

Similar praise is found in a letter to President Kirkland:

I have taken a course of lectures with Schleiermacher on the science of education; it is the most interesting which I have as yet attended. He brings to his subject a mind sharpened by philosophical meditation and enriched with the learning of all ages and countries. He applies to his subject all his vast acquaintance with the different systems of ethics, and with the human mind; his language is luminous, elegant and precise; his delivery is I think almost perfect. I honour Schleiermacher above all the German scholars, with whom it has been my lot to become acquainted. He abounds in wit and is inimitable in satire; yet he has a perfectly good heart, is generous and obliging. I think him acknowledged to be the greatest pulpit orator in Germany.[58]

And again in his letter to Norton:

Schleiermacher is a fine philosopher, a rational, candid, liberal divine, an amiable father and husband, a most industrious, most pious, and most domestic man. Acuteness and sagacity are his grand talents. As a philosopher, he has never suffered himself to be moved by any one of the many systems, which have been gaining admirers and losing them successively for thirty years past. Schleiermacher has never fallen nor changed, but has kept himself from the mysterious speculations and dreams of the day.[59]

While in Berlin Bancroft made quite a study of the public and private schools, to which he was probably directed by Schleiermacher's lectures on education. In November he forwarded to President Kirkland an enthusiatic account:

I need not say, how fine the schools of Prussia are; they are acknowledged to be the finest in Germany. Here in Berlin a great many new ideas are going into application; and the indistinct forebodings of Pestalozzi, and the eloquent discourses of Fichte have not been without lasting fruits. I need not assure you how happy I am in having an opportunity of studying the science of education in a city, where it has been the subject of so much discussion and where the Government have done so much, have done everything they could do, to realize the vast advantages about to result from the reform in the institutions of instruction. No Government knows so well how to create Universities and high schools as the Prussians. . . . Besides the public schools there is at Berlin a private institution, which promises to become very useful. Ten young men, animated by the eloquence and patriotism of Fichte, formed a plan some years ago of establishing a school after the new principles. Each of them chose a peculiar branch, in which he was to perfect himself, and which he afterwards went to teach. Three of them went in the mean time to live with Pestalozzi and become acquainted with his principles from the man himself. An ardour and a perseverance, such as the young men have manifested, deserve to meet with the most decided success. I find it quite instructive to observe their institution from time to time; they know how to unite gymnastic exercises, music and the sciences; and this is the mode of educating, which Plato has extolled as the perfect art. In this way I have excellent means of becoming acquainted with the old and the new ways of teaching in Germany; the subject deserves attention for its practical importance; and becomes highly attracting, when regarded in a philosophical point of view.[60]

The combination of the arts and sciences with gymnastic exercises, and the abolition of corporal punishment for pupils, impressed Bancroft as a system of education which might be introduced in his own country. However, when he discussed with Humboldt the advisability of instituting schools in America after the model of the German system, the philosopher was of the opinion that the plan would not succeed.

You would be able to imitate all the forms [he said], and then would be forced to gaze and wonder how it comes that the effects are so different. The proposition of importing German learned men into America is not a good one. The eminent men, those of very distinguished talents, those who would be able to do good, would never be induced to quit their country. It would be far better to send out young Americans to be trained and disciplined in Germany.[61]

That Bancroft was greatly pleased with his residence in Berlin is seen in the abundant evidence furnished by his letters and journal. He readily contrasted the methods of the University with those of Göttingen, as the following letter to President Kirkland shows:

I have already been here about six weeks, and find abundant cause of joy for having come here. The character of the men of letters is quite the reverse of the character of the Göttingen professors. There an abhorrence is felt for all innovations; here the new, that is good or promises to lead to good, cannot too soon be adopted. At Göttingen the whole tendency of the course is, to make the students learned, to fill their memories with matters of fact; here the grand aim is to make them think. At Göttingen experience stands in good repute, and men are most fond of listening to her voice; but at Berlin experience is a word not to be pronounced too often; speculation is looked on as a prime source of truth. At G. the men are engaged in growing learned and writing useful books, which demonstrate their erudition; at Berlin the professors are perhaps quite as learned, but more accustomed to reflect; and you may find many of their books, to have written which a prodigious degree of erudition was required, and which yet do not contain a single citation. Certainly Göttingen is the best place to gather genuine learning; but I hardly think a man would learn there how to use it properly.[62]

And in a letter to Everett he expressed his praise of Berlin:

In the years spent at Göttingen I certainly had a good deal to endure. It was like living among the dead. The roughness of the students, the cold hearted rudeness and mutual jealousies of the professors made the life there almost as solitary as a hermitage. When I compare the manners, the morals and the ways of thinking at the Georgia Augusta with the kindness and hospitality with which I have been welcomed on all sides in Berlin, I feel very glad that I resolved to pass the winter here.[63]

Further proof of his views on this subject appears in the following interesting summary in his journal:

How glad I am that I left Göttingen to pass the winter at Berlin! What can be more gloriously interesting than intimate communion with the vast minds which are found here? And then too I find that it is quite a different thing to read the German authors separated from the world and shut up in my room, and to read them here in the centre of a most polished and courteous metropolis. Here no exertion is required to transfer myself into the proper state of feeling: everything near me excites in me the elevation necessary to render the German writers intelligible and interesting. No literary enjoyment can perhaps be greater than the reading of a play of Aeschylus, an ode of Pindar, a tragedy of Sophocles; and yet so difficult is it to spell out the sublime effusions of those ancient bards, so hard is it to annihilate the two thousand years which separate us from them, that their grand amplifications of Heathen mythology and their sublime representations of Grecian and of heroic life, often leave the mind wearied — not refreshed, exhausted and not delighted. But the various inventions of Goethe, the rare simplicity and dignity of Klopstock in his odes, the refined manner and pure fiction of Schiller come at once to the heart. We live among them; we feel with them. I am in the midst of the nation for whom they wrote; and understand their allusions, their imagery, their philosophy. I understand the poets themselves and thus draw in instruction and extasy, such as is only to be found again by tasting the pure fountains of Milton and Shakspeare.

I was displeased and disgusted with Göttingen because I found there a want of religious sentiment, an absence of moral feeling. I find at

Berlin eloquent preachers, and hear their friends, and those, too, persons of rank and fortune, talk of them with that love which a holy man ought to inspire into the bosom of confiding devotion. I find at Berlin warm supporters of religion, dignified defenders of Xty, whom the fire from the altar has touched and purified, whom the still small voice of divinity has bid come forth from the darkness which seemed to have enveloped religion in Germany, and to stand forth its pillars, ornaments and propagators. I find society too, where decency is demanded and chastity honoured, and where conversation with friends tends to call forth and confirm the inclination to virtue, to strengthen and support the feelings of devotion.

I was dissatisfied with Göttingen, because I found there nothing which I could fully admire. I longed for a situation which might rouse my faculties to exertion, which might bring into exercise every spring of action in the soul. I longed to be among men to whom I could look up with a wish of becoming like them. I do not find at Berlin any *ideal* of humanity. I find no one who answers to my young notions of mental greatness. I shall find such no where — earth does not bear such; vain is the search after perfection; vain is the hope of ever seeing our early views and expectations realized. But I have found much at Berlin which is admirable. I have found whom I must honour for their genius, revere for their virtues and learning, and love for their hospitality.[64]

After final visits with his friends, Bancroft reluctantly left Berlin at the end of February, 1821. "This kindness was so different from the cold and heartless formality of the Göttingen scholars that I think with a great deal more affection of the place, where I passed but five months, than of that where I lived more than two years," he later wrote to President Kirkland.[65] On his way to Paris, he met various scholars in some of the German towns. At Weissenfels he called on Müller, the author of *Die Schuld*, of whose physiognomy Bancroft says: "I am in doubt whether I found any great signs of genius in it nor not." [66] A visit of four days with young Hedge, then a pupil at Schulpforta,[67] enabled Bancroft to acquaint himself further with German educational methods. His long letter, written from Kösen on March 6 to Levi Hedge, gives an enthusiastic account of the school, its history, organization, equipment, discipline, modes of instruction, and general life.[68] "The whole assembly of the learning and the teaching," he says, "seems bound together by the strongest ties of proximity, and to form one large and well organized family." The physical aspects of the school delighted him, as we observe in the following description:

The situation of Schulpforta is delightful. It lies not in a town or even a village; but inclosed by its own walls, and unpolluted by the vicinity of others, it raises its towers in one of the sweetest valleys I have ever seen. Steep hills, on each side, shut in rich and fertile meadows, and well cultivated fields. These hills seem to have once been the immediate, now the distant banks of the Saale, which gently winds through the vale in a graceful bend, almost rivalling the famed scenery round Dresden. The sunny side is covered with vineyards, and the vintages, spotting the hills, give life to the placid scenery. There is a mixture of grandeur and mildness in the prospect; and if it appears so pleasant now, when not a green leaf is to be seen, how delightful must it be, when sheaves are heaped in bundles, and the fruit of the vine is reddening and growing transparent in the sun. The ruins of two ancient castles crown the proudest eminences, commanding a fine view towards Jena and the plains, which have of late been the scene of such distinctive battles.

During his several days in Weimar Bancroft visited Goethe on March 7 and 12. This time the poet was more carefully dressed and more formal than he had appeared in the autumn of 1819. The first of these visits is fully described in Bancroft's journal:

I was with Goethe for a half hour today. I felt the vast difference between him and the many scholars whom I have lately seen. Goethe has the ease of a gentleman, speaks with loveliness and energy, but does not seem to take any longer a lively interest in the affairs of the world. I tried to bring him to talk of the German poets, and mentioned Tieck, but Goethe remained silent. I mentioned the Schlegels; he observed merely that they had written many pretty things. Byron's *Don Juan* Goethe has read and admired its humour. The humour of the rimes, said he, is capable only in your language where words differently written are often pronounced alike. This peculiarity of your language has been cultivated and exercised by a series of comic writers, Swift, etc. Goethe spoke of Humboldt's *Agamemnon* with high praise. "I still read in it and derive new instruction from it." Goethe asked me about the new hall at Berlin, about the famous masquerade at court, spoke of Sir George Rose and his handsome daughters. I saluted him from Wolf. He added merely, that Wolf had given him the pleasure of his company for a few days the last autumn. Goethe spoke of the progress of colonisation in America and of the agreeable manner we have in America of setting before each advertisement a little cut denoting its subject, as a house, a ship, a horse. He thought it a very excellent custom. He spoke in praise of the riches of Berlin in the arts, the thriving state of sculpture, etc. He spoke of Cogswell, adding that he had sent several little things to him in America by way of Perthes and

Besser at Hamburg. Goethe's appearance is that of a healthy and active old man. His countenance is thin but shows no signs of decay.

Goethe is still very industrious. He dictates often for several hours in succession, lives very secluded, associating with none of the inhabitants of Weimar, appearing neither at Court nor in any parties. When any ideas arise in his mind he dictates them as a fragment, the end of which no one can conceive of, and throws them aside, till accident or inclination brings him again on the same subject. He has by him often works nearly finished, others in good progress and others just commenced on, so that Prof. Riemer says of him, he brings forth like the mice, who carry about in the womb young ones ready for delivery, and others just beginning to exist. At present Goethe has finished a volume of *Wilhelm Meister, Wanderjahren,* and is also engaged in his " Morphologie."

I ought to mention that Goethe praised Schlegel's translation of Shakspeare and spoke of the delight he had taken in a late perusal of Julius Caesar. . . . [69]

The visit a few days later was brief: "I called on Goethe. He was very friendly and manifested an interest in my future welfare. He mentioned, among other things, that he had often sent things to Mr. Cogswell by way of Hamburg, care of Perthes and Besser." [70] Bancroft wrote afterward to Norton, who was constantly warning him against the vice of Europe: "Weimar is the only place I know of, worthy of commemoration for its staid morality"; [71] and many years later, when representing his country at Berlin, he took pride in telling the Queen of Prussia that he had seen Goethe.[72]

From Weimar Bancroft proceeded to Frankfort, then to Darmstadt, and later to Heidelberg, where he spent a month in the company of the university scholars and attending the lectures of Schlosser, the historian. While in Stuttgart on April 21 he recorded in his journal the following comment:

Matthison is a poet, the sweetness of whose verses and the neat sentimentality of his poems may charm many a silly woman or badly educated girl. In his person he is a very plain, ordinary man; nothing marks the poet in his exterior, nor in his conversation. He is now somewhat advanced in life, and indeed I had supposed him long since dead, so seldom is his name now-adays mentioned.

Bancroft arrived in Paris early in May, in time to meet August Wilhelm Schlegel, then preparing to leave for Bonn, and soon established contact with Alexander von Humboldt, Cuvier, Lafayette, Baron de Staël, Washington Irving, Albert Gallatin, and many other notables. To Humboldt he was especially indebted for various interesting experiences during his three months in the city. His admiration is expressed as follows:

The more I see of Mr. de Humboldt, the more I admire him; he does understand the art of talking to perfection. He is at home on every subject that is started; I have heard him talk on philological subjects and what to others seemed dry and uninteresting, when treated by him became pleasant as well as instructive. In politics he is decidedly liberal, and can manage a political discussion even with the great masters of political wisdom. He talks to the ladies with as much ease as if he had passed years in frequenting salons and drawing-rooms, instead of climbing Chimborazo and exploring Mexico; he talks with grace of the news of the day, tells a story charmingly, and relates a current tale of intrigue with unrivalled gaiety and spirit.[73]

A letter which Bancroft carried from Humboldt to Pictet of Geneva commended him as "a young American, who has made excellent study of philology and of philosophic history in Germany." After three weeks in London, which Bancroft seems to have disliked,[74] he started south on a walking tour through Switzerland. Of particular appeal was "all that country," writes Bancroft to Norton, "of which I had so often dreamed in childhood, where the deeds of Tell and the well fought battles of liberty have lent an omnipotent charm to every valley you gaze on."[75] The winter was spent chiefly in Rome and Naples, and from the latter city Bancroft, in a letter to his friend Samuel A. Eliot, then in Germany, paid his respects to the Germans:

I hope you like the Germans; if you do not now, you will learn to value them. The Germans unite in their character, all the elements of greatness and virtue; just as they do in their language, all stores of learning. They alone have not grown tired of reflection, nor weary of industry; they know how to value domestic virtues and enjoyments and feel the necessity of national integrity and firmness. They may be awkward but are sincerely kind; they may be rough but are prodigiously learned, rich in the possessions of unequalled treasures of reflection and intelligence. Poetic invention has grown blunt in those countries where it once was sharpest; in Germany it is bright and general.[76]

In the spring of 1822 Bancroft turned north, and on May 22 had his memorable visit at Monte Nero with Byron. The poet spoke of several Americans, particularly of Ticknor, Everett, and Washington Irving, and the conversation drifted to the subject of Germany and Goethe. Bancroft was much interested in Byron's attitude towards Goethe, as he records in his journal:

> We spoke of Germany. He asked if I knew Goethe. I answered I did, and reported faithfully what I had heard Goethe say of him. I then told him of the translations which have so often been made of his works, and of the great admiration, which all Germans had for him. This B. said was new to him, and would serve as some solace for the abuse which he was constantly receiving from home. . . .
>
> I mentioned Goethe's comparison of *Faust* and *Manfred*; and Byron observed, evidently in earnest, that he deemed it honour enough to have his work mentioned with *Faust*. As to its origin, Lord B. said that some time before he had conceived the idea of his piece, Monk Lewis had translated to him some of the scenes and had given him an idea of the plan of the piece.[77]
>
> Speaking of the immorality of his works, he said: Why, what are Fielding and Smollett and those authors? He seemed to think there were worse things in Smollett than in anything he had ever written. What would they say, too, to the introduction to Goethe's *Faust*? Many of his friends, he said, in Italy as well as in England, had entreated him not to go on with *Don Juan*.
>
> He had dedicated one of his late works to Goethe; but for some reason or other his publisher had omitted to print it.
>
> "Shelley is translating *Faust*: Shelley of whom you may have heard many foolish stories, of his being a man of no principles, an atheist and all that: but he is not."
>
> Lord Byron related to me the late scrape, into which he and his servant got at Pisa.
>
> He laughed at the story Goethe tells of his murdering a man at Florence — hopes Goethe may not hear of this affair of Pisa, lest he should make a famous story out of it.[78]

In June Bancroft sailed from Marseilles, and immediately after reaching New York on August 3 he returned to his home in Worcester, where, yielding to his father's wishes, he was licensed to preach. He had acquired in Europe certain mannerisms and affectations, which made him for some time the subject of ridicule in the circles of Harvard and Boston, and needed, as Emerson stated, "a great deal of cutting and pruning." [79] Andrews Norton had written him in December of the previous year warning him of the state of society in Cambridge, and of the dislike of "ostentation or vanity, anything *outré* or *bizarre*." But one of Bancroft's first acts upon his return was to rush up to his reverend friend and kiss him on both cheeks, whereupon a serious breach between the two scholars followed. The young scholar was severely rebuked by the elder. "I owe it to myself," Bancroft later protested, "to tell you plainly that you have done me great injustice in the estimate which you have made of my manners and feelings. You do not understand my character or you have not taken the pains to consider it." [80] Nevertheless, Bancroft had acquired in Europe certain affectations which were unquestionably offensive to his formal New England friends.[81] On September 24, he disclosed to his friend Eliot the following self-analysis:

I have grown quite estranged from my own country and countrymen; it has been my lot to spend four years in the land of strangers; my ways of thinking are I firmly trust worthy of New England; but my manner of expressing them may have a foreign character; and it is an affair of no small importance to be able to speak our opinions in an impressive and acceptable manner. Having heard for so long a time the accents of foreign tongues, I forget in some measure, that Chatham's language is mine too; and many an unfortunate French or German phrase or sweet Italian is interceding for utterance, when I should in decency talk nothing but plain English. These little difficulties will pass soon, and before winter, I expect to find all the superfluous excitability, which I gathered in Southern countries, chilled to a calmness fit for our colder latitudes.

It was now Bancroft's desire to join his friends Ticknor, Everett, and Cogswell in giving to his country, and especially to Harvard, the benefit of his learning. From Rome, the previous January, he had written to Eliot:

I shall feel very happy in devoting my life to the service of the University, to which I owe so much, and to further communion with those minds, which have embodied themselves in their written works, and which have now so often borne me company and solitude, and comforted me in sadness. But if I am not wanted at Cambridge, I cannot hesitate, I dare not, may not hesitate.[82]

Later he applied for permission to deliver lectures on history at Harvard, but the future historian of his country was denied the privilege,[83] and shortly after his return home he accepted an appointment as tutor in Greek, which position he held for one year, preaching some of the time in the prominent churches in the vicinity of Boston. He entered upon his tutorial duties with great ability and promise, as well as with enthusiasm for European learning. "I do not expect to be a popular tutor, because I intend to require more than has been usual," he had informed Norton in September. It is said that in external matters he imitated German professors, at the same time exacting much of his students, who, according to reports, were accustomed to sing under his windows in the college yard a song beginning "Thus we do in Germany." [84] Bancroft displayed great capacities in his instruction, but sharing with his colleagues of European training the conviction that Harvard needed reforms, he was at once in difficulties with a conservative institution.[85] Early in December he informed Eliot: "I have the satisfaction of knowing that I have carried my points alone, unassisted by any cooperation whatever from any one individual at Cambridge, and supported by no man in any design except Mr. Ticknor." [86] As the year advanced he became more and more displeased with his position and his general environment. "Bancroft is making great exertions to teach Greek thoroughly, and succeeds; but is thwarted in every movement by the President," wrote Ticknor early in February,[87] and on May 10 Bancroft expressed his feelings to Eliot: "For myself, I have found college a sickening and wearisome place. Not one spring of comfort have I had to draw from. My state has been nothing but trouble, trouble, trouble, and I am heartily glad that the end of the year is coming soon." He therefore welcomed his withdrawal from Harvard and the opportunity to establish with Cogswell, as we have noted, the Round Hill School, to which institution we now return for a time, in order to observe Bancroft's connection.[88]

In his letters from Germany to his father, and to Kirkland and Everett, Bancroft had shown that he was undecided as to his career, upon his return to this country, but he had frequently expressed an interest in establishing a school. As early as January, 1819, he had written from Göttingen to Kirkland of a probable choice between an instructorship at Harvard and becoming a clergyman, or setting up a high school. Kirkland replied that he supposed a school of the German character "would be in great consideration and request here," but he would not desire that Bancroft should have the plan in view, unless he actually preferred it.[89] Bancroft informed him some weeks later that his suggestion of a high school appeared to open a fine field for being useful. "I would gladly be instrumental," he said, "in the good cause of improving our institutions of education and it is our schools, which cry out most loudly for reformation." [90] The following August Bancroft wrote to Everett: "Some Gentlemen in Boston are desirous, I should become acquainted with the German Schulwesen, and on coming home set up a high school, on the European plan." [91] He further stated that, while the labor of a school offered nothing alluring, and he would not wish to devote many years to it, the plan appealed to him as the means of doing most good, for which purpose instructors might be imported from Germany — an idea, we recall, which Wilhelm von Humboldt in a conversation later with Bancroft had discouraged. Everett at once forwarded to Bancroft his encouragement:

> Could you have a liberal and proper support, I know no better place for you than a learned School, and the College would be indebted to you, for the most important aid in carrying into execution the projected reforms in education. We can do nothing at Cambridge till we contrive the means of having the boys sent to us far better fitted than they are now. [92]

From Prague in early October of that year Bancroft wrote to his father: "Dr. Kirkland would like to have me return and set up a Gymnasium on the German principles of instruction. How do you like the idea? It might be an important assistance to the cause of good learning, and if a handsome support were given, would be a place of indisputed dignity. Had you rather see me a clergyman or a Professor?" [93] In his supervision of young Hedge's German training, and in connection with his own studies at Berlin, Bancroft had, as we have noted, familiarized himself with methods in German schools, and had given special attention to the educational theories expounded by Schleiermacher. Writing from Berlin on October 20, 1820, to his father of plans for the future and the means of securing financial assistance upon his return home, he said: "If I will assist in erecting a Gymnasium, I may be sure of a bounteous support." Then followed the visit to Schulpforta, with whose system Bancroft was greatly impressed, and while in Milan on October 27 of the following year he entered in his journal his conception of an ideal school. This, in his opinion, should include, first of all, instruction in Greek, then natural history, and prizes should be discouraged. Corporal punishment should not be used, classes should be formed according to each boy's ability, country schoolmasters might be trained by the school at small expense, and eventually a vast printing establishment might be set up in connection with the institution. With these and additional ideas Bancroft had returned home, and had definitely planned during the early months in his tutorship to establish a school. On December 3 he wrote to Eliot, then abroad, of his conferences with Kirkland, Everett, and Ticknor on the subject, of his consideration of schools, the means and end of education, and of his final conclusion:

Now I am going to turn *schoolmaster*. I long to become an independent man, namely a man, who lives by his own labours. Mr. Cogswell has seen so much of the world, that he knows it and its folly; he will join me in my scheme; we will together establish a school, the end of which is to be the moral and intellectual maturity of the mind of each boy we take charge of; and the means are to be first and foremost *instruction in the classics*. We intend going into the country, and we shall choose a pleasant site, where nature in her loveliness may breathe calmness and inspire purity. We will live retired from the clamours of scandal and the disputes of the irresolute. We will delight ourselves with letters, and instead of warring against the Corporation and contending with scandalous reports, we will train up a few minds to virtue and honour, and hope that when we die there will be some hands to throw flowers on our tombs.[94]

From London Eliot replied commending Bancroft for his excellent work at Harvard and urging him to remain.

What is this wild scheme of yours and Cogswell's of going into the woods to give instruction in the classics? [he asked]. The place for you to give instruction in the classics is Harvard College, Cambridge, Massachusetts, and as for establishing a school "the end of which is to be the moral and intellectual maturity of every boy you take charge of," I am afraid it would come to a shorter end than that.

He further advised Bancroft that retirement was to be had anywhere, while independence was never possible.[95] However, Bancroft had reached a definite conclusion, and on May 10 he replied to Eliot: "We are going to establish a Landschule, a regular country school for boys, and we believe we shall be doing our duty as faithful citizens and as scholars."

As has been stated previously, the Round Hill School opened the first of October, 1823. On the evening of the opening day Bancroft wrote to President Kirkland in glowing terms of the new surroundings and of the prospects. "Were I to have a meadow like this of Northampton before me and such *peaceful* mountains," he said, "I should forget that Aetna has its volcanoes and Syria its sands. A few weeks later he wrote with satisfaction to Everett:

We are going on very smoothly and very happily. It is enough to be free from the perpetual interference and unsolicited judgments of others. At Northampton we are left entirely to ourselves; and there is some comfort in shaping one's conduct by one's own inclinations and views, without being obliged to bend to the ignorance of others, who undertake to controul, when they do not understand. Our little family is fast forming habits of obedience and order; and as confinement and retirement are no evils to a scholar, there is nothing which is unpleasant in our situation.[96]

Subsequent letters to various friends are written in the same spirit of optimism. Bancroft was a scholar, not an administrator, and gave practically all his time to teaching. He gave instruction at first in German, as well as in his favorite subjects, the classics and history; but on the recommendation of Heeren, his former Göttingen professor, G. H. Bode joined the staff in 1825 and taught the German classes. Bancroft was of an excentric, romantic, emotional temperament, and lacked a sympathetic understanding of youngsters, though he seems to have accomplished more with the mature ones. Scholarly pursuits interested him more, however, than importing knowledge to others, and he was never eminently successful as a teacher. One of his pupils, George E. Ellis, referred many years afterward to him as follows:

Mr. Bancroft dwelt at a little distance from the school, and so could see but little of the boys except in school hours and at recitations. He was absent-minded, dreamy, and often in abstracted moods as well as very near-sighted. I have seen him come into the recitation room at an exercise before breakfast, with a slipper or shoe on one foot and a boot on the other. More than once he sent me across the road to his library for his spectacles. These were generally to be found shut into a book, which he had been reading before going to bed. The boys, who called him familiarly "the Critter," were fond of playing tricks upon him, which they could do with impunity, owing to his shortness of vision.[97]

Bancroft's unpopularity with the boys was not the only difficulty. Owing to his and Cogswell's differences in temperament, and their views as to methods of teaching, as well as to the management of the school, their relations finally became complicated, and Bancroft, interested more in literary and historical pursuits than in teaching, was glad to dispose of his interest in 1830, though he served one year longer as a salaried instructor. On August 30, 1831, he wrote to Everett: "In one short month I cease to be a schoolmaster. What is to be done? My plan is to maintain my independence if I can. Should circumstances favour, I think I shall succeed; remaining, however, a dweller on the banks of the Connecticut." The experience at Round Hill had afforded him opportunity to put into practice his German training. But he was fonder of society than of retirement in the country, and within a short time he turned to politics and to the writing of history.

Although Bancroft is known chiefly as a historian and diplomat, he devoted much time, especially in his early life, to poetry and to essays of a literary character. His first publication, a small volume entitled *Poems* and dedicated to President Kirkland, "the author's early benefactor and friend," appeared in 1823. It consisted of poems of little value, which he had written in Europe.[98] From now on his pen was busy. He prepared textbooks, adaptations from the German editions of Buttmann's Greek Grammar and Jacob's Greek Reader and Latin Reader,[99] which were used by his pupils and which filled an important need in American education during that period. In 1824 he published a translation of Heeren's *Reflections on the Politics and Character of Ancient Greece*,[100] and two years later a version of Cornelius Nepos. In Germany, as we have seen, he began his studies in German literature, even translating some of the poems of Schiller and Goethe, and in the course of time his private library, rich in historical subjects, contained the works of Herder, Goethe, Schiller, and Heine. During his connection at Round Hill, and for some years afterward, he contributed to some of the leading journals [101] various reviews and articles on German subjects, most of which were collected and published, with slight variations, in his *Literary and Historical Miscellanies* of 1855. His first contribution, a review of *Schiller's Minor Poems*, appeared in the *North American Review* [102] in October, 1823. His early liking for Schiller is seen here in the admirable translation of five of the poems,[103] including comment, and the following remarks:

> The character and feelings of Schiller as an individual appear throughout his poetry. Every sentiment seems to derive its peculiar cast from his own mind, just as certain plants take the color of their leaves from the soil in which they grow. In this he differs remarkably from the poet, who disputes with him the admiration of his country. Goethe reflects in his poems the feelings of others; Schiller feels deeply himself, and knew how to embody his feelings in verse. In whatever age or country Goethe places his invention, he instantly adapts himself to its manners and tone; Schiller always preserves under all changes of scene the peculiar characteristics of his own mind. The person of Goethe is never seen through his verse; that of Schiller presents itself constantly. It is the German poet in Spain, in Switzerland, in France; seizing on all opportunities of paying tribute to excellence, truth, and liberty. We may learn from Goethe what the world is; but Schiller teaches us what it should be.

On February 9 of the following year Bancroft wrote to Jared Sparks, who had succeeded Everett as editor of the *North American*: "I have been cheating myself of my cares by making little translations from Goethe." In March he wrote again: "On Goethe I am seriously employed, and hope to give some translations, which shall at least find their way into the albums of the ladies"; and in June: "Goethe shall be done soon. I have the ideas all warm in my head but must let them ferment a little more, that I may write coolly and judiciously." [104] He was then preparing his well-known essay, "The Life and Genius of Goethe," which was published in the October number.[105] The essay, which is Bancroft's most important contribution on the subject of Goethe, is prefaced by some general remarks on the character of German literature, for which he pleads fair and impartial judgment from foreigners. Pointing out that each nation has a literature with its own characteristics which merit respectful attention, he says of the literature of Germany:

> If on first acquaintance it offend, or seem strange and unnatural, this is nothing more than might have been expected; for the culture,

and consequently the productions of the Germans, have much that is
original and peculiar; and in every peculiarity, both in the forms and
in the subjects of their works, only makes them more worthy of respect, just as reverence is due to any one, who can teach new lessons on
life and the mode of regulating the passions.

Turning to Goethe as the chief representative of their literature,
Bancroft shows that his earlier attitude of condemnation of the
poet is somewhat modified. He reviews the various factors
which have influenced Goethe's poetic development, commends
him for his devotion to the pursuit of letters, and gives unquali-
fied praise to his genius and style. Certain works are cited as
indication of the great power of one who was master in his art,
special reference being made to *Iphigenie*, *Tasso*, and the poems,
several of which he translates with comment.[106] *Faust* is a work
of genius, though it is not of "a purely moral tendency," and in
America the *Elective Affinities*, Bancroft states, would be considered "a false and dangerous libel on human nature." He
closes by stating:

> But the works of Goethe are not without lessons of practical
> morality. Though he makes no boasts of being himself a religious man,
> he acknowledges religion to be essentially the best foundation of a good
> character, and considers cooperation with others in works of practical
> utility, and in the execution of just and righteous designs, the safest
> and the happiest course. He has also drawn many exquisite and ele-
> vating pictures of female excellence, has illustrated the superiority of
> domestic life, and has given the noblest encomiums to that sex, which
> knows how to establish order and economy, to feel, and to endure, "Ye
> call me fickle," says he, " ye err; she but roams in search of a steadfast
> man." Though Goethe has often delineated imaginary woes, and carried
> his readers into a world of fiction, yet it is the tendency of his writings
> to promote a love for the arts, for activity, for truth. They do not
> merely teach us to be satisfied with the world, but to bear with it, by
> showing how rich it is in the means of acquiring virtues, and of perform-
> ing just and benevolent deeds.[107]

The correspondence between Bancroft and his publisher in
connection with this essay is interesting, and leads us to inquire whether, after all, Bancroft's views were accurately presented. He sent his manuscript in July to Sparks, who, it seems,
not infrequently took liberties with his contributors,[108] stating
that it had cost him much time in the making, and requesting
that it should not be altered without consultation before it was

printed.[109] However, the essay appeared with various changes which Sparks explained as "trifling," to which Bancroft replied:

I know not how you can call the changes you made in the unfortunate article so trifling; for while I had been expecting to derive much pleasure from the appearance of it, I have felt only chagrin. And I cannot persuade myself, my disappointment is not well founded. Do you not know, you changed one assertion from a negative to a positive one, thereby saying something, which I do not believe, and which makes the words at least unmeaning. . . . You altered, what you would not have altered, had you understood, why and in what spirit it was written. And the change in two cases out of three, though few, materially affect both the meaning and the style of the most labored parts. I say labored parts, and I am free to add, labored with the most success, and the most *truth and nature*. The matter is of little moment, and my desire to be esteemed as a writer a childish vanity.[110]

George H. Calvert, a young Harvard graduate, who had been studying at Göttingen, arrived in Weimar on March 27, 1825, to interview Goethe. The following day he sent the poet a copy of Bancroft's article, thinking, as he stated, that he might like to read what was written about him in the *New World*.[111] But Goethe had a few hours previously received a copy from a friend in Berlin, to whom he expressed his appreciation:

Your Excellency has put me anew under obligation by the periodical sent me. It is in every case noteworthy to see how the effects of a long life work through the world, and also gain gradually here and there in influence, according to the times and circumstances. I had to smile when I was obliged to regard myself in so distant and besides so republican a mirror.

Moreover, this essay has a good effect upon everybody; so much intellect and insight, joined with a youthfully cheerful enjoyment in writing, excites a certain sympathetic, pleasing feeling. He was able to fill out pleasingly even the gaps where particular information failed him and in general to round out the whole with euphemy.[112]

At Spark's request,[113] Bancroft prepared an article on the *Writings of Herder*, which appeared in the January number of the following year.[114] Although this is very brief, it is probably the first account of Herder to appear in any American periodical. "Of the men of letters in Germany, who contributed to elevate the reputation and improve the taste of their country," says Bancroft, "few were so distinguished for variety of attainments, industry, and the love of morality, as Herder." From this opening statement he proceeds to give an excellent sketch of Herder's life, his services, and his influence, denying him great originality or inventive powers, but emphasizing his work as a translator and collector of songs, his reputation as a prose writer, and his idea of humanity. Importance is assigned to his patriotism and devotion to the welfare of mankind, and though Bancroft would not place him among the "great lights of the world," he informs his American readers that Herder occupied high rank among his German contemporaries, and was a blessing and honor to his age.[115]

From 1827 to 1831 Bancroft contributed to the *American Quarterly Review* a series of papers setting forth the merits of German literature, basing his remarks on various publications which appeared in Germany.[116] He gives an outline of the development of the literature from its early period, and includes the essential characteristics of the most prominent writers. The first of these articles [117] begins with a discussion of literature as an exposition of national character and national peculiarities, in which connection we note Bancroft's opinion:

Other nations have gained higher distinction for melody of verse, for exact and limited elegance; but never did the world behold a nation mature, in a century, a literature so diversified in its character, distinguished by so much learning and so much liberality, so full of thought and imagination, so distinguished alike for specimens of acute philosophical reasoning, and the boldest expression of enthusiastic feeling.

He then traces the history and development of Germany, including its intellectual pursuits and interest in foreign literatures, and passes to a consideration of the independence of German scholars, whose spirit of freedom and research he praises. The second of the series, contributed six months later,[118] follows the development of the literature from the early eighteenth century to 1770, sketching with clear understanding the work of practically every writer of the period. Bodmer receives praise only for his opposition to the theories of Gottsched, while the latter, with "not one spark of genius," and utterly destitute of imagination, is commended for his patriotism. Klopstock deserves commendation for his influence on German literature, and since he confused the spirit of epic poetry with that of the lyric, it is "the

height of folly" to compare him to Milton, while Wieland, according to Bancroft, was full of literary industry, but had "no
elevation of mind, no genuine sublimity of feeling." Ample
tribute is paid to Lessing as a critic, dramatist, and creator of
public taste, and outlines of *Minna von Barnhelm*, *Emilia Galotti*,
and *Nathan der Weise* are included.[119] In September of the same
year (1828)[120] Bancroft sketched the German contribution to the
various fields of learning, and continued his outline of the literature, tracing it from 1770 to the First Part of *Faust*. He gives
his appraisal of Herder, Jean Paul Richter, Bürger, and the
Romanticists, and then passes to Schiller and Goethe. Here, as
during his Göttingen period, he shows his love for Schiller.
Emphasis is given to the poet's popularity in Germany, and a
sketch of his career and dramas is outlined. We note the following praise: "And yet his poetry is marked by dignity, not less
than grace, and the light of philosophy sheds over it a gentle
lustre. He has written in such a manner, that the scrupulous
taste of the most cultivated and speculative minds selects him
as their favourite; and yet he charms the many." After these
remarks Bancroft turns to a consideration of Goethe. He refers
to the poet's position of supremacy in the world, to his sound
judgments, brilliant imagination, wide range of ideas, and his
optimism. Then follows further comment:

The character of Goethe's mind is that of self-possession. No pining
passion prostrates the energy of will; no crazed imagination corrupts
the healthy exercise of judgment. The author of Werther is the very
last man, who would have killed himself for love; the poet who has delineated Tasso's exquisite sensibility, was never a misanthrope or a
hypochondriac. The stream of life came for him from a clear fountain,
and during all its course has reflected the light of day in its natural
splendour. This it is, which distinguishes him from Rousseau and from
Byron, from Tasso and from Schiller.

Nevertheless, Bancroft would condemn certain of Goethe's
works for ethical reasons. The *Roman Elegies*, in his opinion, are
of "heathenish voluptuousness," and *Faust*, though "marked by
a potent intellect and an intimate acquaintance with virtue,"
offers, in the realistic descriptions of vice, details that are "often
gross and offensive." He concludes:

And so at the close, we have but again to concede to Goethe that
quality, which distinguishes Scott, and in which Shakespeare was of

all English writers pre-eminent — Truth in his descriptions. His persons are not creatures of romance and the stage, but are of real life; and as he has drawn his inspiration from the inexhaustible sources of natural feelings, so his reputation will be safe in all the vicissitudes of literary taste.

One year later, in reviewing Henry E. Dwight's *Travels in the North of Germany*,[121] Bancroft recalls with pride his own association with Germany, and especially his personal contact with Goethe:

In his intercourse with strangers, Goethe usually had an air of dignity, which was not wholly free from stiffness. He walked (our remarks have reference to Goethe as he was several years ago) very upright for a man of his years; and this stateliness of manner, joined with a large person, which in youth was very handsome, and in old age was very venerable, hair somewhat long, but fine and perfectly white, left the stranger, on the whole, agreeably impressed with the person of the poet, who is surpassed in genius by none of his contemporaries. But he has long since ceased to take any very lively interest in passing events. He has for a great while spent his time in retirement, hardly associating with any of the inhabitants of Weimar, and appearing neither at court, nor at parties in the city. Yet he still retained vigour to dictate, and would sometimes do so for hours in succession. He never wrote anything except readily. If a new thought struck his mind, he would forthwith dictate it as a fragment, and throw it aside, until accident or inclination brought him again upon the same subject. Thus he often had by him works nearly perfect, others in good progress, and others but just sketched; so that one of the Weimar men of letters compared him in his habits of production to the mice.

We have said that ordinarily Goethe had for many years been indifferent to passing events; but he regarded America with a lively curiosity, and possessed a good knowledge of our country. He would sometimes receive an American with more than hospitality, with open cordiality, and detain him as a guest for the whole evening, till nearly midnight. On such an occasion he would get into fine spirits, and be as familiar and playful as if with a friend of his youth. He would then talk with considerable freedom of the character of his contemporaries. "Lord Byron," he would say, "Lord Byron is the greatest, and indeed the only great living poet." And again, "there is a very large party in Germany, who regard Byron with unbounded admiration. I belong to that class, and swallow everything greedily that comes from him." He would then enlarge on the various poems of the illustrious English bard, allude with satisfaction to the manifest reference to his own Faust in the English Manfred, and admire the satirical humour of Don Juan. This again led him to an allusion to Dean Swift, and Goethe believed he discerned in the poetry of the Dean, the same caustic, misanthropic humour, and a similar, though inferior comic effect, produced by singular and unexpected rhymes. Goethe had less to say of Walter Scott; of Wordsworth and Southey he knew nothing; of Coleridge, the name, but had forgotten his works.

After some hours of good humour, he said of himself, what indeed his appearance very clearly indicated, that he had grown fastidious and morbid in his feelings; and that it required something uncommon to excite his attention in any degree. Bright days were then rare with him; and there are probably few hours, in which it would have been pleasant to be in his company.

Thus the rule of *nil admirari* would seem to gain further confirmation by one more illustrious example. Old age and disease are almost as great levellers as death itself. To have sat at the same board with the great patriarch of literature, or to have taken a morning's walk along with him, is an agreeable reminiscence for life; but while the homage of the lettered world has exalted him permanently in the eyes of men as a mind of a superior order, and even during his lifetime securely entered his name on the register of those forms and whose works mankind will never consent to lose; and while every cultivated person among the many millions of his countrymen is constantly expressing an interest in his health and life, the octogenarian poet is himself not spared by the stern law of nature; and it is the office of those who are near him, to smooth his descending steps with affectionate reverence, to watch the last glimmerings of the light of that inventive mind, which in its noon-day dazzled the world, and, in the presence of one of the most powerful geniuses that have ever appeared on earth, to stand in the relation of the strong, soothing the pains of decline, and ministering to the infirmities of age with anxious assiduity.

In 1830–31 Bancroft contributed a long review [122] of the first two volumes of William Taylor's *Historic Survey of German Poetry*, a work which he pronounced "singular in its merits and its deformities." He concedes to Taylor mature scholarship, and in general discrimination in his judgments, but states that the greatest fault which can be charged against him is "a wanton and officious exhibition of his indifference to religion." Further exception is taken also to some of Taylor's laudatory comment on certain authors, especially on Bürger, Wieland, and Kotzebue. In Bancroft's opinion, Bürger's *Lenore* is to be commended for its style and its rapidity of narration, but nothing further. "We would ask," says Bancroft, "is not the 'Bride of Corinth,' a poem which is not the most conspicuous of Goethe's, a finer production than the best of Bürger's? Let it be further remembered, that after two or three ballads, the works of Bürger have doubt-

ful claim to praise, and most of them hardly rise beyond medi-
ocrity." Wieland's works, Bancroft claims, offer "neither a wise,
practical philosophy of life, nor the proof of poetic genius," and
are to be condemned on the ground of immorality. "Strike from
literature the entire work of Wieland," he says, "and nothing
would be lost to the world." Even in *Oberon*, writes Bancroft,
the best things are borrowed, though he admits it has a good
plot, and Agathon, the author's most famous character, "is
Tom Jones turned philosopher." In reviewing the third volume
of Taylor's work,[123] Bancroft states that there is "still the same
amiable and funk garrulity on the part of the old gentleman, the
same fondness for strange opinions, and the same variety of
critical remarks." According to Bancroft, Taylor retains his
former indifference to positive religion, but "in the midst of
oddities" there are signs of good judgment and rational understanding. Especially is this true of the translations, which reveal
a power of reproduction "truly extraordinary," of which the
version of *Iphigenie* is a splendid example. Bancroft pronounces
Taylor's remarks about Kotzebue "ludicrously extravagant,"
stating that Kotzebue's plays are "a repertory of moral curi-
osities, a museum of moral monsters," the characters being
"neither Christian, pagan, nor man." Exception is taken to the
scant attention given by Taylor to Herder and to Schiller. "Of
all the German writers," declares Bancroft, "Schiller will most
surely obtain enduring admiration: he is always noble, pure, and
dignified."

In all his discussions of German poets, Bancroft has shown a
decided preference for Schiller, who seemed to him the embodiment of idealism, morality, and dignity. However, if he had
written nothing further on Goethe than the publications thus
far included, we should credit him with an intelligent appreciation, at times even a scholarly analysis, of Germany's greatest
poet. But as we have observed, there is often, in his opinions of
Goethe's personality and some of his writings, a discordant note
which is distinctly emphasized in the course of years. In 1839
John S. Dwight, one of the most enthusiastic exponents of German literature, published his *Select Minor Poems from the German
of Goethe and Schiller*.[124] This was favorably reviewed by Bancroft in the July number that year of the *Christian Examiner*,[125]

but it gave him opportunity for one of the most scathing attacks on Goethe's personality and character in the history of criticism. Contrasting Goethe and Schiller, he writes:

> Goethe and Schiller are an antithesis. Schiller, though ennobled, remained in sympathies essentially plebeian; Goethe had "the predicate" and the indifference "of an Excellency"; Schiller was proudly independent, exhausting his life in strenuous, unrelenting industry, rather than receive a pension; Goethe had no scruple in accepting from a prince enough for wants which he declares were not little. Schiller had a heart which would throb, and a mind which would utter itself freely; to Goethe the affections were inanimate subjects for dissection, and he always considered before he spoke. Schiller's writings bear evidence of discipline in the sublime philosophy of Kant; Goethe had no philosophy, no creed, no principles.

In youth, Bancroft points out, Goethe was "indifferent to God, and reverential only toward rank and the Bourbons"; in maturity, when his country was invaded, he "quietly studied Chinese, or made experiments in natural philosophy," and is the representative of the morals and character of the "broken-down Aristocracy." On matters of public opinion he was silent, being "one of the most wary, calculating, circumspect people of his times." He is "far inferior" to Voltaire in genius, industry, and morality. His conception of freedom, as expressed particularly in three lines of *Tasso*, is his reply to Jefferson and the doctrines of the American Revolution. His works bear evidence that he had "no faith in reason, or in the affections, in God, in man, or in woman." *Wilhelm Meister* and the *Elective Affinities* are products of a poet who "not only had no morals, but scarcely a knowledge of what morality consists in." The denunciation continues:

> It is this ignorance of morals, which gives to Goethe's works one of their peculiarities: insincerity. He is an artist, and not a man. He imitates, he reproduces, he does not create, he does not build up.
> In this want of sincerity lies also the secret of his want of popularity. Goethe is at once dissolute and illiberal. The poet knew in his old age, that he never could become popular. His chances at popularity are diminishing. Twaddle will not pass long for wisdom. The active spirit of movement and progress finds in his works little that attracts sympathy. The conservative loathes him; for there is nothing fixed and permanent and vital in his principles. To rest on him is like trusting in a gale to a dragging anchor, that has caught only in a quicksand.

In everything that relates to firmness of principle, to love of truth for truth itself, to humanity, to holiness, to love of freedom, to virtue, Goethe holds perhaps the lowest place. What man of his genius is comparable to him for baseness? Byron, Voltaire, we had almost said Shelley, soar far above him in moral worth and generous feelings.

After his long tirade, Bancroft admits that Goethe has no superior in the art of writing, of which his prose and shorter poems furnish the best illustration. "Bancroft has written a violent article against Goethe," wrote Longfellow to his friend Greene,[126] and all lovers of Goethe might infer that Bancroft had never read Goethe at all, so completely has he misunderstood him. But if not always consistent in his views, and changing decidedly his attitude between 1824 and 1839, it is evident that Bancroft had unlimited admiration for Goethe's genius and his commanding position in the world of letters. It was, however, the moral aspect of the poet, as revealed in some of his writings, that created the deepest impression on Bancroft. This point of view was manifest, as we have seen, in his journal when he first began reading Goethe, and remained with him throughout the years. He did much to make Goethe known in America, but the poet's views of life and those of the young New England Puritan were essentially different.

As the years passed, Bancroft led, from the time of his retirement from Round Hill, an active life, devoting his time principally to politics, diplomacy, and writing.[127] His *History of the United States*, in ten volumes, appeared at different intervals over a period of forty years. He served, it is well known, as Secretary of the Navy for one year, and as minister to England for three years. As the representative of his country at Berlin during a critical period, 1867 to 1874, including the successive changes from the Kingdom of Prussia to the North German Confederation, and finally to the German Empire, Bancroft, because of his training in former years, was enabled to bring to his post a sympathetic understanding of German life, as did his successor, Bayard Taylor. In his home in the Thiergarten assembled statesmen, scholars, poets, artists, and men of science, including Bismarck,[128] von Moltke, Mommsen, Ranke, Helmholtz, Herman Grimm, and others. In 1868 he received from the University of Bonn the degree of Doctor of Laws, and in September, 1870, the University of Göttingen, in accordance with its custom of renewing degrees on fiftieth anniversaries, sent a special deputy to Berlin to present Bancroft a new diploma. "I answered him in German," says Bancroft, "giving an account of Göttingen in my day." He recalled also his student days at Berlin, and his associations with Schleiermacher, Humboldt, Hegel, and Wolf. The previous June he had announced his intention to endow a scholarship at Exeter Academy,[129] and two years later he wrote to President Eliot of Harvard offering to establish a scholarship in memory of President Kirkland, his former benefactor, and to make possible for deserving young Americans the advantages of study abroad.[130] Knowing his scholarly attainments and the unusual advantages of his position, Bayard Taylor wrote requesting information and assistance in his Goethe studies, to which Bancroft cordially replied:

I shall certainly lend you all the encouragement in my power in the great undertaking on which you have entered. Enclosed is a review from the Journal des Débats, which shows how the interest in Goethe is extending. Of course you know that there is an enormous mass of material in Weimar; and Goethe's grandsons have stores which as yet have remained unused. Here there is little or nothing new.

Of course, the deeper thought you put into your writings, the more you demand *reflection* and high culture in your readers, the narrower will be the number of those who resort to you. But your own internal satisfaction and reward are the greater.

The Masque of the Gods I know only from reviews which have reached me; I shall read the whole poem with close attention and expect it with eagerness.[131]

On his departure from Berlin Bancroft was honored by a farewell dinner given by the Royal Academy, of which he had been elected by a corresponding member as early as 1845. Tributes were paid him by the aristocracy of German letters, including greetings from the Universities of Berlin, Munich, and Heidelberg. When he returned to this country Bancroft adopted Washington as his residence, and continued his interest in things German. He was one of the original members of the Goethe Club of New York City, which was organized in 1874 and played an important role in the literary and cultural life of the country during the seventies of the last century.[132] Throughout the years Bancroft never ceased to manifest a deep interest in German life. He was fond of reading and speaking German, and retained until his death in January, 1891, his faithful servant Hermann, whom he had brought with him from Berlin. In his manner and personal dress, it is said, Bancroft often suggested in later years the appearance of a German, even to the extent of wearing on his pedestrian tours and on horseback a Prussian military cap. A story was current in Washington that when he was accustomed, in the course of his daily exercise, to ride past the Soldiers' Home, a stranger, who had observed him frequently, once asked who was the old gentleman with a military bearing. The guard replied: "That is an old German named Bancroft." [133]

Henry Wadsworth Longfellow

It is sometimes stated that Ticknor was the first American scholar to achieve an international reputation. However, neither he nor any of these ambassadors of learning between Europe and their own country was so important and potent an interpreter as Longfellow. Ticknor, Everett, Cogswell, and Bancroft had preceded him by several years in their sojourns abroad, but coming later, he had the advantage of their experience and the benefit of their enthusiasm. They had blazed the trail; he broadened the path. By nature, he was the most cosmopolitan of all; by temperament, too, he was perhaps the most sensitive to impressions.

As an undergraduate at Bowdoin College, Longfellow gave brilliant evidence of his talents for languages and literature, distinguishing himself in the translation of Latin verse.

> I expected, when I got here [he wrote to his parents on September 22, 1822], that I should have to study very hard to keep on good footing with the rest of the class; but I find I have sufficient time for the preparation of my lessons and for amusement, and that I am not more deficient than the rest of the class. I have not been "screwed" at recitation yet and shall endeavor not to be. So much for egotism.

His letters record the reading and study of Greek and Latin authors, the private reading of English literature, and of French, in which he had had some private instruction in Portland. Moreover, he found time to contribute brief essays and poems to the Portland papers, to the *American Monthly Magazine*, and to the *United States Literary Gazette*. He was graduated in 1825, the fourth in a gifted class of thirty-seven members, which numbered Nathaniel Hawthorne, George Washington Peirce, and others of unusual ability.

In his senior year Longfellow conceived the idea of spending a year after graduation at Harvard principally in the study of general literature. "Whether Nature has given me any capacity for knowledge or not," he wrote to his father in December, "she has at any rate given me a very strong predilection for literary pursuits, and I am almost confident in believing that, if I can ever rise in the world, it must be by the exercise of my talent in the wide field of literature." And again, "Let me reside one year at Cambridge; let me study belles-lettres; and after that time it will not require a spirit of prophecy to predict with some degree of certainty what kind of a figure I could make in the literary world."[1] His chief object, he stated, was to gain as perfect a knowledge of foreign languages, especially French and Italian, as could be had without the advantages of travel abroad.[2] After that year he would decide whether he would elect literature or the law as his calling. His very wise and sympathetic father, then a member of Congress, assented, but the plan for a year at Cambridge was abandoned. In 1825 it was voted to establish a chair of modern languages at Bowdoin, and Longfellow, who, it is said, had made a very favorable impression in his senior examinations by an excellent translation of an ode of Horace, was presented for the new position, with the suggestion that he first go to Europe to prepare for his duties. Longfellow received the proposal with delight. He read law in his father's office during the autumn and winter of 1825–26, and made his preparations for his European journey. In the spring he conferred with President Kirkland in Cambridge, and dined with Ticknor in Boston, "a little Spanish-looking man, but exceedingly kind and affable," who gave him letters to Göttingen professors, to Robert Southey, and to Washington Irving, and strongly recommended that he spend a year in Germany. At Northampton, Cogswell and Bancroft seconded Ticknor's suggestion and also armed him with letters of introduction. Longfellow wrote to his father on May 5 from Albany:

Mr. Ticknor says that the expenses there will not be so great as at Paris, and that it is all-important to have a knowledge of the German language. The lectures on literary history, which he wishes me to attend there, commence in October, and he says I could before that time become sufficiently advanced in the language to understand them. I should take rooms there as at Paris, and should pay about one guinea for a course of lectures. It will, he thinks, be removing me from a great deal of temptation, and moreover be laying a solid foundation for future literary requirement.

For my own part, I must confess that this change in my original plan did not strike me very favorably at first, but the more I reflect upon it, the better I like it. I wish you to write me, at New York, as soon as you receive this, and tell me what you think of the change in my plans. Mr. Ticknor and Mr. Bancroft have both studied at Göttingen, and of course their opinion upon the subject is of much weight.

On May 15 Longfellow sailed for Europe. After a month's crossing he landed at Havre, and immediately settled in Paris for a residence of more than eight months, before proceeding to Spain for the same length of time, and later to Italy for a year. In the course of this entire period the question of his plans, especially for study at Göttingen, was the principal subject of various letters which passed between him and his parents. He was disposed to substitute a residence in Germany for that in Spain, "inasmuch as the German language is infinitely more important than the Spanish, being infinitely more rich in literary resources," and furthermore he did not relish the idea of entering Spain, a country filled "with the horrors of Civil war." He wrote to his father of his disappointments concerning the immediate advantages and of his slow progress in learning French. He proposed a change in his plans:

I am convinced that if I remain here but two years I had better relinquish the Spanish language for the German, since I cannot acquire a thorough knowledge of four languages in so short a time. This was the advice which Mr. Bancroft and Mr. Cogswell gave me, who of course are well qualified to judge upon the subject. If you are of the same opinion, the plan which strikes me as being most plausible is to pursue the French most vigorously for a few months, then to commence Italian — learn its principles thoroughly — spend the Spring in Italy to speak the language, and spend the summer and succeeding winter in Germany. This to be sure is changing our plans, from the very foundation, since the year which I intended to pass in Paris, will be essentially shortened.[3]

Further change and indecision are indicated in a letter later in the same month:

The question then will be which is the most important for me as a scholar, the German language or the Italian? All those who have spoken to me on the subject in America have told me by all means to become a German scholar — that the language was rich in literary resources — and that no student ever regretted a year's residence at Göttingen. Mr. Ticknor said "give up the Italian for the German" and moreover urged me very strenuously to go first to Germany — tho' for my own part I am well satisfied with learning the French first.

Mr. Bancroft and Mr. Cogswell both said that the German was all-important and advised me to lengthen my residence in Europe rather than return without a knowledge of it. So much for our own counselors. For my part I do not imagine that I could learn to speak the German with correctness and fluency in the space of a year — but if I go there in the spring instead of to Italy, I shall learn the language perfectly enough to read it, and to understand the literary lectures which commence in November or the last of October. I must confess that this is the course which I wish to adopt. I had rather be master of the German and French than to know them superficially together with the Italian and Spanish, and I make this proposition to you as the one which of all others I should choose — though in my last letter I proposed going into Italy in the spring. But let us take all possible suppositions and propositions into view, and then decide. Spain I must give up — which then to choose — the German or the Italian. If I can have but one, it should be German; if both, the Italian last. Hence I am for remaining here in my comfortable winter quarters until March or April and then for passing into Germany to remain a year.[4]

He suggested that his father confer with Ticknor, or Cogswell, or Bancroft on the subject of Göttingen and "the advantages of the German literature and language." His mother, who had felt from the beginning that his European journey meant "going into a thousand perils," had read that Göttingen students were "very licentious, unrestrained by the government, extremely addicted to duelling," and was of the opinion that such association would be neither pleasant nor profitable. "As to acquiring the German language," she wrote him, "I think you will not be able to acquire it without extending the length of your absence beyond the year and a half, as we contemplated. I am told it takes a great deal of time and is a very difficult language to attain correctly." Moreover, she advised against the danger of "the confusion of Babel" in the acquisition of so many languages. Longfellow promptly assured her that there was no cause for fear, since he had never had any particular fondness for a duel, but he added: "It would be useless to go to Germany unless I could remain at least a year." He had hoped, he stated, to learn the language and to acquire some knowledge of the literature within a few months, but on being informed that more time was necessary to devote to it, he was reverting to his original plan of proceeding from France to Spain and Italy, though to the latter country first, in view of the dangerous state of affairs in Spain.[5] His father, who had suggested that he might eventually visit Göttingen, "if it should be thought advisable to visit that place," urged his attention, first of all, to French and Spanish. In his opinion, Spanish was of more importance than Italian or German, owing to the relations developing between the United States and South America. But, he adds, "I consider the German language and literature much more important than the Italian; and if you can learn only one, the former is to be preferred." [6] However, in February of the next year he wrote urging his son not to expose himself to the unsettled conditions in Spain. He suggested that he might have good advantages for learning Spanish, as well as German, at Göttingen. [7] After conferring with Ticknor on the subject, he forwarded in August a letter to Longfellow, then in Madrid:

I have recently seen Mr. Ticknor, who appears very anxious that you should go to Germany. He says the acquisition of the German language will be of more importance to you as a literary man than any two other languages within his knowledge, as it unlocks a vast store of learning and you find in that language the best treatises on French, Spanish, and even English literature that are to be found in any language. Although you may be correct in your supposition that generally speaking a situation in a private family in a retired town would be better than a university, I should doubt whether a seclusion of that kind in Germany would be so advantageous to you as a residence at the University at Göttingen. Mr. Ticknor says the advantages there for perfecting your knowledge of all the languages are very great, and the expenses are much less than at any other place in Europe. The Lectures also are of very great advantage to a literary man. I am disposed to do all in my power to make your education as perfect as possible, and as you are now abroad, I should be sorry for you to omit anything which could occasion regret hereafter. [8]

In another letter, however, written within a few days, he advised his son not to relinquish entirely the idea of visiting Italy, even for a brief period, though he considered it much less important to learn to speak the Italian language than the French or Spanish. Again, we note the further influence of Ticknor:

It seems to be the opinion of literary gentlemen that the German language will be more important for you than the Italian, and if you can acquire but one, it should be the former. Mr. Ticknor says you will be able to obtain a good knowledge of the Italian at Göttingen, at the same time that you are learning the German. As there is no gentleman in this State who is master of the German language, it is desirable that you should learn it, if you can do it without too much time and expense. I suggested in my last that probably you would enjoy more advantages at Göttingen than any other place, and this appears to be the opinion of those who are better judges than I am. But you must get the best information you can and pursue the wisest and best course, keeping constantly in view the object which you are pursuing, sensible of my solicitude for your health, morals and literary improvement. I am sure you will do all in your power to improve your advantages and avoid temptations.[9]

Meanwhile, Longfellow had proceeded to Spain and to Italy. In the course of his year he was drawn more and more to the idea of studying in Germany. "I feel anxious to get into Germany, at least as much so as I do to see Rome and Naples," he wrote from Florence on January 23, 1828, to his mother, and in April a letter to his brother Stephen referred to Göttingen and expressed the hope that he might yet see its venerable walls. On December 19 he wrote to his father: "I intend leaving Venice in a few days for Dresden, where I think of remaining until the opening of spring. I do not wish to return without a competent knowledge of German. All that I can do to acquire it shall be done." On reaching Dresden, he would decide whether to remain there or to hasten to Göttingen. A week later he adds: "I can hardly reconcile myself to the idea of relinquishing my studies at a German university. I become daily more and more impressed with the importance of it. My familiarity with the modern languages will unlock to me all those springs of literature, which formerly would have been as sealed books to me."

From Venice Longfellow journeyed to Vienna, then to Prague, and entered Germany the middle of January, 1829. On April 9 his father wrote:

It gives me great pleasure to learn that you have at length arrived in Germany, are diligently pursuing your studies there, and above all that you are enjoying good health. . . . At Dresden, under the duties of a good private instructor you will probably make more rapid progress in learning the German language than you would at a university, as you may not be so subject to interruptions as you would at Göttingen. But if you had more time to devote to German literature, your advantages would undoubtedly be much greater at the latter place than the former, and the reputation of having studied at Göttingen would have considerable weight with those who are influenced by *names*. On the whole, I hope you will be able to spend some time at that university, as it will make you acquainted with the system of education and the modes of instruction, which may be useful in after life, especially if you should connect yourself with a similar institution. . . . It is very desirable that you should remain in Germany long enough to obtain a competent knowledge of the language . . . for it will be of great importance to you as a literary man.

However, the father's advice was belated. Longfellow had spent about a month in Dresden in observing the customs of the people, frequenting the concerts, opera, and balls, and enjoying the social advantages of the city, having brought with him letters of introduction from Washington Irving. Also, he did a little work on Spanish in the Royal Library, and received private lessons in German under an instructor, who, Longfellow says in his journal for February 9, "is a very fine specimen of the 'shabby genteel' and would be an acquisition to almost any cabinet of natural history." After two days in Leipzig Longfellow arrived on February 22 in Göttingen, where he joined his friend, Edward Preble, and continued his studies until the following June.[10]

On February 27 Longfellow wrote to his father informing him of his safe arrival in Göttingen and of his happy meeting with his friend Preble. He gave his impressions of his new environment and requested permission to extend his Göttingen residence through the summer:

I find living at Göttingen very cheap. As I have just arrived, I cannot give you any just idea of what my expenses will be monthly; but as soon as I have been here a little longer I will send you a continuation of what my last letter contained. The Library here is the largest in Germany and is full of choice rare works; and the advantages for a student of my particular pursuits are certainly not overrated in the universal fame of the University of Göttingen. . . . I brought letters to several of the professors here from Bancroft and Ticknor, and have been well received. Göttingen is a small city, and there are no amusements here whatever; so there is no alternative but study. With regard to duelling, for which all the German universities are more or less notorious, you will find a description of them in the North American for July 1828, page 87. They are considered by the students as sport; and it is not uncommon to hear of six being fought in one afternoon on the same spot. There is, however, no possibility of Preble or myself being engaged in these affairs, as we do not know the broad-sword exercise, and are of course *hors de combat*. There are about fourteen or fifteen hundred students; as in all universities, some are scholars, and others high, wild fellows. He who wishes to be distinguished must fight his way to distinction; but he who wishes to pursue his studies quietly is no more molested here than at one of our colleges.

A letter to his sister on March 28 says: "With Göttingen I am much delighted, though I have no other society than my books. My studies, you already know, are modern languages and modern literature." A few days before he had informed his father that he had established acquaintance with some of the leading professors, with Eichhorn, Heeren, Blumenbach, and Bode, and that he liked Göttingen more and more. He had of late been "reading a little and thinking much" on the subject of education, and was moved to draw certain comparisons between the foreign educational system and that of his own country:

Germany and France may well boast of their schools and universities. Good Heavens! what advantages have they not in these countries! Here indeed the gates of wisdom may be emphatically said to be swung wide open. There is a voice of free grace crying to all, that the fountains of their salvation are open. — May it soon be heard in our own happy land, swelling above the voice of worldly gain, and the roar of political strife.

What has heretofore been the idea of an University with us? The answer is a simple one: — Two or three large brick buildings, — with a chapel, and a President to pray in it! — I say University, because with us University and College, have till now been almost synonymous terms. Mr. Jefferson it is true made a bold attempt — but it failed — if not totally at least in part — it failed — and why? — Because, with all due respect, he does not seem to have begun right. He began where every body else in *our* country would have begun — by building college halls, and then trying to stock them with Students. — But that is not the way to found an University. European Universities were never founded in this manner. Indeed, as far as regards University buildings — one might live in Göttingen from one year's end to the other without having the slightest idea of its being the seat of a University. — No — it was by collecting together professors in whom the spirit moved — who were well enough known to attract students to themselves, and after they had assembled them capable of teaching them something they did not know before. It was so with the Italian, Spanish, German and French Universities — and when there is an American University, it must and will be so with that. Then, instead of seeing a new College ushered into existence every winter by a petition to the Legislature for funds to put up a parcel of Woolen-Factory buildings for students — we should see capital better employed in enriching the libraries of the country and making them *public*! — and instead of seeing the youth of our country chained together like galley slaves and be "scourged to their dungeon" — as it were — our eyes would be cheered by the grateful spectacle of mind throwing its fetters off — and education free from its chain and shackles.[11]

He would like to see a university on the European plan established in Portland, and also a public library liberally supported by the town. On this subject he wrote:

The Library too should be furnished with books in foreign languages as well as in the vernacular. As much attention has of late been given to modern languages in Portland, — the means of pursuing those studies — and of investigating more or less the literature of different nations, is of great and vital importance. In order to preserve a knowledge of any language, one must have constant exercise in it. This exercise of course consists in conversation and in reading. Now in Portland opportunities for conversation in French, Italian, Spanish and German are comparatively rare — hence in order to preserve a familiarity with a language in whose acquisition we have passed months if not years — and of course would not willingly forget — tho nothing is easier than to forget a language — we have no other resource than books: at all events, upon books we must place our principal reliance. If these books be not within our reach — there is no remedy. We must forget what we have learned by laborious study. Indeed — one month, when our thoughts are turned into other channels, will do more toward forgetting a language than the labor of six toward its acquisition. The importance of furnishing our library with standard authors becomes at once evident. — I mean authors in the four principal foreign languages.

A tour of one month during the spring, which took Longfellow as far as London, gave him an opportunity to enjoy a trip down the Rhine — "a noble river," he said, "but not so fine as the Hudson." He traveled in parts of Belgium, France, and Holland, and on returning to his studies he wrote to his father on May 15:

I am now very much occupied with my studies. But unfortunately there are no lectures on modern literary history. The courses I attend are Wendt on Natural Law, Heeren on Ancient History, and a third on Modern History by the same. This occupies three hours of the day; the remainder is occupied in study of the German language under the guidance of an able professor, and in pursuing other branches of literature.

The professor of German was of course George Benecke, who had given instruction in the subject to all the other Americans at

Göttingen. Longfellow found the language "beyond measure difficult," not to read, he reports, but to write, and he deemed correct writing necessary in order to teach. "I can only promise you to do my best," he wrote his father. "I can assuredly lay a good foundation, and much more I cannot expect to do." Furthermore, at this time he was writing "a kind of Sketch-Book of scenes in France, Spain, and Italy," which was a preparation for *Outre-Mer*, and was reading in the classics in Spanish, French, and English writers. His journal contains notes on various subjects, and "The Old Dominion Zeitung," a manuscript journal which he and Preble edited weekly in their playful moments, is a miscellaneous collections of quotations, descriptions, drawings, puns, and nonsense, probably included as much for the amusement of their respective families as for themselves.[12] The "Prospectus to the Public" which accompanies the first number states:

A Journal, that should be at once a vehicle of amusement and of Foreign Intelligence, has long been a desideratum in the literary world. It is to fill up this hiatus, that the Editors of the Old Dominion Zeitung have determined to issue their Journal. In making it worthy of themselves, no time nor pains will be spared by them — they are resolved to 'go the whole hog.'

But it does not become us to boast the merits of our paper — let it speak for itself. Coming from the University Press we hope it may be an acceptable offering to the Public. There is a literary atmosphere about the walls of Göttingen which breathes new life into the nostrils that inhale it. Something of this we hope to communicate to our readers through the medium of our columns; and if we can amuse one listless hour — cheat the heart of a moment's care — or chase one cloud from his thoughts — our labors are not in vain. — We hope at least to amuse our readers and that the Zeitung like 'kerchief checker'd with heavenly blue' may wipe all tears from their eyes!

There is no evidence that Longfellow, during this Göttingen period, made any extensive study of German literature. The list of books which he drew from the library deals chiefly with the literature of France, Spain, and Italy. His notebook contains brief quotations from Byron, Wordsworth, Luther, and Heine, and a line from Voss's *Luise*. A short note referring to the influence of poetry on character, with quotations from *Iphigenie*,[13] furnishes the one reference to Goethe.[14]

While on his London tour he passed through Frankfort, and was there again on June 8, on his return home. He may have seen Goethe's house on one or both of these journeys, though he makes no mention of it. Nor is there any evidence that, like his American predecessors at Göttingen, he was inspired to travel the road to Weimar. Early in May his generous father had consented to his remaining at Göttingen through the summer, but had insisted on his return in the autumn. "It is unfortunate," he said, "that your visit to Germany has been so long delayed, but regrets on that subject are unavailing, and we must make the best of improvement of the short time which remains." However, a feeling of homesickness rather than orders from parental authority probably curtailed Longfellow's residence abroad, and he departed from Göttingen on June 6. From Paris a few days later he wrote of Göttingen to his friend, George W. Greene: "I can only say, do not on any accounts omit studying there, if your health will permit. I never saw so great advantages for a student — and living is moderate." [15]

The following July he sailed from Liverpool and arrived home on August 11, to begin his duties at Bowdoin, where he remained for the next five years.

This, the first of Longfellow's four trips to Europe, had come at a fortunate period in his career. As a result of his contact with foreign countries he returned considerably less the Puritan, with enthusiasm, and with his horizon widened, ready to give evidence of his training.[16] "I am thoroughly persuaded, that in no part of the world, could you pass two years more profitably than in Germany," he writes in October of the next year to his friend Greene, who was then on the point of sailing for Europe. "I will send you letters to my friends and instructors in Göttingen, and will procure you others to Schlegel, the celebrated philologist at Bonn, on the Rhine, which place I hope you will not fail to see." After the first few weeks of his work at Bowdoin, Longfellow wrote to Lieutenant Slidell of the Navy:

How unstable and precarious an acquisition is that of languages! — I refer to the facility of speaking them. My foothold is slipping from under me daily; and it is a subject on which I feel pretty sensitive now, having placed myself in a situation peculiarly liable to animadversion. The only consolation I have is that at some future day I shall be forced to go back to Europe again for nobody in this part of the world pretends to speak anything but English — and some might dispute them even that prerogative.[17]

Although the young professor served as college librarian, the greater part of his time was devoted to romance languages, in connection with which he prepared several textbooks. He also gave some instruction in German, after the subject was introduced in the curriculum in 1831, and continued his private readings at random in German literature. In addition to his regular college duties he delivered public lectures and contributed to various journals. On June 2, 1832, he informs Greene: "I now have a strong desire to tread the stage on which I can take longer strides, and speak to a larger audience." Cogswell, as we have noted, proposed that he take charge of Round Hill, but Longfellow's friends discouraged his acceptance. The possibility of a professorship of Spanish at New York University and of modern languages at the University of Virginia made strong appeals. His course was determined when, on Ticknor's recommendation of him as "an accomplished general scholar, particularly in modern literature," [18] he was chosen in December, 1834, for the famous Smith Professorship at Harvard, with the understanding that, if he wished, he might reside a period in Europe "for the purpose of a more perfect attainment of your German." [19] The proposal was immediately accepted. "The intelligence communicated by Mr. Ticknor and in your last letter has given me more delight than I know how to express," wrote Longfellow's friend, Cornelius C. Felton, "and I devoutly hope we shall hear no more of your going into the Cimmerian region of New York Presbyterianism." [20]

On April 10 of the following year Longfellow and his wife, the former Mary Storer Potter, and two friends embarked for a period of eighteen months abroad, armed with letters of introduction from Emerson and Jared Sparks.

The party reached Portsmouth on May 8, and were soon in London for a three weeks' visit. Longfellow made the acquaintance of many distinguished figures, among them Hayward, the translator of *Faust*, who was "interesting and intellectual looking,"[21] and the Carlyles, to whom Emerson had given him an introduction. Writing of his call on Mrs. Carlyle at Chelsea, he states:

Speaking of Hayward, the prose-translator of Goethe's *Faust*, she said she did not like the book, and did not think the translator equal to his task.

"But in his Preface he animadverts harshly upon the defects of other translators."

"Oh yes, indeed; detraction is the element in which he moves and has his being." [22]

His journal for the evening of May 30 records a visit with Carlyle, whom he describes thus:

He is a tall man — with coal-black hair — brown complexion, and a face that reminds you of Burns. His dress, an old blue coat, worn trousers, and carpet socks upon his feet. His manners awkward, almost clownish. But his conversation is glorious — so natural — and bearing the stamp of so free and original a mind.

Subsequently we read in the journal:

Passed this morning over a coal fire, reading Carlyle's Life of Schiller; a work of rare merit, written by one who entered *con amore* into his subject. It is altogether a fine biographical sketch; though the author speaks slightingly of it, and "wonders how anyone can read so tame and colorless a production." It is nearly two oclock in the morning, and I have just finished The Life of Schiller, a truly, noble delineation of the life, character and writings of that great and good man. I shall lie down to sleep with my soul quickened, and my good resolutions and aspirations strengthened. God grant that the light of morning may not dissipate them all. [23]

Of his visit three days later at Chelsea, when he breakfasted with the Carlyles, he writes:

He stepped out of the room for a few minutes and I asked his wife if he considered Goethe the greatest man that ever lived. She replied:

Oh yes, I believe he does indeed. He thinks him the greatest man that ever lived, excepting Jesus Christ."

Mrs. Carlyle is also a German scholar. She told me her husband was much pleased with what she said of her own impressions of Schiller and Goethe. "What I read of Schiller makes me shed tears; but what I read of Goethe, I read a second time." Her husband wrote this to Goethe, who expressed himself much gratified; as his aim was to make people think, and not to move their sympathies. Goethe she thinks the greater man, Schiller the most lovable. [24]

From London Longfellow journeyed to the Scandinavian countries for the summer months. "I have given up the plan of passing the winter in Berlin," he informed his father from Copenhagen. "I prefer some place upon or near the Rhine, both on account of climate and expense. Heidelberg on the Neckar, a few miles from Mannheim, will probably be the place." [25] A part of the autumn was spent in Holland,[26] where his visit was saddened by the death of his wife. He proceeded up the Rhine, and at Bonn called on August Wilhelm Schlegel. He gives this vivid description of his visit:

> I was shown up into a small room, furnished with a desk or two, a table, sofa and chairs. On one of the desks was a bust of Schlegel. The servant maid threw a few fagots into the chimney, and kindled a fire. In a few minutes enter Schlegel: an old man, stooping under the burden of some three-score years. He wore a little black skull cap; a frilled shirt, without cravat; a loose, brown or rather clarat surtout, drab pantaloons and clock slippers. His forehead broad and high, eyes large, and the expression of his countenance intellectual and pleasant. He rather lectured than conversed: — so I shall not pretend to record what he said. He was, to tell the truth, rather discursive; and I could not get him upon any topics of interest to myself. Still I was much gratified to see the translator of Shakespeare. He is very much of a gentleman — and takes snuff from an ornamental box of tortoise shell.[27]

On the evening of December 11 Longfellow arrived in Heidelberg, at the Prinz Karl. Some days later he was comfortably settled in the home of Frau Himmelhahn, from which he had a commanding view of the surrounding country:

> The rooms they have given us look upon the market place, and towering up almost perpendicularly rise the mountains covered by the ruins of Heidelberg Castle. A pathway leads from the square up the hill-side to this magnificent relic of the past. The view from the terrace down into the valley of the Neckar, with the roofs of the town thick crowded beneath, the arches of the bridge of stone, and the huge form of Heiligenberg on the opposite side of the river, is magnificent. The whole reminds me of the Alhambra and the valley of the Darro.[28]

His journal and letters for the winter and spring in Heidelberg, as for the remainder of his travels, record his various activities and experiences, some of which were later embodied in those of Paul Flemming in *Hyperion*. Although he found the climate disagreeable, and the people in general "rather limited in their notions," he was charmed with his new environment. He made sundry excursions through the country, became intimate with some of the professors at the University, formed an acquaintance with Gervinus, the historian of German literature, who was "quiet and friendly in his manners," saw much of Clara Crowninshield, who had accompanied the family to Europe, and met here for the first time William Cullen Bryant [29] and Samuel Ward.[30] The University, consisting of 400 students, "smoking in the streets, and even in the lecture rooms," included a distinguished law faculty, but a literary faculty "null and void," though Longfellow found the library large and especially rich in old manuscripts, which were shown him by Dr. Umbreit, "a worshiper of Goethe." He heard lectures by Thibaut on the Pandects, by Schlosser on modern history, and by Reichlin-Meldegg on Shakespeare and Schiller. His greatest progress, however, was derived from private discussions and the incessant reading of German literature. At the beginning of the year he planned a careful and systematic study of the literature from the early periods to the close of the fifteenth century,[31] and like Paul Flemming "buried himself in books, — in old dusty books," while assembling his materials. "I have already accumulated six centuries of German literature in this way," he informs his friend Greene.[32] In the preparation of this proposed publication he read the *Nibelungenlied*, *Till Eulenspiegel*, and various collections of early literature. But the journal for the greater part of the period indicates that he was particularly interested in the literature of the eighteenth and nineteenth centuries. Early in January he heard Reichlin-Meldegg lecture in "barbarous German" on Schiller's *Don Carlos*, and Schlosser discourse on the Romantic School and young Germany.[33] During the month he was reading *Heinrich von Ofterdingen*, "wild and singular," with its "strangely beautiful thoughts," a biography and some of the ballads of Bürger, with their "peculiar and musical" style,[34] and stories by Tieck, Jean Paul Richter, Grimm, Musäeus, Chamisso, and Hoffmann.[35] The remaining four months he read intensively various writers — Hölty, Salis,[36] Schiller, Goethe, Lessing, Madame de Staël, Heine, Herder, Klopstock, the Stolbergs, Fouqué, Uhland, Görres, and more than any other Jean Paul. The sermon of the Friar in *Wallensteins Lager* impressed him as "curious enough"; the *Piccolomini* was interesting, though as in *Don Carlos* "too much is said and too little done," while *Wallensteins Tod* is "fine, in parts magnificent"; [37] *Emilia*

Galotti is a "horrible tragedy . . . not written with much art, nor is there much development of character"; [38] *Nathan der Weise* is not a masterpiece, does not close satisfactorily, though the story of the three rings "is beautiful and as good as a sermon"; [39] Heine's *Romantische Schule* is "a pungent critical sketch containing too much vituperation," but "what he says of Goethe is beautiful." [40] There are numerous references to Jean Paul, whose brilliant wit, comparable, in Longfellow's opinion, to that of Sterne, kindled his imagination. He thinks that the *Flegeljahre* ends most unsatisfactorily, and that the plan of *Titan* is very defective, though the description of scenery and the drawing and development of character are masterly. [41] The journal furnishes the following general observations:

> He is difficult to understand — intricate — strange — drawing his illustrations from every by-corner of science, art, and nature — bold and daring in his style — a comet among the bright stars of German literature. Among this all, to him may be applied the title of "glorious." — To read his writings is like climbing a high mountain in merry company to see the sun rise. At times you are enveloped in mist — the morning wind sweeps by you with a shout; — you hear the distant thunder. Wide beneath you spreads the landscape — field, meadow, town and winding river — the ringing of distant church-bells, or the sounds of solemn village clock reaches you — then arises the sweet and manifold fragrance of flowers — the little birds begin to sing — up comes the glorious sun — the vapors roll away. You revel like the lark in the sunshine and bright blue heaven — and all is a delirious dream of soul and sense — when suddenly a waggish friend at your elbow awakes you from your trance by a bad joke, and offers you a piece of Bologna sausage. — As in real life, so in his writings, the serious and comic — the sublime and the grotesque — the pathetic and the ludicrous are mingled together. It is strange that a man whose soul was so full of poetry should have worn a yellow Nankeen coat and get maudlin on beer.
>
> Jean Paul runs into so many foolish extravagances in his style, that I get out of humor with him. This eagle of German literature is not content to sweep through the bright fields of pure air and bright sunshine — but he must dart into the thunder clouds, — and hide himself in mists and vapors. He soars beyond our ken, and we only hear his scream. It is not because he is so far above us, that we cannot follow him — but because he is enveloped in a cloud. [42]

According to the journal, Longfellow during his Heidelberg period was more interested in Goethe than in any other writer except Jean Paul. A few days after his arrival he engaged in an argument with Fräulein Hepp upon the merits of Goethe and Schiller.[43] "Goethe is the idol of her poetic devotion," he writes, "and the *Sorrows of Werther* lie near her heart. I told her I thought the moral impression of Goethe's works was not good, to which she replied: 'Das ist das allgemeine Irrthum.'" He read Schiller's *Don Carlos*, "a tragedy of great interest," purchased on December 23 from an antiquarian an edition of fifty-five volumes of Goethe's works, and six days later wrote in his journal:

Read the *Sorrows of Werther* in German. The language and imagery are beautiful. In England and America the book is sneered at, I think it is not understood. In one or two places the author has suffered the love for simple homely virtue to carry him a little too far; as Wordsworth has done in his poetry. They have both been laughed at by persons who have intellect without tenderness of heart, and by those who have neither; but not by the few who have both. Thus, for example, when Goethe describes the delight his Werther felt in going into his garden at sunrise to gather green peas — in sitting down to shell them — while he read his Homer — in choosing his sauce-pan — buttering his pea pods, and stirring them over the kitchen fire, it required a mind of peculiar tone to enter into the *ideal* of such a scene, and with the hero "powerfully feel how the superb lovers of Penelope slew oxen and swine, hewed them piece-meal and roasted them." To the great majority of readers the whole transaction is ridiculous in a romance; a very few only will see therein a forthshadowing of simple, patriarchal life.

The book is the history of a young man of fine intellect, and a heart overflowing with a love for the good and beautiful — full of the religion of Nature—of violent passions—unrestrained by Christian principle. He is weak, like a little child. He has the intellect of a man, with the heart of a child. He suffers himself to be swept away to self-destruction, by a fatal passion for the betrothed — and afterwards the wedded wife of another; till at last, the balance of his mind destroyed — in a cool kind of frenzy and despair he shoots himself "in a blue frock-coat and yellow waistcoat." He believes that a man has power given him over his own life — to resign it when he will. But his reasonings on this head are very weak. To a man placed in a similar situation with Werther — and like him without a fixed Christian rule of conduct—they might seem powerful. His reflexions are demons grim and terrible — like those that of old in bodily shape beset the saints—and like them they vanish at the sign of the cross.

After all such books are not favorites with me. The impression they leave in the soul is one of unrest and pain. This is not the company

I love to keep. I should shun the society of a person, who with all Werther's admirable qualities of heart and mind, talked and acted as he does. Therefore such books do not lie "close to my heart and mine eye." [44]

The following day Longfellow was reading various books, among them *Wilhelm Meister*, especially a few pages in the "History of a Beautiful Soul." He writes: "The effect which Wilhelm Meister produced upon me, when I first read it, was not that of a good book: — it was decidedly bad. I mean to read it again, and if the effect be the same, it seems a fair conclusion, that the moral impression of the book is not good." [45] Evidently, in his early readings of Goethe, he was deeply concerned with the moral aspect of the poet's writings. In later years he arrived at a different conception of the novel, and something of his interest in it is seen in *Hyperion*, when, writing of the Heidelberg experiences, the Baron says to Paul Flemming, "Why, the women already call you Wilhelm Meister." [46]

On Saturday, March 5, we note the following: "Commenced Goethe's autobiography. He lingers with the garrulity of old age on the most trifling recollections of his childhood, and records with a minuteness which is tedious." Three days later he read *Die Geschwister*, "which though trifling as a literary production, has one or two touches of pathos." [47] In April, while on a four days' excursion to Frankfort, he saw the annual fair, the statue of Ariadne, heard his favorite opera, Don Giovanni, and on Tuesday, April 12, visited for the first time, it would appear from his journal, Goethe's house.[48] It was the house in which Goethe was born, and the scenes he frequented in his childhood and remembered in his old age, we learn later in *Hyperion*, that interested the Baron and Paul Flemming most. "Thus, O Genius: are thy footprints hallowed, and the star shines forever over the place of thy nativity." [49] In May the journal continues: "Began Goethe's *Egmont*; and read the first act, which begins to be interesting towards its close. The character of Clärchen interests me. She is gentle and interesting; but one sees from the beginning that she is to be a victim in the Tragedy." [50] At the close of this month [51] he began reading *Faust*, and in June Eckermann's *Conversations with Goethe*. Of Eckermann he writes: "He is another Boswell — a jackall to this German lion." [52] Meanwhile, Longfellow mentions meeting a few days earlier at the hotel a gentleman who, in his remarks on Jean Paul and Goethe, passed severe judgment on the latter,[53] to which Longfellow adds:

There is some truth in the fat man's criticism of Goethe. He certainly loved to describe the painfully interesting scenes of human frailty, and they take a strong hold upon our sensibilities, because we also are human. There is a living reality and truth about the works, which none can deny. Human nature is seen there in a mirror, but alas! only in its degradation; not in its brightness and strength, and purity. His admirers say this is a true picture of life; and when they have said this, they think that they have said all, that all objections are answered. But who has told them that books are to be nothing more than an exact reflexion of what passes in real life? There is enough misery in the world to make our hearts heavy; in books let us have something more than this — something to strengthen and elevate and purify us. Schiller, the beautiful Schiller, does this. He is the prophet of the ideal, Goethe the prophet of the real.[54]

Ticknor wrote from Dresden to Longfellow that the training in a German university was superior to that of any other place for the teaching of literature, as there was more "absolute learning in Germany than in all the rest of the world besides." [55] In the course of time, however, Longfellow became lonely and restless, critical of his environment,[56] and longed for home. In May he writes: "I am growing tired of being cooped up here in Heidelberg, beautiful as it is. I feel a strong desire to be once more on the wing." [57] In June, following an excursion of several days to Ems and neighboring cities, he states: "My mind has lost its sensibility and does not feel the spur. I cannot study, and therefore I think I had better go home." [58] Concluding that he would journey to the Austrian Tyrol and to Switzerland for the summer before his return home, he left Heidelberg on June 25. At Stuttgart he heard music in the gardens and recorded his impression of the people: "Even the ladies drink beer; and on every table was a row of foaming glasses. The Suabians are generally considered to be a rough and even a stupid people; I do not pretend to say with how much justice." [59] He called on the sculptor, Dannecker, but was unable to find Uhland anywhere. In the neighboring village of Kamerstadt he endured a lengthy sermon on the Reformation and first heard sung "Ein

feste Burg." Munich, where he spent three days, created a favorable impression, with its attractive women, its English Garden,
its art collections, and especially the Royal Palace, containing
paintings of subjects from Bürger, Goethe, Schiller, and other
poets. He made a sketch of Count Rumford's monument, which
he thought looked neglected. "It was with a feeling of pride and
pleasure," says Longfellow, "that I thought that the man who
planned and executed the beautiful works around me, was an
American. Yet here he seems to be known only as the patron of
a Soup-house." [60] One of his three companions in the stage-
coach from Munich to Salzburg was Grillparzer, "a poet from
Vienna, an insignificant man in appearance; but a very pleasant
one in reality." [61] He passed through the Tyrol to Switzerland,
and at Thun on July 20 first became acquainted with the family
of Mr. Nathan Appleton, whom he later joined in part of his
travels. "Mr. L. gave us a lesson in German, pretty ballads of
Uhland, 'Der junge König,' and 'Das Schloss am Meer,'"
writes Frances Appleton in her journal for August 3 at Inter-
lachen. A few evenings later, in Zurich, Longfellow tells us he
translated Uhland's "The Castle by the Sea," with "the assistance of Lady Fanny, who was scribe on the occasion, and
made some of the best lines." [62] At Schaffhausen he read *Modern
Characteristics*, a work on German writers of the day, and noted,
"The sketch of Hoffmann von Fallersleben is capital." Here
Ticknor fell in with the party, and Frances Appleton listened
with interest to the discussion of the educational system in German universities. After an absence of two months Longfellow
returned to Heidelberg for a week, and arrived early in September in Paris, where, in observing the varied throng on the boule-
vards, he was reminded of Goethe's description of nature in
Werther.[63] On October 10 he sailed from Havre, and returned to
his home in Portland the following November.

In December, 1836, Longfellow settled in Cambridge, preparatory to assuming the duties of his Harvard professorship, which
he held until 1854, when he was succeeded by Lowell. "I have
not yet entered upon my college duties; nor shall I this term,"
he soon informed his father. "What these duties will be seems
quite uncertain, though I think I shall have nothing to do but
lecture. I have already begun my preparations for a course on

German Literature, which I hope to deliver next summer." [64]
Of his plan for lectures he wrote to Greene: "I do not write
them out, but make notes and translations. I think this the best
way, decidedly." [65] On February 3 President Quincy officially
notified him of the formal approval of his election the previous
day by the Overseers, and later in the month he received from
his father the following letter:

I rejoice, my dear son, that you are at length established in so very
eligible a situation. With your literary tastes and habits, I can hardly
conceive of a more pleasant location, and I most sincerely hope and
pray it may remain permanent, and that no unfortunate circumstances
may occur to mar your enjoyment or diminish your usefulness. I think
your ambition must be satisfied, and your only object now will be to fill
with eminence and distinction the office in which you are placed, and to
become distinguished among the literary men of the age. [66]

Harvard College was still the conservative institution which
Longfellow's predecessor had formed many years before, though,
as we have seen, Ticknor had instituted certain reforms, especially in his own field of instruction. "Into this snug little
coterie," writes Edward Everett Hale, "came Longfellow. . . .
He was fresh from Europe. He could talk in French with French-
men, Italian with Italians, and German with Germans." [67] The
resignation of Ticknor and of Follen had left the department
over which Longfellow was to preside with four instructors,
among them Hermann Bokum, instructor in German. [68] Meanwhile, the professor had his views on the methods of teaching
German and proceeded, during the early months of 1837, to give
instruction in the language to a small class which met informally
in the "Corporation Room" in University Hall, where he later
delivered his lectures. In his undergraduate diary for April 26,
Edward Everett Hale says: "We recited in German for the first
time to Prof. Longfellow. The recitations, or rather the exercise, for we had no lesson set before us, was very easy. I think
we shall like the study very much." [69] In May Longfellow informed his father that he would soon commence his lectures, and
gave a list of the subjects to be covered. Of the twelve lectures
he will offer, seven deal with German. One of these is on the
history of the language, another provides for a sketch of the
literature, while three are devoted to Goethe, and two are on

Jean Paul. Some are to be written lectures, while others will be delivered from notes, he announces,[70] to which the father replies urging him to prepare in "most elegant and appropriate language" all his lectures in writing, in order "to have something to rely on, if any perturbation or embarrassment should arise."[71] A few days afterward the lectures were begun, and the young professor was much pleased with his success.[72]

Among Longfellow's papers are notes providing the materials for lectures which he delivered from time to time during the years of his professorship. The notes on Jean Paul include a sketch of his life, which, Longfellow states, appealed to him as being more interesting, instructive, and encouraging than that of any other author. He urges his students to read Jean Paul's romances for their descriptions, their power and beauty, and their superb language, which, he says, "is almost as elaborate as poetry. It has the march of lofty hexameters. At times he is as gorgeous as an autumnal forest, at times as simple as the green leaves of summer." If his students are unable to read the author in the original, he suggests that some conception of his style may be gained by reading the *Sartor Resartus* of Carlyle, an author of kindred spirit. Also, there are outlines of the lives and principal writings of Hoffmann and of Matthison, with comments included. The former, according to Longfellow, had a lively imagination, a keen relish for all the pleasures and excitements in life, which resulted in his acting from impulse, and of his works, the "Fantasy Pieces," expressing "humor, poetry, and brilliant fancy," are the most finished and successful. The characteristics of Matthison, says Longfellow, are "a quiet melancholy tone," a mourning for the dead, as illustrated particularly in "Adelaide," "Die Vollendung," "Der Frühlingsabend," "Die Kinderjahre," and "Elegie in den Ruinen," which Longfellow read to his class. But there are more copious notes on Goethe than on any other writer. Follen, who was interested in the cause of political freedom, had concentrated in his lectures on Schiller and Körner, his favorite poets, and it remained for Longfellow to deliver the first lectures at Harvard on Goethe. In August, 1837, after he had taken rooms in Craigie House, he wrote to his father that he would soon commence the autumn term lecturing on *Faust*, "of which I shall probably have an edition printed

here — *not* at my own expense — which is something unusual." [73] On the morning of September 18 he delivered his first
lecture on *Faust*. Edward Everett Hale, a member of the class,
records his impressions:

At 11 a.m. went to Prof. Longfellow's first lecture on Goethe's
Faust. The lectures are to be extemporaneous translations of the German with explanations; as he called it, recitations in which he recites
and we hear. He made a long introduction to the matter in hand, very
flowery and bombastical indeed, which appeared to me very much out
of taste. I believe, however, that it was entirely extemporaneous and
that he was carried away by the current of his thoughts. In fact, he
appears to say just what comes uppermost. The regular translation and
explanation part of the lecture was very good. [74]

The First Part of *Faust* was covered by October 27, and lectures
on the Second Part were given the remainder of the term to only
a part of the class. Again, young Hale says:

We had our last lecture in Professor Longfellow's course on *Faust*
today; that is, the last in the first part of *Faust* which is all we were
obliged to attend. A volunteer section will have lectures on the second
part, but the whole cannot, on account of difference in books, all the
editions not having the second part in them. I shall not go. The lectures are tolerably interesting, but not enough so to compensate for the
time taken up by them. [75]

In a letter to a friend at the close of his first year, [76] in which
Longfellow mentions just having finished his lectures on the
Second Part, he says:

I shall, however, write out, and very soon, (I intended to do so last
week) a Lecture upon the Faust. I think one will be enough; and this
you shall certainly see, if you think it won't bore you to death. There
is only one impediment in the way. I was imprudent enough to take up
Dante the other day; and he excites me more than any other poet. I
hate to turn back to Goethe. But the lecture must be written; and I
think I had better settle with the *Adversary*, while I am in the way with
him. Tell me, how can I stop mid-way in an Introductory Lecture on
Christian Dante to take up Heathen Goethe.

Various references in the course of the next two years show
that Longfellow was much occupied with his German studies.
On June 7 he was reading *Die Wahlverwandtschaften* and preparing a lecture on Goethe's character and works. Three days later
he was reading *Hermann und Dorothea*, "a very simple, singular,

and beautiful poem." September 8 he refers to an "introductory lecture on *Faust* for Monday," and the evening of November 13 he thought over his "last lecture on *Faust* for tomorrow." After his lectures during the autumn of 1839 he was comparing several translations, noting that all the poetic ones were "heartily poor," and that Hayward's prose version was "incomparably the best." Meanwhile, as his biographer points out,[77] he had read to his class at the close of a lecture on Goethe the previous year the "Psalm of Life" before it received publication.[78]

The lectures on Goethe's life and works which Longfellow delivered were of an informal character, and were accompanied by translations, quotations, and general comment, a method which was pursued throughout his eighteen years of instruction. As we have seen, he spent much time from the beginning in preparation, and among his manuscripts are numerous miscellaneous notes which, with extracts from various publications, especially from *Dichtung und Wahrheit*, Eckermann, and Mrs. Austin's *Characteristics of Goethe*, served as the basis of his lectures. In spite of their fragmentary form, these may be read with special interest for Longfellow's interpretation of Goethe during a period of divided American opinion of the poet's personality and attainments.[79]

The first lecture opens with a reference to Goethe's death and its effect upon Germany and the world, and gives a detailed sketch of his career to the Weimar period. A translation of "Wanderers Sturmlied" is included, and the importance of Weimar as an intellectual centre is emphasized. In the course of his remarks Longfellow makes the following observations:

> It seems to me very strange that any one should deny to Goethe the attribute of genius. Yet this has been done. Persons have not been wanting, who would fain have dethroned the Monarch of Letters. Friends and foes have waged fierce war together, and so great is the dust of the battle, that we cannot see clearly how the victory goes. And here, it seems to me, lies the difficulty of estimating justly the character of this extraordinary man. There is such a din in our own ears and such a smoke before our own eyes, that we are blinded and confused. From the midst of battle we hear the shouts and war-cries of the combatants on one side: The dear, dear Man, The Life-enjoying Man, The All-sided One, The Representative of Poetry on Earth, The Many-sided Master-mind of Germany; and on the other, the fierce epithets of Old Humbug, Old Heathen, Magnificent Impostor![80]

Subsequent lectures resume the narrative of Goethe's life, which Longfellow is compelled to present as briefly as possible, since he is desirous of bringing before his students certain conflicting opinions of others, before passing to a consideration of the poet's character and writings. He divides Goethe's life into three principal epochs, each of which he briefly characterizes. The first, ending in 1776, when he carries Goethe to Weimar, is one of "infinite longings after some unknown good — unsatisfied, stormy, impetuous, head-long," and the second, 1776–86, is "an age of romantic manhood, in which passion assumes the force of strength, and is useful, not destructive." In neither of these periods, he says, are we to form an estimate of Goethe's character, the final result and termination of his actions and opinions, but in the third, from 1786 to his death in 1832, which is the "age of classic repose, of ripe and perfect manhood and sublime old age." He then quotes from Menzel's severe criticism [81] of Goethe, which he calls "truly ferocious," and whose entire accusation amounts to saying that Goethe "was utterly selfish, that he was wanting in enthusiasm, and in politics was aristocratical and conservative." He is glad that the criticism was offered by a native German; otherwise it would have been received as evidence of foreign prejudice, for "if ever a great man were mistranslated, misunderstood, and calumniated out of his own country, that man was Goethe." After these general statements, Longfellow proceeds to give his own impressions, which are intended as an answer to the poet's critics.

He first points out that self-culture was Goethe's great study from youth to age, and that he strove to develop and to improve whatever faculties nature had given him, "always going forward in perfecting himself into a complete man, as he thought man should be, perhaps occupied too exclusively in this great work of self-culture." Furthermore, Goethe was a philosopher in search of truth, and though, in consequence of his commanding position in German intellectual life, some traces of selfishness and egotism may be found in him, the result of this rigid system of self-culture was that he became a philosopher, or "world-wise man," whose spirit dwelt in its own allotted element, and who beheld beauty in everything. "This was his religion, to busy himself with the present, fulfilling his destiny. . . . This was his idea of human perfectibility, and he seems almost to have realized it in his own person." In his mature years the impetuosity of youth, the "wild excitements" which found an explosion in *Werther*, gave place to a more calm and dignified character of mind, to "a quick perception of every pleasant sensation." This, Longfellow believes, kept Goethe too much aloof from other men, from all "their vast plans and movements, and joint-stock companies for the improvement of the human race," all of which was contrary to his nature. He was the calm, philosophic observer of the political world and of great events, "a conservative — not a radical," standing upon the vantage ground of Truth, while self-possessed and smiling at the indefinite aspirations of minds less clear-sighted than his own, as many of his epigrams illustrate. This state of philosophic indifference Longfellow also finds pleasantly expressed in Goethe's "Vanitas," [82] and for his attitude toward politics and patriotism we have his "wise and true" words as reported by Eckermann. Of Goethe's moral and religious character it is "difficult to say anything definite," though from the famous passage in *Faust*,[83] and from significant statements elsewhere,[84] it is evident that the subject of religion and immortality often occupied his mind from childhood to the close of his life. After treating these various aspects of Goethe, Longfellow presents in conclusion his estimate:

This man, then, was a man of comprehension and commanding intellect, of rich imagination, and strong, simple, healthy common sense. In character he was calm and dignified; of great gentleness and benignity in his judgments of other men; of great sensibility to all the forms of beauty, and great love for all the forms of truth. He seems to me, indeed, to be strikingly like Franklin, though with more imagination. The practical tendency of his mind was the same; his love of science was the same; his benignant philosophic spirit was the same, and a vast number of his little poetic maxims and soothsayings seem nothing more than this worldly wisdom of Poor Richard versified and idealized.

Having dealt with Goethe's personality and character, Longfellow now turns to a discussion of Goethe as a writer. In the handling of his subjects, he states that Goethe had no rival in Germany. Considering all things as objects of art, he treated them as they exist in reality. The most striking characteristic of his style is naturalness, which gives no evidence of effort or struggle for effect, and is at all times sustained and dignified, though occasionally "this extreme naturalness degenerates into puerility and silliness, as in Wordsworth." His plastic style is only an index or outward sign of the changes in his character. Therefore, critics have with reason distinguished three epochs in his art. The first, which is designated as the sentimental or intense, produced *Götz von Berlichingen* and *Werther*; the second, that of the ideal, gave us *Wilhelm Meisters Lehrjahre* and *Faust*; and to the third, the period of the elegant, belong *Iphigenie*, the *Wanderjahre*, and *Westöstlicher Divan*. Observing further that the biographers have said much of Goethe's many-sidedness or objectivity, confusing the two in the same connection, Longfellow explains the difference between objectivity and subjectivity, and is astonished that Goethe is spoken of as an objective writer only. In *Götz* and *Iphigenie* he is objective, but in *Werther* and *Faust* he is subjective; and the fact that he could be either is evidence of his genius. Following this, Longfellow outlines the story of certain works and passes his judgment. *Götz von Berlichingen* is pronounced "an able, interesting production . . . wonderful as the handiwork of a young man." The facts upon which *Werther* is founded, the effect of its publication, and its fame throughout the world [85] are related, after which Longfellow writes:

I have read the book several times, both here and in Germany. The effect was different. The state of society in Germany lifts one up near to a level with the book. But in this country the difference between our daily feelings and those described in the book is far greater. Above all the work should not be read in a translation. One of its great charms is its style; and the sentiment seems less factitious when seen through the dim veil and twilight of the German language. . . .

Looked upon as a work of art merely, the book deserves high praise, particularly when we remember that a young man of twenty-four wrote it in the short space of a single month. The workings of the hero's mind are truly and powerfully sketched, and the insight into human life and character, altogether remarkable in so young an author.

As to the moral effect of the book, I cannot think it is bad, unless upon minds weak and willing to err. It is a portrait, no more; and though in the days of popularity many young people became infected with its hypersentimentality, or what Franz Horn called *Wertherismus*, the blood-stained and evil death of the hero rather terrifies than attracts.

The more obvious moral lesson which it teaches is, that every human being must have some object for his thoughts and affection. There must be some outlet for the vast energies of the soul. The electricity of the mind must be carried off by something, by the point of a pen, or the point of a sword, or the point of a needle: — some lightning-rod must there be, or from that overcast and clouded heaven the burning thoughts will strike down, into the heart, and consume it.[86]

Apparently Longfellow was more impressed with *Werther* than with either of Goethe's other novels. A brief mention of *Wilhelm Meister* refers to Carlyle's translation and estimate, and to the unfavorable review of the novel in the *Edinburgh Review*.[87] *Elective Affinities*, it is explained, is "merely an illustration of human sympathies, to which the language of chemical science is applied, . . . a romance of character, not of incident, a cool and artist-like sketch of compound adultery in imagination only," but significant of the truth that "if you bring fire and gunpowder too near each other, an explosion will be very likely to follow." For this part of his treatment we find in the notes various quotations from Goethe on the subject of originality, appropriation, his method of procedure, and his impressions of the literary world,[88] all of which were conveniently incorporated in the lectures. Finally, Longfellow is convinced that the recent publication of Goethe's correspondence and reminiscences have done much to remove the prejudice against him. "I doubt not," he says, "that ere long the voice of calumny will wholly die away, and that hereafter, with all his errors and short-comings, he will be recognized in the light of historical truth as a simply great and good man — a glorious specimen of humanity."

Other works of Goethe are mentioned only by title, as Longfellow wishes to turn his attention to *Faust*. Besides his interesting private copy of the drama, which will be considered later, his manuscripts contain an abundance of material on this subject, with which, as we have seen, he was much occupied from the first year of his professorship. Separate notebooks include outlines of all the scenes and references to English translations and to various theories of *Faust*, all of which shows a carefully planned study from the very beginning. A lecture which he delivered before his class in the summer term of 1838 opens with comment on the "beautiful and wondrous" story which was told by German peasants, was enacted as a puppet-play, and made its way from Germany to England.[89] The legend, he says, furnished Goethe a glorious theme for his wild, youthful imagination. It gave him an opportunity for presenting the motley scenes of human life, the contrasts of human character, and shows, as does Cyprian of Antioch, how man by his errors may be led to truth and holiness. Goethe never had any intention other than that Faust should be saved, as the Prologue in Heaven shows. This was the great doctrine taught likewise in *Wilhelm Meister*, and had Madame de Staël seen the conclusion of the Second Part she would never have misunderstood the drama. At this point a resume of the story is given, and we read:

When a great poet is at work all his life long upon a single poem, we have reason to expect something extraordinary. Nor are we disappointed in this great masterpiece of modern German poetry. It is indeed a wonderful production; a poem which probably will live longer, and be more universally read and admired than any other of the age. The second part is, however, every way inferior to the first. Notwithstanding the author's own opinions, you see the wrinkled hair of age upon it. The continuous power and glowing imagination of early manhood are no longer there.

To Longfellow *Faust* is Goethe's autobiography. It presents the poet's longings, his struggles, aspirations, and disappointments, and ends, as did Goethe, in useful service. In it is enacted the three-fold life, "the life and world of passion, the life and world of ideal art, the life and world of practical activity." The two principal characters are admirably drawn. Faust is portrayed in all the aspirations of youth, passing through despair and enjoyment, grappling in spirit with the highest and deepest, and "longing to heap the weal and woe of the human race upon his own breast," all of which is carried out nobly in the First Part; but in the Second Part he steals away from us; he is not prominent enough, and we begin to feel less interest in him. Mephistopheles is the spirit that denies, "cold, bitter, sarcastic, full of irony and mockery, an impersonation of the skeptical spirit of the last century, a Voltaire, half monkey, half eagle," whose repulsive visage affects the reader as it does Margaret, and in whose presence "we feel as if we could not pray." But as with Faust, Mephistopheles loses, in the continuation, much of his strength and becomes "a kind of *bon diable*." The drama was not written for "weak and sickly minds, but for healthy, manly, and strong minds." Nor is the work without defects, especially in certain details. There are too many trivial and local allusions, particularly the witticisms in the "Walpurgis Night's Dream," which we can no longer understand and interpret.

Of particular interest is Longfellow's interleaved copy of the First Part of *Faust*,[90] containing his assignments to the class,[91] outlines of scenes, translations of significant passages, comments, and miscellaneous references which he added from year to year. We observe first his notes on the chronology of the drama, on the prevalence of popular traditions, and on the historical Faust,[92] together with a list of English versions and of various other dramas on the subject.[93] Attention is called to some of the "desperate blunders" made by Hayward and Gower, and included are translations of a part of the peasants' song in "Before the Gate," of Faust's monologue in "Forest and Cavern," and of the whole of "König in Thule." The scene in "Auerbach's Cellar" impressed him as "one of the best, perhaps the very best"; the Cathedral scene is "grand," and the prison scene is "dreadful." In addition to interpretations and comments usually given in any course on *Faust*, there follow, in the progress of his study, many notes from Hayward's prose rendition, various citations, and numerous references to parallel or kindred passages in other literatures. The song of the archangels in the Prologue recalls Bryant's "Song of the Stars" and Milton's "Hymn on the Nativity." With Faust's first monologue may be compared Marlowe's *Faustus*, Byron's *Manfred*, and Goethe's remarks on his own restless life.[94] The "goldnen Eimer" refers to "the mid-gard of old northern mythology — the great serpents that enriched the earth, holding all things together"; the Earth-Spirit is Shelley's "Nature's vast frame — the web of human things"; and Faust's second monologue, as well as that in "Forest and Cavern," suggests certain lines in Wordsworth's "Excursion." [95] Mephistopheles must be studied in relation to the corresponding figure in Dante, Milton, Calderón, Byron, and Bailey, while the character of Margaret, suggested by Goethe's Gretchen, Frederica, and Lili, may be compared with one of the same name in the old English play of "The Countree Girl."

The magic mirror of the "Witch's Kitchen" is an old tradition used elsewhere, especially in the *Gesta Romanorum* and in Cervantes. Public penance [96] was likewise required by English law as a punishment for adultery, and instances are on record of it having been enforced in colonial times in this country.[97] The remaining pages contain references to Shelley's translations from the "Walpurgis-Night" and to Heine's description of the Brocken, and notes on some of the allusions in the "Walpurgis-Night's Dream."

As we have observed, Longfellow considered the Second Part of *Faust* quite inferior to the First Part. A few notes, with outlines of the scenes, give us his impressions. The defect in the "Carnival Masquerade," he points out, is "a want of driving tendency and movement toward an end." He admits that there are brilliant passages, that the language is "musical and magical," but holds that the scene, with its want of movement, of life, and of interest, does not warm the reader's imagination. He finds the scene too long, too much of "a throwing together of fantastic scraps of song from a portfolio, tied by a silken thread of half-meaning," though the close is exquisite.[98] The "paper money" scene he calls prosaic and commonplace in every respect. "Its dulness," he writes, "is not even redeemed by a good jest, but rather increased by attempts thereat, which are platitudes." Although Longfellow continued throughout his professorship to lecture on both parts of *Faust*, and to manifest his interest in the subject, it is evident that he gave far more time to the First Part.[99] Motley's article in the *New York Review*[100] impressed him as the best thing on *Faust* that he had ever heard or read, and later in the same year (1839) he was examining Stapfer's edition, with engravings which he liked better than those in Retzsch. His "Book of Suggestions" for 1847 includes plans for "A New England Faust. The old tradition of selling one's soul to the devil." At the close of his lectures on the First Part, May 27, 1851, he states: "I am more than ever struck with the greatness of this poem," and in a note which he made many years earlier he probably had more in mind this part, when he calls *Faust* "truly a wonderful tragedy! Truly, the work of a Titan!" The lectures were popular and were much in demand, especially during the years when Longfellow became less inter-

ested in teaching and wished to devote his time to creative writing. On March 1, 1844, President Quincy wrote him: "Many if
not all (of the Juniors) wish to attend your lectures on Faust."
Some years later [101] this entry appears in Longfellow's journal:
"Today a new class in college wanting to read *Faust*. And I
cannot in conscience say No. Inclination to do everything for
the youngsters prompts me to say Yes; accordingly I do say Yes.
It is only one impediment more between me and the real work
I have to do." One of his students recalls with pleasure Longfellow's gift in reading poetry, especially the refrain in the
"Shepherd's Song" from *Faust*, which "he recited with such
effect that one imagined he heard the touch of the bow upon the
'cello, with the mellow, long-drawn cadence." [102]

In August, 1839, appeared *Hyperion*, the publication of which
brought to the American public an expression of Longfellow's
love for German life and literature and a wealth of German
romance. In praising the book in an exposition of things German, Felton stated: "We have no hesitation in claiming for our
countryman the foremost rank among German translators." [103]
Writing to Greene some months after its appearance, Longfellow
says: "It contains my cherished thoughts for three years." [104]
However, in much of its content the work extends farther back
than this period. It is a composite, containing not only a record
of many of Longfellow's experiences in Germany, Austria, and
Switzerland, but materials which he had offered in his journal
and in his Harvard lectures. We turn to it for the author's excellent renderings of various German poems, and for his criticism of a number of writers, particularly Jean Paul, Hoffmann,
Goethe, and Uhland. Here, as later, we note to what extent
Longfellow continued to express in various ways his interest in
Goethe and in other German authors. In *Hyperion* he is impressed with the similarity between Horace and Goethe.[105] We
note that on one occasion Paul Flemming found the Baron playing and humming "Der Fischer," his "favorite song from
Goethe." [106] Further, we observe acquaintance with Goethe's
views of Tiedge's *Urania* and with Bettina von Arnim's *Goethe's
Correspondence with a Child*, "a very singular and valuable
revelation of the feelings which he excited in female hearts,"
and familiarity with "Über allen Gipfeln," which Longfellow

translates, and with *Faust*.[107] The conversation between Paul Flemming and the Baron in the chapter significantly entitled "Old Humbug," [108] a caption changed in the later edition to "Goethe," contains some of the principal points which had been covered in the lectures during the summer of 1838. It is stated that Goethe's philosophy is the old ethnic philosophy proclaimed by Horace, and that while objection to his sensuality may be met by the cold purity of *Iphigenie*, it is supported by the *Roman Elegies* and "that strange book, the *Elective Affinities*." Again, Goethe was an artist who considers all things as objects of art which he describes as a realist. Both praise and condemnation are included throughout the discussion, which gives Longfellow an opportunity to express not only his qualified admiration of the poet, but some of the opposition and defence which Goethe encountered in England and America during the first half of the nineteenth century.

About the time *Hyperion* was published, Bancroft contributed to the *Christian Examiner* his bitter criticism of Goethe, which, as we have noted, Longfellow pronounced a "violent article." [109] Menzel's *History of German Literature*, with its "ferocious" attack, was translated the following year by Felton, and was favorably reviewed by Longfellow,[110] though he could not agree with the estimate of Goethe and of some of the other great men of Germany. He deplores the fact that a large portion of the English public seem to think that German literature consists only of ghost stories, sentimental novels, and mystic books of philosophy, with absurd titles.

Many [he says] have formed their idea of this literature from a poor translation of the *Sorrows of Werther*; others from some of Hoffmann's wild tales; others from *Faust* and the Philosophies. Not finding these to their taste, they lose all patience; call their whole literature silly, rhapsodical, absurd and immoral, and finally exclaim with Danton in the French Assembly, "Gentlemen, in the future, let us have prose and decency."

Meanwhile, in his journal, he ridiculed the idea of Margaret Fuller or any woman writing a life of Goethe. "I wonder," he says, "if this lady ever read the *Elective Affinities*." [111] Being considered one of the foremost champions of Goethe, Longfellow was informed on June 7, 1839, by the Goethean Literary Society,

founded at York, Pennsylvania, in June, 1835, that it had taken
the liberty of enrolling his name on its distinguished list of honorary members. Appreciating his devotion to German literature,
the committee wrote: "We are aware that it is only by securing
the influence and cooperation of such persons as yourself that we
can give character and influence to our institution." [112]

Throughout the years Longfellow continued to read widely in
German literature, adding from time to time various translations, some of which were included in *Voices of the Night* in 1839,
and in various periodicals. [113] His journal for March, 1838, records the reading of Tieck's *Phantasien über die Kunst*, "a pleasant, poetical, deep-feeling, reverential book"; of *Franz Stern-
balds Wanderungen* he later comments: "Some passages are fine;
as a whole not great. My admiration for Tieck, which was never
high, is rather diminished." [114] In March, 1842, he contributed
to *Graham's Magazine* [115] his "Heinrich Heine," which includes
a sketch of "Young Germany," and of Heine's career, together
with passages translated from the *Reisebilder* and comments.
Heine's style, according to Longfellow, is remarkable for its
vigor, wit, and brilliancy, but is wanting in taste and refinement.
With the ruthlessness of Byron is combined the sentimentality
of Sterne. Longfellow comments:

> He is always in extremes, either of praise or censure; setting at naught
> the decencies of life, and treating the most sacred things with frivolity.
> Throughout his writings you see traces of a morbid, ill-regulated mind;
> of deep feeling, disappointment and suffering. His sympathies seem to
> have died with him, like Ugolino's children in the tower of Famine.
> With all his various powers, he wants the one great power — the power
> of truth. He wants, too, that ennobling principle of all human en-
> deavors, the absorption "after an ideal standard, that is higher than
> himself." In a word, he wants sincerity and spirituality.

Referring to Heine's minor poems, Longfellow states that,
though they possess the highest lyric merit, they deal too often
with the trivial and commonplace, and reveal at the same time
the exaggerated tone and sentiment of his prose, where the lofty
aim is wanting. "We listen in vain," he says, "for the spirit-
stirring note — for the word of power — for those ancestral
melodies, which amid the uproar of the world, breathe into our
ears forever more the voices of consolation, encouragement and

warning. Heine is not sufficiently in earnest to be a great poet."

In 1842 Longfellow obtained a six months' leave of absence from Harvard to go abroad for the improvement of his health. He settled in June at Marienberg, near Boppard on the Rhine, where, as he tells us, he at once found himself surrounded by "desperate looking patients." [116] At St. Goar he made the acquaintance of Freiligrath, who became his intimate friend and translator.[117]

He is a youth of about my own age [writes Longfellow to his sister], and the best of the young poets of Germany. His wife is a very genteel person, and quite American in her manners and looks. They are very agreeable people and are a great resource to me. He has translated a good many of my poems into German; which I shall not copy here, as they would not benefit you much. We make excursions together to old castles and ruins.[118]

During the summer Longfellow continued his devotion to German literature, reading the *Nibelungenlied*,[119] Freiligrath, Herwegh, Immermann, Geibel, Anastasius Grün, Lenau, and Heine. His request for an extension of his leave was discouraged by President Quincy, who appreciatively remarked that his work "illustrated the College." [120] His department needed his services. Therefore, after visiting several German cities, among them Frankfort, Nuremberg,[121] and Heidelberg, he journeyed to London, where he was the guest of Dickens, and returned in November to resume his duties.

In the autumn of the following year Longfellow began the preparation of one of America's representative anthologies,[122] *Poets and Poetry of Europe*, which appeared at Philadelphia and London in 1845, bringing together the translations which most appealed to him from several hundred European poets. The section devoted to German contains sketches of the literature and of representative poets, together with poems selected from the earliest period to 1844. While the collection includes Longfellow's renditions of poems by Dach, Tiedge, Salis, Uhland, Müller, Heine, Mosen, and Pfitzer,[123] it omits his translations from Goethe.[124] However, a new edition, published in 1871, with a portrait of Goethe as the frontispiece instead of one of Schiller as in the earlier edition,[125] has a supplement containing a scene,

"The Death of Faust" by Bayard Taylor,[126] and Longfellow's excellent translations of the two "Wanderer's Night-Songs," which are later and more literal renderings than the versions included in *Hyperion* and in his letter to Ward of September 17, 1841.[127]

While performing his duties as a professor, Longfellow became increasingly restless in his desire to do creative work. During the next few years he produced *Evangeline* and *The Golden Legend*,[128] using in the latter work, as is well known, the theme of Hartmann von Aue's *Der arme Heinrich*. The journal for 1846 and 1847 records further reading of Jean Paul, Zschokke, Fichte, Heine, Hoffmann, and the political poets, as well as Goethe. On January 22, 1846, he heard Emerson's lecture on Goethe, which was "very good, but not so pre-eminent as some of his discourses," and shortly afterward he had with Sumner and Hillard a "long discussion on Goethe,—his art in poetry."[129] In reading the *Italian Journey* the following June he noted the poet's usual lucid, simple style, resembling the conversation of an "elegant and very intelligent man" with keen powers of observation. He found it interesting to read in connection with Dickens's *Letters from Italy*. "One is all drollery," he writes, "and the other all wisdom."[130] A delightful touch appears in his journal under date of June 21 of that year:

> I dreamed last night that Goethe was alive and in Cambridge. I gave him a supper at Willard's Tavern. He had a beautiful face, but his body was like the Belgian giant's, with an immeasurable black coat. I told him I thought Clärchen's song in *Egmont* was one of his best lyrics. The god smiled. This dream came from reading the Italian Journey no doubt; or from comparing it in my mind with Dickens's which we read this evening.
>
> It would be curious to view these two books together; the authors having been about the same age when they wrote them, and about sixty years having elapsed between them, Goethe's tour having been made in 1786. If I had eyesight, I would do it.

The journal further records the reading of the *Campaign in France*,[131] of Edward Keneally's *Goethe*, "a very imaginative but fantastic book with much poetic power,"[132] and of *Wilhelm Meister*. "What a gallery of portraits!" he declares. "What variety! What richness of coloring,—and what a collection of tainted ducks! If this be, as I suppose it is, a picture of German society at the close of the last century, it was the most promiscuous thing imaginable." [133]

With the close of the academic year in 1854 Longfellow resigned his professorship, and shortly afterward he received a letter from the Harvard Corporation expressing its appreciation of his services and its regrets "at the retirement of one whose reputation has, for so long a time, made part of the reputation of the College." [134] Longfellow was now free to go forward with his private studies, which, with the exception of his final journey to Europe in May, 1868, for a period of fifteen months, remained almost uninterrupted. Many references in his journal for these remaining years express his continued interest in German literature. Grillparzer's *Ahnfrau*, he notes, is "the concentrated form and quintessence of the German ghost and Robber-of-the-Rhine style of tragedy, but extremely effective." [135] Lessing's *Emilia Galotti* he calls very tragic, but dramatically of great power,[136] and another old friend, Jean Paul's *Titan*, is pronounced "wild and wonderful." [137] Then followed, in later years, the reading of Luther's *Tischreden*, Strodtmann's *Life of Heine*.[138] Schlegel's lectures on the German drama, Grimm's *Michael Angelo*,[139] and Voss's *Briefe*.[140] In February, 1872, he was reading Schiller's *Don Carlos* and comparing it with Alfieri's *Filippo*; "Schiller's is a very noble poem, affluent in thought and diction," writes Longfellow to Greene, "but too long and too intricate for a tragedy. The real Tragic Muse hardly stops to pluck so many flowers by the way." [141]

But Longfellow never ceased to be interested in Goethe. On December 16, 1855, he is reading Lewes's *Life of Goethe*, which impressed him as "a very clever and judicious book. The best we have as yet, giving the great German as he really was." Writing to Sumner of it, he says: "Have you read it? If not, do so; it will interest you." [142] Some years later he concludes that certain parts of Goethe's *Tag-und Jahreshefte* and Schiller's *Correspondence with Körner*, with extracts from similar works, would make the best life of Goethe. These two works, he states, "give a very different view of Goethe from the one usually given, and show a man not holding himself apart from others, but longing for sympathy, and very lenient in his judgments." [143] In a discussion of *Faust* with Agassiz in January, 1871, the relation between literature and science was well illustrated when the scientist drew a diagram showing the relation of the pentagram to the frequent arrangement of leaves on stems.[144] Having shown a personal interest in Bayard Taylor's version of *Faust*, the first part of which appeared in December of that year, Longfellow joined a distinguished group which met in the home of James T. Fields to do honor to Goethe and to his translator. A few years later he was associated with Taylor, Bryant, and other notable figures in the Goethe Club of the City of New York.

The history of Goethe in the New England of the nineteenth century is a record of struggle and achievement. When Follen began his instruction at Harvard in 1825, New England was still stumbling over the correct pronunciation of Goethe's name. The Göttingen group, to be sure, had expressed their appreciation, though Bancroft later adopted a hostile attitude. But with the influence of Carlyle's essays, and the work of Longfellow and others, especially the *Dial* coterie, Goethe became a vital force, the central figure in the introduction and progress of German letters. His genius, achievements, and poetic mastery were universally recognized, but intolerant and provincial puritanism found it difficult to accept what it considered his laxity of morals. Channing, Alcott, Theodore Parker, and a few others were either unbiased in their judgments or accepted Goethe with reservations, while Cogswell, Calvert, Motley, James Freeman Clarke, Frederic Henry Hedge, and Margaret Fuller were among his enthusiastic admirers. To Calvert, Goethe was the most complete man of his time, the richest specimen of humanity since Shakespeare; and to Margaret Fuller, his staunchest defender, he was a spiritual guide, the real liberator of her soul. Emerson had always a partial understanding of Goethe, though, owing chiefly to Carlyle's influence, he gradually became more tolerant and made him one of his master-minds. Writing to Herman Grimm in 1871 he stated: "For Goethe I have always an ascending regard." Longfellow, like Emerson, gradually arrived at a saner and more comprehensive knowledge of the poet and his work. He endeavored to present Goethe in an impartial light. While he objected to his sensuality, he maintained, as we have seen, that Goethe, with all his errors and shortcomings, was a glorious specimen of humanity. Goethe became, as did Dante, one of his great life experiences.

As a teacher, Longfellow made Goethe a living figure in academic halls, thus serving to counteract the hostile attitude of Follen. Referring to the introductory period of his career, Higginson called him one of the two prime influences through which the treasures of German literature, and especially of German romance, were opened to English readers. He further observes that Longfellow undoubtedly shared with Carlyle the function of interpreting Germany to America, first in *Hyperion* and later in his *Poets and Poetry of Europe* and his numerous translations.[145] Longfellow's interest in Goethe is an evidence of his interest in all great literature. For his scholarly mind literature had no national barriers. He did honor to the genius of great masters without regard to their nationality. It mattered not in what language they wrote. In this respect he was akin to Ticknor, his predecessor, and Lowell, his successor. Fortunate, indeed, was America in having these three men to interpret to the public the great modern European writers. At a special meeting of the Cambridge Historical Society on February 27, 1907, celebrating the one hundredth anniversary of Longfellow's birthday, President Eliot spoke in high appreciation of Longfellow's services to the University, mentioning especially that for eighteen years he taught the noblest authors before a somewhat prosaic and utilitarian youth, doing steady, assiduous, painstaking work of instruction.

In the valuable library of Craigie House is to be found a wealth of books on German literature, particularly those referring to Goethe. The collection contains many first editions presented by the authors and intimate friends. Peculiarly appropriate is the compliment which James T. Fields [146] pays when he speaks of being struck "with the likeness of his private rooms to those of a German student or professor, — a Goethean aspect of simplicity and space everywhere." The reader of the chapter on Goethe in *Hyperion* will recall that Paul Flemming, discovering in a window a full-length cast of the poet, says to the Baron, "But let us step in here. I wish to buy that cast." It is of interest to note that on the desk in the corner of Longfellow's study, where he did most of his creative work, stands a plaster statuette of Goethe, clad in a long great-coat, with his hands folded behind him.

The "Old Humbug" of 1839 had become vital in Longfellow's intellectual life.

John Lothrop Motley

In THE preceding studies we have seen five men who helped in the slow and gradual process by which European scholarship obtained recognition in this country during the first half of the nineteenth century. Ticknor, Everett, Cogswell, Bancroft, and Longfellow each had made, as we have stated, important and distinct contributions to the development of our early intellectual life. But the story would be incomplete without a consideration of one who, in every respect, is worthy of an honorable place in this company, and who, unlike his predecessors, never held an academic position.

As a pupil at the Round Hill School from 1825 to 1827, John Lothrop Motley distinguished himself by an uncommon interest in historical and literary subjects and by a remarkable facility for learning foreign languages. "I am reading Hume's 'History of England,' which Mr. Cogswell lent me, and think it very interesting. I have commenced Spanish, which I like very much," he wrote to his mother on May 29 of his first year. Two days later he informs her: "I study 'Charles XII' in French, which I think very interesting, and it is much more by its being in French; I can read French books very easily, which I do very often." There was instruction also in German, and in Greek and Latin. His knowledge of the German language and literature undoubtedly made a favorable impression on Bancroft, who was his instructor, and who, as Oliver Wendell Holmes points out, could hardly have dreamed that the handsome youth of ten years was to take rank with his teacher in the field of historical writing.[1]

In the autumn of 1827 Motley entered Harvard, and was graduated four years later, the youngest member, with one exception, of his class. It is reported that he did not take his college responsibilities any too seriously, though he attained Phi Beta Kappa rank. He was gifted with handsome appearance, rare intellect, and natural ability, which made here, as in school, a deep impression on his instructors and classmates. As a de-

claimer and as a writer he gained quite a reputation in college, and was associated for a time with Holmes and John Osborne Sargent in editing an undergraduate publication called the *Harvard Register*. It is evident that he was interested more in literary and historical matters than in any other subjects. Among his various projects were sketches of his favorite authors and characters, soliloquies, fragmentary poems, and scenes of plays. Shelley, Byron, and Goethe were among his favorite poets. "You have forgotten, or perhaps never knew, that Motley's first appearance in print was in the 'Collegian,'" wrote Sargent in later years to Holmes. "He brought me one day, in a very modest mood, a translation from Goethe, which I was most happy to oblige him by inserting. It was very prettily done, and will now be a curiosity." [2] The interest in Goethe was real and bore fruit. Although Follen, Motley's instructor in German, gave but little attention in his lectures to the great poet, Motley was inspired to deliver at the college exhibition on May 3, 1831, his senior year, the following essay on "The Genius and Character of Goethe," which is preserved in manuscript form in the Harvard library:

The German Muse had not been behind the rest of the choir in the art of inspiration. The harp of the North had already rung to the songs of chivalry; and the softer and sweeter strains of melody had sounded in its chords — it had been found that the atmosphere of that Country which had proved the very promised land of religion and philosophy, was not too Boetian for the wings of poetry to float in.

But it was reserved for the present age to behold the foundation of a German literary dynasty, by one whose single genius enabled him to maintain it during a period long enough to witness the crumbling of many more substantial thrones and sceptres.

The history of German literature is short and interesting. It presents an appearance so rich and various — it has sprung forward so rapidly — and has about it so much of grotesqueness and originality, that it savors more of the rapid vegetation of Fairy Land, where golden palaces and princely gardens are reared in a night, than of the regular, but comparatively stinted growth of this "banknote world."

Previously to the appearance of Goethe as a writer, the poetry of Germany had been divided into two orders — the works of the followers of Wieland and of Klopstock. The poetry of the one is romantic and national — the other consists in the efforts of an imagination ever reaching beyond its own sphere. Wieland's is an impassioned, stormy music; the other's is quiet, contemplative, sublime. Both have been followed as guiding stars by innumerable writers; and both are as splendid and influential on their followers as they are different from each other.

But Goethe like every other splendid genius, apprenticed himself to no particular artist. His efforts in every kind of literature have been equally successful; and there is hardly a path through which he has not freely wandered, not a strain of music which has not sounded in his shell; and thus with the delicate finger of genius and taste, he has gathered from all things the requisite aroma of beauty and fragrance and melody and has thus impregnated every work of his hand with the very essence of genius. In so limited a space as this, it would be utterly impossible to enter into any thing like an inquiry into the peculiarities of the genius and character of Goethe; and it will be accordingly attempted merely to mention briefly some of the most prominent characteristics of his mind.

In the first place — one of the most striking and the very pleasantest of the attributes of Goethe's mind, is its faculty of diffusing itself over every thing which emanates from it. In taking up one of his volumes, we are invoking by means of a spell he has himself woven, not his shade, but himself, and that in the very first bloom of his genius and manhood. And after all, this is the only true immortality — or rather it is something better — it is the possession of a power to render imperishable those elements of our nature and those only, which we are anxious should be preserved — and feeling this to be the case, we needs must be surprised that so splendid an object for ambition should be so often lost sight of. Salathiel, when the blow struck on Mt. Carmel rendered him imperishable, might lament that immortality, which was the prerogative of sin — for the one burning crime of his life was all beside his body that would not die — but it is much to be lamented that the most splendid poet of modern times (I mean Lord Byron) should have neglected to have extinguished by a single effort of this function, those unfortunate productions of the earthly part of his nature; those motes in the rich sunlight of his other poetry, whose brightness serves but to illuminate their ugliness. . . . I believe that there is but little need of any such excision in the works of Goethe. As I have noticed, they are all stamped with the impress of his mind; which he has diffused, like a rare essence, over their whole surface; and it is this power of breathing into his volumes the breath of his own life — of conversing with his reader face to face in every country or age, which is the one of the sublimest attributes of genius and is peculiarly so of Goethe.

II. The next great characteristics of his mind that we shall mention are its simplicity and generousness. He is altogether innocent of inflation. The treasures of his mind which he often throws open to us, like an eastern magician, by a single word, are displayed as carelessly, and in appearance with as little effort, as the pearls and diamonds into which the words of the fairy in the fable changed as they were uttered. He has no marking out of set points for effect, accompanied with a suspension of all vigorous exertion till the grand dramatic explosion — there is no visible pluming of wings and preparation in his most arduous flight. His mind is as clear and reposing as the heaven — but like it, is filled with suns, and stars and light. In a word he is a poet — and we can give him no higher praise, than when we say that Poetry unveiled herself to his adoration and love, on the infantine altar whose fire he first kindled — for, in the words of old Ben Jonson —

> "Indeed, if you will look on Poesie
> And view her in her glorious ornaments
> Attired in the majesty of art,
> Set high in spirit with the precious taste
> Of sweet philosophy, and, which is most,
> Crowned with the rich traditions of a soul
> That hates to have her dignity profaned
> With any relish of an earthly thought;
> Oh then how proud a presence does she bear,
> Then is she like herself; fit to be seen
> Of none but grave and consecrated eyes."

Joined with the simplicity of Goethe is to be observed his fairness and openness of mind — the candor of his criticism is perfect. In his examination of the efforts of others, there seems never to have been a thought of his own comparative excellence, nor the fear of the overthrow of his own literary sovereignty, however probable such an event might have appeared. His candor in expressing his private and printed opinions of other men's efforts is well known, and it is told of him, that when Byron was in the zenith of his popularity and taking with him the lion's share of the admiration of the world that he asserted that Byron was not only the greatest living poet, but the only one. Thousands of instances of this generosity might be unnecessarily mentioned, and on his noble criticism of Shakespeare it is too late to comment.

III. Another quality, which might perhaps be included in the simplicity of his mind, is its freshness and unstained purity of which there is no finer evidence than his fondness for dwelling on his own childhood. The possession of manliness and wisdom is often obtained by a melancholy barter — by an exchange of the clearness and truth of youthful feeling — the bright sheen of the soul is too often apt to be dimmed by the rust of the world — "the wing of the dove has been soiled and broken by keeping company with the owl" and it is therefore doubly refreshing to find the excellence and fullness of manhood united with the brightness of youth. In the autobiography of Goethe, there are many instances of this fondness for dwelling on his childhood — and the simplicity accordingly which dispenses such a charm over his writings is all natural and healthy.

IV. But his genius never shows a sublimer power than when it is exercised in the investigation of the human mind, of pourtraying human character. The mind is a world, and a fairer one than any whose laws its own cunning has adjusted — it is in his definition when he called a man a microcosm. The mind is indeed an universe — it contains a heaven and an earth and a hell and perhaps it is only in the mind that they all exist. It is in vain for us to reason on the real position in which we are placed. Perhaps our existence, nay perhaps this rounded atom which we call a world, may be in all its myriads of properties, but a thought, a passing idea in the mind of an immensely superior power — for who shall say, that in every minute atom which floats by us on the air, and which perishes even while we are observing it, there be not millions of thinking and reasoning inhabitants, generations after generations of whom shall have rolled away, during the very moment in which the thought of the atom shall have entered and left our superior and duller mind? Speculation is useless on such a subject, but perhaps not the least reasonable of all theories on the subject is that the mind is the only universe — that the pure, benevolent and righteous propensities of human nature compose heaven, the sensual part of man earth, and the degrading, unnatural and criminal feelings form the only pandemonium. If there be any thing reasonable in this theory, certainly the knowledge and the mastery of human nature is the sublimest attribute of genius. It is for this that we worship Shakespeare, as if really kneeling at the shrine of a Deity and it is for this too, that the splendid subject of our remarks is elevated to honor, if not equal in degree, yet the same in kind.

In conclusion, we would only remark as we did in the beginning that there is no attribute of Goethe's mind more admirable than its versatility. He has pourtrayed almost every passion of the human soul from the most tempestuous emotions, to the quietest and gentlest feelings, and all with equal success; and it is pleasant to reflect that the same mind, which can by its efforts stir the full grown soul to the most tumultuous enthusiasm, is willing to descend from its heights and sound those chords which wile more with pleasure the heart of childhood — even as the ocean, before whose waked wrath, navies and nations disappear like bubbles, will in its peaceful rippling to the shore, sing a pleasant and quiet song to glad the souls of the young and the simple.

This juvenile but pleasing production of an undergraduate at the age of seventeen years is interesting as showing the views of Goethe by one who early in life made the poet one of his masters and who, years later, was to play a significant role in interpreting Goethe to the American public. The essay made an impression on his audience, but on none more than Motley's former teacher, Cogswell, who was present. It is recorded that Cogswell found it so excellent that he later sent a copy of it to Goethe's daughter-in-law, Ottilie, who, after reading it, is quoted as stating: "I wish to see the first book that young man will write." [3]

It was due to the influence of his former association with Cogswell and Bancroft at Round Hill that Motley, after his graduation from Harvard, was inspired to sail in April, 1832, to
Europe for three years of study and travel. The ocean passage
was stormy. "I contrived, however," wrote Motley to his
mother just before landing, "in the course of the voyage to learn
a good deal of German, by talking and reading and writing, and
I have been talking all day with the German pilot (who speaks
very little English) and have acted in some sort as an interpreter
between him and the captain." 4 On reaching Hamburg, he proceeded to Göttingen,5 where he devoted more than a semester to
the study of law and history. As was true of his American predecessors at Göttingen, Motley's first task was to improve his
German by an intensive study of the subject under the instruction of Benecke. On June 23 he informed his father of his plans:

> This term (about ten weeks are left) I intend to devote to German,
> for I have not enough of the language to understand the lectures well,
> and as it is, of course, useless to take them. I, however, attend one
> lecture (five times a week), of Professor Hugo, as the introduction to
> a course of Civil Law — of which I am able to understand the general
> drift, by taking the textbook with me to the lecture-room. Next term,
> however, I shall have a lecture in the Pandects, a lecture on the Insti-
> tutes, a lecture on Natural Law, a lecture on the history of Roman
> Law, which, with the introductory lecture of Hugo — which I now
> attend, and which I shall hear again next *Semester* — form a complete
> course of Civil Law. Besides which I shall probably attend Heeren's
> lectures on History, Saalfeld's Political lectures (he is a tremendous
> Liberal, and lately a member of the Diet), which altogether will be
> quite a sufficiency. . . .
> My first object at present, as I said, is to possess myself of the
> language, and I study it five or six hours a day, and, as I said, have a
> lesson from Professor Benecke from seven to eight every other morning.
> As soon as I have acquired enough of the language to write it and speak
> it and understand it, I shall feel at my ease and ready to begin my lec-
> tures, and that will undoubtedly be by the end of this *Semester*.6

Within a few days Motley matriculated, and after signing an
immense list of promises, which he states are never in the slightest degree kept by any of the students, was formally admitted to
the University. He was soon introduced to Hugo, whose lectures he found "dull and stupid," and whose great peculiarity
Motley discovered to be "an unbounded passion for thermom-

eters," as was evident by the number observed in every room of
his home and in his lecture-room. Göttingen itself impressed
Motley as an unpleasant town, and the country about it uninteresting, but he was fascinated by the ruined castles in the
vicinity, the views of the Harz mountains, and the traditions of
the Brocken. Many of his experiences in Göttingen, as well as
those on excursions during vacation periods, were later incorporated in his earliest novel, *Morton's Hope.* He gives the following description:

> Göttingen is rather a well-built and handsome looking town with
> a decided look of the Middle Ages about it. Although the college is new,
> the town is ancient, and like the rest of the German university towns,
> has nothing external, with the exception of a plain-looking building in
> brick for the library, and one or two others for natural collections, to
> remind you that you are at the seat of an institution for education.
> The professors lecture, each on his own account, at his own house, of
> which the basement is generally made use of as an auditorium.[7]

The University library, Motley states, is a vast collection of
books, approximating 400,000 volumes, and contains but few
rare books, manuscripts, or splendid editions, though everything
is for use and students are not restricted in the number of books
which they wish to take out. Elsewhere we note his general
observations:

> The principle that has been adopted in the construction and col-
> lection of the German libraries is a good one. They buy the cheapest
> editions that are to be had of everything; but they buy everything. . . .
> The consequence is that you find in all the university towns and in all
> the capitals libraries varying in numbers from 150,000 to 400,000 vol-
> umes, and it is very difficult for a man of any science, or any profession
> to find himself in a situation where he has not within his reach all the
> assistance that a library could afford him for his labours.[8]

The following extract from one of Motley's letters, written to
his mother shortly after his arrival, gives a picture of German
university students a century ago:

> But I have said nothing yet of the students because I am afraid of
> attacking such a boundless and inexhaustible subject. The German
> students are certainly an original and peculiar race of beings, and can
> be compared to nothing.
> The University towns are the homes of *"outré-ness,"* or rather, they
> are places where it is impossible to be *outré*, except by dressing or be-

having like "a Christian or an ordinary man." You can hardly meet a student in the streets whose dress would not collect a mob anywhere else, and, at the same time, you hardly meet two in a day who are dressed alike, every man consulting his own taste, and fashioning himself according to his *beau ideal*.

The most common outer garment is a red plaid or a blue velvet frock-coat, twenty of which you find to one of cloth. The head is covered with a very small cap with the colours of *Landsmannschaft* to which the individual may belong. The boots are garnished with spurs universally, albeit innocent of horse-flesh; the forefinger of the left hand always with an immense seal ring (often of iron or brass); and the upper lip and chin fortified with an immense moustachio and beard (in fact, I have seen several students with a depending beard more than four inches long, and there is hardly one who does not wear moustachios). A long pipe in the mouth, a portfolio under the arm, a stick in the hand, and one or two bull-dogs at the heels, complete a picture not in the slightest degree exaggerated of a Göttingen student! The most promising article in the formation of a German student's room is the pipe. There are generally about twenty or thirty of different kinds hanging in his room — of porcelain, meerschaum, and stone, all ornamented with tassels, combining the colours of his *Landsmannschaft*; and you have no idea how beautifully some of the pipes are painted with landscapes, portraits (there are often beautiful miniatures painted on them), or coats of arms. Pipes are a favorite present among the students (and you have anything you wish painted on one when you wish to give it away). Every one smokes, and smokes at all times, and in all occupations (except that they are not allowed to smoke in the streets), reading, writing, talking, or riding. I prefer a pipe now to a cigar, and I am hardly ever without one in my mouth (for instance, I have been smoking a great meerschaum all the time I have been writing this), and I always breakfast at half-past five o'clock (!) on a cup of coffee and a pipe, and continue the "cloud compelling" occupation through the day. I find I grow fat on it, for I never was in such health in my life. I find that I have said nothing as yet about the German duels. These things are such a common and every-day occurrence that I have ceased to think at all about them. I must, in the first place, tell you that the accounts you have read in Dwight, etc., of the frequency of these things is not in the slightest degree exaggerated, in fact it is entirely impossible to exaggerate them. I have been here now about three weeks, and during that time as many as forty have been fought *to my knowledge*, and I know of as many as one hundred and fifty more that are to take place directly. . . .

There is also a regular code by which the different offences are meted, and the degree of sabre satisfaction determined. The most common and slightest insult is the "Dummer Junge" (stupid boy), which demands a duel of twelve Gangs. (A "Gang" I cannot exactly describe. It is the closing of the two combatants and a certain number

888

of blows and parries.) The parties have each a second at his side to strike up the swords the moment a wound is received. The doctor then steps in, examines the wound, and if it proves to be "*Anschiess*" (a wound of a certain length and depth), the duel is discontinued.

A more gross insult demands twenty-four Gangs, and a still more important one, forty-eight. But the most severe duel is that of one "Gang," in which, as I have said, the duel continues until one drops.

You need be under no apprehension about my returning with a disfigured visage, for as a foreigner is seldom or never insulted, and if he be, has the right of choosing his own weapons (which in my case would be pistols or rifles, and the Germans have an aversion to gunpowder), in which event the offender generally makes an apology and backs out of the business. I assure you I have not at all exaggerated this duelling business. If you cannot have faith in it, you have only to say —

"Travellers ne'er did lie,
Though folks at home condemn them."

And though it is beyond all contradiction a brutal state of things, yet I cannot help thinking it is not without its uses. For instance, some of the students are perfect knights-errant, and if they hear of a lady being insulted (for it is not uncommon for a German student, who wishes to manifest his independence, to push a lady off the side-walk), are sure to seek out the offender and salute him with "Dummer Junge," in which case twelve Gangs of the Schläger must necessarily ensue. . . .

The Germans are certainly the most musical nation on earth. It is almost impossible to meet a student who cannot sing a thousand songs and play at least one instrument. We have at dinner a full band of music playing, and there are concerts in the public gardens here as often as once a week. The Germans appear to me the most affectionate and (but you will not think it) the most enthusiastic people on earth. Certainly they are infinitely the most industrious and studious. Almost all the students study somewhat, and the greatest part of them immensely, besides writing off at the lectures nearly every word the professor says.[9]

Motley entered more than any of the Americans who had resided at Göttingen into the life of the German students. He naturally formed close contacts with two of his fellow-countrymen, Amory Coffin and Mitchell King, both from Charleston, South Carolina, and was intimate with a number of native Germans, whose habits and customs he soon adopted.

I have formed very agreeable acquaintances among the German students [he informs his parents near the close of the first semester], and I have mixed with them on all occasions and in all places, like one of them. I believe I told you in my last letter about the ceremony of drinking "Schmollis" or Brotherhood. It is a very pleasant way of sealing a friendship, and I have drunk it with several of the best students here.

Among others,[10] he knew well Graf Alexander Keyserling, the later distinguished natural philosopher, and it was at this time that an affectionate friendship was established between Bismarck and Motley, which continued until the end of Motley's life.[11] Bismarck had entered the University in May of that year and was soon termed "the mad Junker," owing to his reckless, daring conduct in defiance of all authority. A few weeks after his matriculation he became a member of one of the most prominent corps, the "Hanovera," and in a short time was famous for his successful roles in student duels and in the "Kneipen." Political questions made but little appeal at this period to the future statesman; he welcomed instead Motley's interest in literary matters, and companionship with the three young Americans, whom he joined in celebrating the Fourth of July, 1833. Motley, a slight, delicate youth, impressively handsome, affected, in accordance with the custom of many young Englishmen and Americans of that period, the Byronic cynicism and turned collar. "Although not having mastered yet the German language," says Bismarck, "he exercised a marked attention by a conversation sparkling with wit, humor, and originality." [12] From the young American Bismarck learned his favorite songs, "Good Old Colony Times," and "Auld Lang Syne." These friends were a picturesque couple as they wandered down the streets of Göttingen, discussing various literary and philosophical subjects, Bismarck in a ridiculous costume, with his cane and huge pipe, followed by his dog. In *Morton's Hope* a vivid portrait of Bismarck is presented in the hero, one Otto von Rabenmark, whom Motley describes:

Rabenmark was the "fox" (the slang term for a student in his first year) who had just been challenging the veteran students to drink. He was very young, even for a fox; for at the time I write of he was not yet seventeen; but in precocity of character, in every respect, he went immeasurably beyond any person I have ever known. As to his figure, I certainly have seldom seen a more unprepossessing person at first sight, though on better acquaintance I began to think him rather well-looking. He had coarse, scraggly hair of a mixed color, something between a red and a white brown. His face was peppered all over with freckles and his eyes were colorless in the centre and looked as if wedged with red tape. An enormous scar, the relic of an ancient duel, in which, like a thorough fox, he was constantly engaged, extended from the tip of his nose to the edge of his right ear, and he had been sewed up with fourteen stitches, every one of which (as the "Pauk-Doktor" had been a botcher at his trade) was distinctly and grotesquely visible.

As every one of the students was tattooed and scarified in the same way, like so many New Zealand chiefs, his decoration of itself hardly excited attention; but as, to heighten the charms of his physiognomy, he had recently shaved off one of his eyebrows, his face certainly might lay claim to a bizarre and very unique character.

His figure was slender and not yet mature, but already of a tolerable height. His dress was in the extreme of the then Göttingen fashion. He wore a chaotic coat, without collar or buttons, and as destitute of color as of shape; enormously wide trousers and boots with iron heels and portentous spurs. His shirt collar, unconscious of cravat, was doubled over his shoulders, and his hair hung down about his ears and neck. A faint attempt at mustachios, of an indefinite color, completed the equipment of his face, and a huge saber, strapped around his waist, that of his habiliments. As he wrote "Von" before his name, and was descended from a Bohemian family which had been baronized before Charlemagne's time, he wore an enormous seal ring on his forefinger, with his armorial bearing.

Such was Otto von Rabenmark, a youth who in a more fortunate sphere would have won himself name and fame. He was gifted with talents and acquirements immeasurably beyond his years. He spoke half a dozen languages — Heaven knows where he picked them up — was an excellent classical scholar, and well read in history; played well on the violin and piano, and if not a dexterous was at least a desperate and daring swordsman. He was of undoubted courage, and a little of a renomist (or swaggerer), a defect which his extreme youth excused, and from which he very soon recovered.[13]

At the close of his first semester in Göttingen Motley wrote to his parents:

This term I cannot pretend to have done much in the way of studying law, because it was impossible for me to attend lectures with any profit before I knew enough of the language to understand them perfectly. But I have studied German a great deal this term, and by mixing a good deal with the students on all occasions, I have made some progress in speaking and understanding the language. By reading a great deal of German every day, too, I have become able to read it almost as easily as English.[14]

Vacation followed, and Motley, in company with three German students, journeyed, chiefly on foot, to the Tyrol, to parts of

Switzerland, and through the Rhine Valley. The following
semester he attended a full schedule of lectures, but concluded
afterward to pursue his studies in another university. In 1832
the Göttingen faculty was not so distinguished as it had been
during the residence of Ticknor and his immediate successors.
"It is at all events not worth one's while to remain long at
Göttingen," Motley wrote home, "because most of the Professors who were ornaments of the University are dead or decayed,
and the town itself is excessively dull." [15] Berlin, with distinguished scholars, notably Savigny, offered more attractions, and
therefore he settled there the following year. He was soon
joined by Bismarck and Keyserling, with whom he lived in
closest intimacy in the same house.[16] Here they continued their
discussions, the favorite theme being whether Byron could be
compared with Goethe. It is reported, doubtless with some
truth, that Bismarck had now adopted a more subdued personal
appearance and conduct, and that he entered more into the
social and intellectual life of the city. However, says one writer,[17]
it is not well known that the future statesman and the future
historian and diplomat were once arrested and lodged in the
same guard-house for loud singing and disturbing the peace
while returning from a students' festival. Of his young friend
Bismarck later stated:

> Motley by that time had arrived at talking German fluently; he
> occupied himself not only in translating Goethe's poem "Faust," but
> tried his hand even in composing German verses. Enthusiastic admirer
> of Shakespeare, Byron, Goethe, he used to spice his conversation abun-
> dantly with quotations from these, his favorite authors. A pertinacious
> arguer, so much so that sometimes he watched my awakening in order
> to continue a discussion on some topic of science, poetry, or practical
> life, cut short by the chime of the small hours; he never lost his mild and
> amiable temper.[18]

The lectures which Motley followed during his one semester
in Berlin covered the same subjects which Göttingen had offered, principally law and history. His letters to his parents
describe with enthusiasm his new environment. He enjoyed the
advantages of Berlin society, particularly the home of Savigny,
the theatres, the opera, the galleries, and the libraries. There
were excursions to Potsdam, where he was invited to a military

ball. "It was rather dull," Motley wrote his father, "but it must be confessed that the Germans are very polite to strangers, and I have experienced nothing but kindness and civility in every town that I have been in." [19] He concluded that the Germans could generally be conveniently divided into two classes, "the Vons and the not-Vons," and that their opinions of America were singularly erroneous. The first class believed that both a democratic people and demagogues existed in the United States, while the second class, particularly those of the lowest stratum, were convinced that the people were plutocrats and that the streets of New York were paved with gold. Of the Berlin theatres Motley wrote home:

Shakespeare's tragedies are seldom given, and notwithstanding the richness of the modern German literature, they have very few fine-acting tragedies. The *chefs-d'oeuvre* of Goethe and Schiller are not adapted to the stage. Some of them are occasionally given, but seldom with success. The other evening the drama of "Goetz von Berlichingen with the Iron Hand," a magnificent picture of the old time in Germany, and one of Goethe's masterpieces, was given, but with so many stage alterations, that from a serious martial tragedy it was metamorphosed into a farce or a sort of Tom Thumb melodrama, full of scenes excellently fitted "to amuse the ears of the groundlings," and to disgust everybody who had read a line of the original. The character of Goetz von Berlichingen, the best possible portrait of a knight of the middle ages, part robber, part soldier, and part *preux chevalier*, was given by a thickset, periwig-pated fellow, whose sole effort was to represent Goetz as a lusty knight "most potent at potting," who could never keep his fingers from the flask of Rhenish, except when he was slaughtering legions and committing unheard-of exploits with his iron fist.[20]

In the spring of 1834 Motley's brief residence in Berlin came to a close and he started on his travels, which included first brief visits to several German cities. In Weimar he was cordially received by Ottilie, but was disappointed, he tells us, in not having arrived in Germany before Goethe's death "that I might have seen this Nestor of German literature." However, he felt partially compensated, for in Dresden he met Tieck and formed an acquaintance with some of his writings. He wrote afterward to his mother:

I do not know if many of Tieck's works have been translated into English. If they have, you will get them at the Athenaeum. Inquire for

"Fantasas" or "Puss in Boots" or the "World upside down," or Tieck's novels (which last are a set of exquisite little tales, novels in the original meaning of the word), full of old German legends and superstitions, and the authorship of which will entitle him to the title of German "Boccaccio." The other works are the old nursery tales of "Fortunatus," "Puss in Boots," "Blue Beard," etc., etc., done into plays (not for the stage) and as full of playful and sharp satire, poetry and plain sense as they can hold. If they have not been translated we shall have a chance of reading them together one of these days. I was invited by Tieck to tea on Sunday evening, when there was a small party. He is at present just about finishing his translation of Shakespeare (in company with Schlegel), and is in the habit of reading a play aloud to a party of select auditors. I did not hear him, and rather regret it, because he seems to be rather vain of his elocution. His head and bust are fine, and it was not till he got up from his chair that I observed he was slightly deformed (humpbacked). His conversation was like his books, playful, full of *bonhomie*, good-natured sort of satire, and perhaps a little childish vanity. He spoke of Cooper, Irving (whom he knew in Dresden, and whom he admired very much), steamboats, homoeopathism, himself, elocution, with Shakespeare and the musical glasses. His conversation was pleasing and quiet, but without any great show or brilliancy. . . ." [21]

From Dresden Motley proceeded to Vienna, then through the Tyrol and southern Germany, and arrived in Paris in July. Later he turned southward, and after spending the winter principally in Rome and Naples, the spring in Sicily, and the following summer in the British Isles, reached home in the autumn of 1835. On his return he was much in Boston society, and was married two years later to the charming Mary Benjamin. During the next few years he gave slight attention to the reading and practice of law, for which he had no special liking, but had all the while literary and historical ambitions which form the principal evidence of the training and knowledge he had acquired in Germany. In 1839 he published his first novel, *Morton's Hope*.[22] This is a crude piece of work, destitute of plot, but in its autobiographical character it furnishes an excellent record, disguised under a series of incidents, of Motley's early life, his love of languages, literature, and history, and his character, ambitions, and aspirations. Furthermore, it is not only a partial record of Motley's experiences in Germany, corresponding in a sense to the position of *Hyperion* in Longfellow's career, but is a faithful picture of many aspects of German university life. One hesitates, however, to accept, even for that period the following severe impressions:

It is a singular anomaly, — the whole German student existence. The German students are no more Germans than they are Sandwich Islanders. They have, in fact, less similarity with Germans, than any other nation. You see in them a distinct and strongly characterized nation, moving in a definite, though irregular orbit of its own, and totally independent of the laws which regulate the rest of the social system of Germany. It presents the regular phenomenon of a rude, though regularly organized republic, existing in the heart of a despotism. In fact, every one of the main points of the German character is directly opposite of those of the German student. The German is phlegmatic — the student, fiery. The German is orderly and obedient to the authorities, — the student, ferocious and intractable. The German is peaceable, — the student, forever brawling and fighting. The German is eminently conservative in his politics — the student, always a revolutionist. The government of all the German states is despotic, — the student's whole existence is Republican. The German is particularly deferent to rank and title. In the student's republic, and there alone, the omnipotent "Von'" sinks before the dexterous schläger, or the capacious "beerbummel." Lastly, the German is habitually sober, and the student invariably drunk.[23]

As the youthful product and the first literary adventure of a young man of twenty-five, this novel did not give much promise for the future eminent literary historian, nor was it well received.[24] In May of the year of its publication, Longfellow wrote to Samuel Ward:

When does Morton of Morton Hope make its appearance? Do you know, I have this design: if I can get the sheets of the book, to write a notice for the July North American, provided the book is to appear *before* July, and provided, likewise, I can praise it heartily and warmly; ... because I have no idea of doing such a thing unless I can praise it with a relish. Then I will most gladly; for it would be a grateful welcome to a young author to have *early* laudation. I am on very friendly terms with the author, and like him, and wish to do all I can to give him a fair start in the field.[25]

However, the *New York Review* commented:

The story is a tissue of wild and extravagant adventures, drawn with boldness and vigor by a masterly and facile pen; the incidents and portraits are remarkably graphic, and with the exception of an occasional caricature, and dark improbability — we should pronounce them faithful delineations. The German scenes especially are wrought up with great skill, and the reader we are sure will leave Göttingen with regret.[26]

There is further tangible evidence of Motley's contact with Germany and of his continued interest in the literature of that country. In Dresden, as we have seen, he had made the personal acquaintance of Tieck and had interested himself in his writings. In December, 1840, he contributed to *The New World* [27] a fairly acceptable translation of Tieck's five-act drama *Blue Beard*, prefaced by the following "Advertisement":

Tieck is the most popular living author of Germany; his writings are upon a variety of subjects, and his critical essays, particularly upon topics connected with the five acts, rank very high in German literature. But his popularity is chiefly derived from his lighter works. His tales, poems and satires are considered by his countrymen to be full of wit, humor, and a lively fancy, and have produced for him the title of the German Boccaccio.

But more satisfactory and more valuable to American scholarship is Motley's continued interest in Goethe, which, as we have shown, began during his undergraduate days at Harvard, if not at Round Hill. As a student in Germany he had visited Leipzig and Weimar, and perhaps Frankfort. A rollicking scene in one of the chapters in *Morton's Hope* carries us to Auerbachs Keller, of which Motley gives a description. "Goethe had not yet written *Faust*," he says, "but the wild fable which was the foundation of that wonderful drama, was as well known as now." [28] In October, 1838, and in July of the following year, Motley contributed to the *New York Review* two excellent articles on Goethe which not only stand as a reminder, were there nothing further of Motley's mature scholarship, but also rendered valuable service to the history of Goethe studies in this country. In the first of these, a review of *Dichtung und Wahrheit*, and of Mrs. Austin's *Characteristics of Goethe*,[29] he praises the poet for the interesting, detailed, and vivid history of his development, as well as for a picture of the age in which he lived. A splendid sketch of Goethe's career, including extracts from his own narrative for the purpose of supporting Motley's views, and the essential traits of the poet's genius, personality and character are given. He defends Goethe against the absurd charges of egotism presented in the *Edinburgh Review* in 1816, as one "whose reputation has been steadily increasing for nearly a century, and who, during the successive generations, sustained the *first* rank in the republic of letters." Championing Goethe against those who had accused him of indifference to political questions, Motley says:

It was the sense of obligation to bring out all that was in him which could benefit others, that led him to shun so sedulously a "mere negative and polemical direction of talent." He thought it better to build than to destroy. He preferred to create the beautiful, rather than combat the ugly. Any one can do the latter — how few comparatively are capable of the former.

Again we note his conception of Goethe's procedure:

Goethe eminently constrained and moulded his circumstances. In the midst of his multifarious life, of his apparently ever changing and transient purposes, the germ within was unfolding in obedience to the law of its nature, and drawing congenial nourishment from the manifold elements in which it grew. Even while he appeared to float at the mercy of every shifting current and fickle breeze, this inward, guiding principle was always active. If we compare the close of his life with his earliest tastes and purposes, we shall find that he *was* what he *meant* to be, spite of all obstacles — we might almost say through the means of these obstacles; for the assimilative power of his mind drew nourishment from the most uncongenial elements.

Referring to the accusations of Goethe's disregard of morality, Motley offers his views:

In so far as this charge rests on the want of a distinct moral aim in his works, we regard him as fully justified, on this ground . . . that morals and aesthetics constitute two distinct provinces. A work of art is perfect, when it is perfectly conformed to the rules of art. With the laws of morality it has nothing to do, except so far as they are implied in those of art. It is absurd to demand of an artist that his work should inculcate *a moral*. . . . But on other grounds we do not know that Goethe can be entirely justified from the charge of "lukewarmness of moral sentiments."

It is here only that Motley fails to take a definite attitude. "We will leave to our readers," he says, "to decide how far Goethe has been justly charged with a criminal indifference to the moral welfare of mankind." Finally he approaches the question of Goethe's universality of interests and presents what might be called a summary of his impressions of the poet:

We are therefore struck with astonishment when we encounter a mind like Goethe's, equally at home in the real and the ideal; equally interested in the laws of poetical criticism and the theory of colors; equally attentive to a drawing of a new species of flowers and the plan of a railroad or a canal. With an imagination of boundless fertility, he combines the powers of judging, so seldom found in connexion with it, and is at once a great artist and a great critic. In short, with the most delicate sense of the beautiful, the most accurate perception of the mode of representing it, and the intensest love for it, he combined a fondness for observation, a love of the actual in nature, and a susceptibility to deep impressions from objects of sense, never before perhaps found in such a conjunction.

The second of the reviews,[30] which is practically a continuation of the first, emphasizes more of what appears to Motley to be the peculiar characteristics of Goethe's mind and writings. Considerable attention is paid to the poet's intellectual egotism, independence, pursuit of truth, sincerity, placidity of temperament, universal interest, and industry. We note the following appraisal:

It will accordingly be observed that every one of his works forms the result of a painful observation of himself. Whether it be the revelation of a tormenting passion, the promulgation of a cherished theory, the prosecution of an intellectual nosology, it will still be observed that the subject matter is drawn out of himself, out of his own observations, passions, misfortunes or success. The productions through which he is immortal, have been spun from himself as the web from the spider; and every succeeding day involved him more deeply in the intricate but accurately woven and exquisitely developed production, which it was the natural instinct of his existence to weave. Whether, as in *Werther*, he lays bare his own bosom to the scalpel, and surrenders himself to a spiritual autopsy; whether, as in *Wilhelm Meister*, he unfolds a vast plan of universal education; or whether, as in *Faust*, he expresses with a master's hand, the longing which tempts man beyond the confines of his inferior nature, till he destroy himself against the adamantine barrier which restrains him in his allotted but unsatisfying sphere; whether we examine the one or the other of these various works of art, we shall find them each and all the result of an elaborate and systematic observation of his own individuality. It is this, and this alone, which entitles these productions and these studies to take rank with the purest physical sciences. He has, without a paradox, treated of the intellectual physically; and thus we may consider the whole mass of his poetry and fiction as forming one great museum of natural history — the natural history of the human mind.

After pointing out the various excellencies and defects of Goethe, which form, in Motley's opinion, one great characteristic, namely universalism, he passes to a consideration of the poet's style and of *Wilhelm Meister, Die Wahlverwandtschaften*, and *Faust*, as illustrations of his views. Goethe's prose is graceful, natural, and lively, for with him, more than with any author of modern times, says Motley, literature was an art. From this he proceeds to a lengthy analysis and discussion of the three works mentioned above. *Wilhelm Meister*, Motley declares, is not so much a novel as a treatise upon, or rather a digest of, universalism. It contains a dull mass of egotistical and technical details upon many subjects which will always prevent its popularity with readers of novels; but the varied experiences and development of the hero illustrate the rule of the author's life. Turning to *Die Wahlverwandtschaften*, which Motley calls one of the most remarkable and decidedly the most characteristic of Goethe's productions, though one of "those moral monsters" inconceivable in any country other than Germany, we note the usual early American impression of the novel:

There is nothing in any other of his works to be compared with this, as an exemplification of the scientific and experimental mode of examining the human passions to which his genius addicted him. . . . It is a tale of crime, suffering, and death; but crime, suffering, and death, are investigated and discussed, as it were, physically. We do not think it necessary to enter into an elaborate castigation of its immorality; it is enough for us to say, that it is a story of extremely pernicious tendency, however innocent the author may have been of any such design. It is a proof of mental rather than of moral obliquity, a distorted picture drawn by one accustomed to treat the intellectual physically, to regard virtue and vice, happiness and anguish, bad passions and holy impulses, purely as phenomena; and we have already observed that the different phenomena of nature were to Goethe equally important, equally interesting, equally respectable, and except as subjects of investigation, equally indifferent.

The germination, the expansion, the gradual and at last perfect unfolding of the guilty and disastrous passions which form the theme of the story, are watched, investigated, experimented upon, and discussed, with the same calm and passionless attention, with which the naturalist regards the process of crystallization, or (to look into the book itself for an illustration) the combination, separation, and reunion of an alkali, an acid, and a gas. This is the singular idea which it is one of the great objects of the work to develop. The *Elective Affinities*, in short, is a novel in the chemical taste — its subject is adultery.

Finally Motley pays his respects to *Faust*, which he calls the greatest poem of the age. He shows an intelligent understanding and appreciation of the work, though he confines his remarks to the First Part. Evidently he had little acquaintance with the Second Part. He gives his conception of the philosophy of the poem, and an analysis of Faust and Mephistopheles, carefully supporting his interpretation by citing certain passages in his own fairly adequate translation, which, he tells us, he has rendered with no attempt at versification or elegance. It is first stated that Faust is the eternal type of a mind in which the equilibrium between human ambition and human ability is destroyed, a mind which is disgusted with the insufficiency of all human knowledge. "Faust, in a word," says Motley, "is a man who is disgusted with the insufficiency of man." Faust and Mephistopheles are contrasted as the embodiment of the two opposing principles existing in humanity, the angelic and the bestial. Faust, with his aspirations and ambitions thwarted, represents the first of these, while Mephistopheles, the unrivalled creation, the greatest conception in poetry since Shakespeare, is the quintessence of the second, and "the only portrait of the devil which mortal ever drew." According to Motley the great principle of Mephistopheles' character, and one which is developed in the most masterly manner, is contempt. He despises all things equally, the good and the bad, but is incapable of hate. Being the essence of good nature and tranquillity of mind, he forms a delightful, lively, and agreeable companion for Faust. After quoting certain lines in translation from the first and second "Study" scenes and the "Witch's Kitchen," Motley gives his final estimate of the poem:

There is not in fact, in the whole range of literature, a work which contains a sounder, deeper, or more healthy moral than this drama. It is, moreover, as we stated in the commencement, a poem, which embodies, as it were, the result of all Goethe's studies, actions, life. And it is for this reason that a study of this single work would give the reader a very comprehensive notion of his genius.

To make the most of present life, of present knowledge; to develop to the utmost the human intellect as it exists; and to look forward to their complete expansion, to their perfect development, in some future existence, with faith, with placid and unrepining hope; to be *universal* within the present limits of humanity, and to trust for an universal and unbounded existence in a future sphere; this, as we have repeated again and again, was — Goethe. The reverse of this — the embodiment of man, over-ambitious, disgusted with humanity, and "cursing patience";

invoking and devoting himself to the fiend which slumbered as yet unformed and chaotic within his own nature — this is Faust.

Motley regrets that he is compelled to leave unnoticed many other productions of Goethe, but states that his purpose has been to generalize and to deduce, as far as possible from a careful study of certain writings, the principles and laws of the poet's genius. His review was received with interest. On April 25 Ward informed Longfellow, "The New York Review is to open with Lothrop on Goethe — a most excellent article"; on July 13, after the publication appeared, Longfellow, who shared Motley's views, replied, "Please tell Mr. Cogswell that his last number is *excellent*. Motley has said the best thing on Faust (so far as it goes) that I have heard or read." [31] It is striking that in the very month and year when Bancroft published in the *Christian Examiner* his absurd criticism of Goethe, his former pupil at Round Hill, who had begun the study of German under him, wrote so intelligently on the subject. We turn with pride and satisfaction to Motley as one who, like Longfellow, understood and appreciated Goethe and adopted a sane attitude when the poet was the central figure in American study of German literature.

In 1841 Motley began his diplomatic career, serving for a few months as secretary to the American legation at St. Petersburg. His journey through Prussia led him to observe that he was in a country with no history, "an artificial patchwork, without natural coherence, mosaiced out of bought, stolen and plundered provinces, and only kept together by compression." [32] It seemed to him a land of mild despotism, but a land where the colors black and white were everywhere in evidence and everything was regulated by the Government. On his return, early in 1842, he made brief visits to several German cities. He spent two days at Weimar, principally in Goethe's house, as the guest of Ottilie. Of this experience he writes to his wife:

She is the same lively, agreeable and intelligent person that she was eight years ago; but she has grown much older, her hair is entirely grey, and I fear she is in a decline. She thinks so herself, and is going to Italy in the spring. Her sons are neither of them in Weimar. I gave her my article on Goethe, which she read and was pleased with; but I refused to tell her even the name of my unfortunate novel, of which she had heard and about which she was curious.[33]

But Weimar was no longer "a little Athens," says Motley, and all that he found remaining of its former illustrious literati, "that splendid army of genius," were the coffins of Goethe and Schiller. He left with regret, however, and proceeded to Frankfort, where he spent a day looking at Goethe's house, Dannecker's celebrated Ariadne, and the picturesque Römerberg. His travels carried him to Paris and to London, and he soon returned home to devote his time to politics and to writing.

The essays which Motley contributed to the *North American Review* during the next few years were of a historical and critical character, and were favorably received. In "The Novels of Balzac," [34] published in 1847, he again shows his interest in Goethe when he draws the following comparison:

> In all this calm and conscientious study of nature, he often reminds us of Goethe. Balzac, however, is only an artist. He walks through the world to observe, but he observes phenomena only to furnish materials for his art. Goethe we have always considered a great naturalist. His pursuit is always truth, natural truth, which he delights to teach, through all its manifestations, up to its living principles. He, too, was no moralist, but a student of universal nature, both physical and metaphysical, who watched the sprouting of a hyacinth or a passion, the combination of an alkali and an acid, and the conflict of the affections, the efflorescence of a carnation, the revolution of a people, the eruption of a volcano, all with equal attention, and classed them all as natural phenomena, each as worthy to be studied as the others. To your true physician, the development of a cancer is as beautiful as the flowering of a rose. To Goethe, all manifestations of nature were interesting, for he studied truth. He gave to the world the results of his investigations with the most scrupulous fidelity to truth, so far as he could reach it, and let consequences take care of themselves. It is for this reason, among others, that many people have discovered that he is a very immoral writer. . . . Balzac stops short of Goethe, however. He is no naturalist except to serve the purpose of his art.

Another essay, "Polity of the Puritans," [35] which appeared in the October number, 1849, and which was based upon a German publication, gives us Motley's comment on the German language:

> We consider the German language to be less adapted to narrative, and particularly to historical narrative than any language of Europe with which we are acquainted. Hardly any German, even among the acknowledged classical authors, writes a good prose style. Taking out

Goethe and Schiller, we hardly know an individual whose style is to our taste. German prose is, to the intensest degree, prosy. . . . But the Germans have to contend with the structure of their language, as well as with a slight natural propensity to be tedious. . . . German prose, in short, is so formidable and elaborate a language that a German *Bourgeois gentilhomme* might well be more astonished than M. Jourdain, if informed that he had been speaking it all his life.

For some years Motley had been working on his first great project in the field in which he established his reputation. In order, however, to do justice to the history of the Dutch Republic, he found it necessary to have access to the libraries and archives of Europe. He therefore sailed with his family in 1851, and spent the next five years in several countries collecting his materials and preparing for publication his *History of the Dutch Republic*, which appeared in three volumes in 1856. Several months of this time were spent at work in Dresden, where, owing to letters of introduction from Ticknor, he enjoyed the advantages of the Court and particularly the friendship of Prince John of Saxony. He reveled in the opera, the galleries, and the Royal Library.

And now add to the advantages here enumerated [he writes to his mother] a magnificent library of 450,000 volumes, and very excellent opportunities for education, besides a very beautiful and picturesque country surrounding the city in all directions, and you will understand why Dresden is so often selected as a residence. It is a dull little place, no doubt, but I like it the better for that.[36]

Passing through Frankfort in July, 1855, he was cordially received by his old friend Bismarck, then Minister to the Diet of the German Confederation. It was their first meeting since the Berlin student days. "The Bismarcks are as kind as ever," writes Motley. "Nothing can be more frank and cordial than their manners. I am there all day long. It is one of those houses where every one does what one likes." [37]

After a short visit home, Motley was again abroad, 1857–60, preparing his *History of the United Netherlands*, the first two volumes of which appeared in 1860, and the remaining two eight years later. During a few days in Frankfort in May, 1858, he was constantly in Bismarck's home. Several months of that year and the following one were passed in London, where, in

much the same way as had Ticknor, Motley mingled in distinguished society. He saw much of Mackintosh, Thackeray,
Carlyle, Macaulay, Hallam, Lady Byron, Lord John Russell,
Palmerston, Clarendon, and many others. He returned home in
1861, but was soon appointed by President Lincoln as minister
to Austria, which post he held for the next seven years. When,
first presenting his credentials he spoke so fluently in perfect
German that the Emperor was led to inquire whether he was a
native German. On being assured that he was an American the
Emperor seemed relieved and exhibited satisfaction.[38] The
period of Motley's service in Vienna was of course a critical one
in the history of America, as of Europe. Referring to our Civil
War, he wrote in August, 1862, to Holmes:

> Do you remember that wonderful scene in *Faust* in which Mephis-
> topheles draws wine for the rabble with a gimlet out of the wooden
> table; and how it changes to fire as they drink it, and how they all go
> mad, draw their knives, grasp each other by the nose, and think they
> are cutting off bunches of grapes at every blow, and how foolish they
> all look when they awake from the spell and see how the Devil has
> been mocking them? It always seems to me a parable of the great
> Secession.[39]

Motley's letters during these years in Vienna contain a full account of his experiences and of his many problems as a diplomat,
and throw considerable light on the important political questions
which then confronted European countries. His continued intimate friendship throughout the years with Bismarck is unique
in American history. Bismarck had high regard also for Bancroft, but the relations between him and Motley were those of
personal affection. The voluminous correspondence exchanged
between them is full of affectionate praise and admiration for
each other.

> I never pass by old Logier's House, in the Friedrichstrasse [wrote
> Bismarck in April, 1863] without looking up at the windows that used
> to be ornamented by a pair of red slippers sustained on the wall by the
> feet of a gentleman sitting in the Yankee way, his head below and out
> of sight. I then gratify my memory with remembrance of "good old
> colony times" when we were roguish chaps.[40]

A letter in May of the following year from Bismarck reads:

> Jack my Dear, — Where the devil are you, and what do you do that
> you never write a line to me? I am working from morn to night like

a nigger, and you have nothing to do at all — you might as well tip me a line as well as looking on your feet tilted against the wall of God knows what a dreary colour. I cannot entertain a regular correspondence; it happens to me that during five days I do not find a quarter of an hour for a walk; but you, lazy old chap, what keeps you from thinking of your old friends? When just going to bed in this moment my eye met with yours on your portrait, and I curtailed the sweet restorer, sleep, in order to remind you of Auld Lang Syne. Why do you never come to Berlin? . . . When can you come, and when will you come? I swear that I will make out the time to look with you on Logier's quarters and drink a bottle with you at Gerolt's, where they would not allow you to put your slender legs upon a chair. Let politics be hanged and come to see me. I promise that the Union Jack shall wave over our house, and conversation and the best old hock shall pour damnation upon the rebels. Do not forget old friends neither their wives, as mine wishes nearly as ardently as myself to see you, or at least to see as quickly as possible a word of your handwriting.[41]

Motley soon replied, addressing him "My dear Old Bismarck" and assuring him that he would come to Berlin as soon as he found a good opportunity. "As to Logier," he said, "I am sure that his ghost still haunts the Friedrichstrasse No. 161, and will not be laid until you and I go up into the first floor front together and exorcise him. After that we will proceed to Gerolt's, and put our legs on all the chairs in the restaurant." [42] He urged him to come to Vienna, and in the summer of 1864, when Bismarck was in Vienna to settle the terms of peace with the Emperor, following the war between Denmark and Austria and Prussia, he and Motley reviewed their youthful days together as students. In October, 1869, when Motley was minister to England, Bismarck insisted that he pay him a visit. "Then we will sit down again to a game of chess at Logier's house," he said, "and dispute as to whether Byron and Goethe can be compared to each other." [43] Finally, in July, 1872, Motley was the guest of the Chancellor for several days at Varzin, which was their last visit together. "The truth is, he is so entirely simple, so full of laissez-aller," wrote Motley, "that one is obliged to be saying to one's self all the time, This is the great Bismarck, the greatest living man, and one of the greatest historical characters that ever lived. . . . He is the least of a poseur of any man I ever saw, little or big." [44] In Berlin Motley was entertained by Bancroft, and soon departed for an excursion to the Harz, to view once more the Brocken, though not from the summit. "I have 'Faust' in my bag," he said, "and can read the 'Walpurgis-nacht' over again comfortably in bed, which will be much jollier." [45]

In 1874 Motley published *The Life and Death of John of Barneveld*, which is not a biography but rather a continuation of his historical studies, bringing the annals of Dutch history down to the beginning of the Thirty Years' War. With the exception of a few months in this country during the next year, he spent the years prior to his death in 1877 chiefly in England, the land which, as Dean Stanley stated in alluding to him in a service in Westminster Abbey, he passionately loved, and whose mother tongue was that of the literature which he made his own. However, John Motley was pre-eminently a cosmopolitan man of the world. If, as his intimate friend Oliver Wendell Holmes suggests, he had disappointments in his diplomatic career, he had more than enough to console him in his brilliant scholarly triumphs. As was true of Bancroft and of Prescott, he combined with his historical studies a love of good literature and of the great human spirits, regardless of age and nationality. He holds a prominent place in the annals of American scholarship.

NOTES

Notes

GEORGE TICKNOR

1. *Life, Letters, and Journals of George Ticknor*, 2 vols., Boston, James R. Osgood and Co., 1876. The work was partly edited by Ticknor's intimate friend, George S. Hillard, and completed by Mrs. Ticknor and her eldest daughter, Anna Eliot Ticknor. A new edition containing an interesting introduction by Ferris Greenslet was issued by Houghton Mifflin Co., Boston and New York, 1909. While for purposes of this study I have used with freedom this publication, I have followed available manuscripts and other sources, particularly the manuscript journals of Ticknor's first and second journeys to Europe, containing much unpublished material.

2. March 24, 1876. *Letters of Charles Eliot Norton*, ed. by Sara Norton and M. A. DeWolfe Howe, Boston, 1913, ii, 62–63.

3. His instruction in Greek was given by Daniel Webster's elder brother, Ezekiel, and that in French and Spanish by Francis Sales, with whom he was associated many years later at Harvard.

4. He records (*Life*, i, 7) that he enjoyed calculating the great eclipse of 1806, and making a projection of it, "which turned out nearly right." Something of his artistic ability during this period may be seen in his sketch of the college buildings, which adorns the walls of the present Graduate Club in Hanover.

5. Manuscript letter, February 18, 1807, Dartmouth College Library, a copy of which has been kindly forwarded to me by Professor Howard Dunham of the Dartmouth faculty.

6. *Life*, i, 11.

7. December 20, 1814. Jefferson mss., L. C. In the same letter Adams mentions giving letters of introduction also to Edward Everett and Francis C. Gray. Everett, however, was compelled to return home from Washington without visiting Monticello. For Gray's account of the visit to Jefferson, as given in his journal discovered by Henry S. Rowe of Boston, cf. *New York Times*, April 10, 1927.

8. February 7, 1815. *Life*, i, 34–38.

9. February 5, 1815. Jefferson mss., L. C.

10. June 10. L. C.

11. February 14. L. C.

12. February 11, 28, March 2. These letters, as well as those to Lafayette and Adams, are published in the Library edition of Jefferson's *Works*, Washington, 1903, xiv, 239, 254–267, 301.

13. American peace commissioner abroad, who took a leading part in the peace negotiations between England and America which resulted in the Treaty of Ghent.

14. March 19. L. C.

15. March 6. Mass. Hist. Soc.

16. Jefferson mss., Mass. Hist. Soc.

17. March 21. Mass. Hist. Soc.

18. Mr. and Mrs. Samuel G. Perkins of Boston and Mr. Nathaniel A. Haven of Portsmouth, N. H. The sons of John Quincy Adams were on their way

to join their father, then United States minister at St. Petersburg, and Everett entered, with Ticknor, the University of Göttingen. Cf. *Life*, 1, 49.

19. The manuscript journal for these four years abroad, which Mr. Philip Dexter kindly placed at my disposal, consumes nine good-sized volumes and contains copious accounts of Ticknor's many interesting experiences, including detailed descriptions of all the places which he visited.

20. Ticknor's journal records meeting many prominent figures, among them Lord Byron, whom he found, contrary to all expectations, affable and gentle, simple and unaffected, and delighted to discuss various topics, particularly America and Greece.

21. June 18. L. C.

22. July 5. L. C. On August 7 the father gratefully replied: "All I ask is, that he may merit your confidence and approbation and receive your blessing, and transact your business as becomes a wise, judicious, and prudent young man." Mass. Hist. Soc.

23. Polybius, Reiske's edition of Dionysius of Halicarnassus, Catesby's Natural History, Bruncke's Aristophanes, Suidas, Dugdale's Monasticon, Hakluyt's Voyages, Hollingshead, Hall's Chronicle, Horsley's Britannia, Hume's History, Johnson's Dictionary, Milton's Poetical Works, Purchas' Pilgrimage, and an edition of Rapin.

24. In this and a subsequent letter of August 16, Jefferson states that for this purpose he has arranged with his banker in Philadelphia, Mr. Girard, for a credit of $350 on his correspondents in Paris.

25. July 4. L. C.

26. "It was our purpose to remain there a year. But the facilities for study were such as we had never dreamed of. My own residence was, in consequence, protracted to a year and nine months; and Mr. Everett's was protracted yet six months longer," says Ticknor in his tribute to Everett, at a meeting of the Massachusetts Historical Society, January 30, 1865.

27. Journal, August 5.

28. Journal, August 7.

29. In his journal, August 9, Ticknor gives his address as 66 Weenderstrasse. During most of his Göttingen period, he resided in the home of Bouterwek, the literary historian, and a favorite professor in the University.

30. August 10. *Life*, 1, 74 f.

31. In his journal for October 4, 1815, Ticknor records: "The people about here are a strange people. They are certainly very orderly and moral in their lives; but in their conversation, they are extremely extravagant and profane. The practice of swearing is universal." He states that some of the professors, particularly Eichhorn and Blumenbach, swear "abominably," that even the ladies are grossly profane, and the clergy are "inattentive to the injunctions of the apostle." He also complains of the way Sunday is observed. The professors never attend church, and Eichhorn "does not even know where the church is."

32. Joseph Green Cogswell, who joined the American group in Göttingen in 1816, writes to Stephen Higginson of the high esteem in which Ticknor and Everett were held in Germany and of their importance in creating more respect among Europeans for American scholarship. March 8, 1817, Cogswell mss., N. Y. Pub. Lib.

33. December 17, 1815. *Life*, 1, 84 f.

34. The second volume of Ticknor's journal opens with a long account of the history of the University and the liberal basis on which it was founded and

administered. He states: "Münchhausen knew well what must be the central point of a good university and from the moment he founded Göttingen, he determined to give it a Library, as nearly as possible, perfect. It was commenced with a collection of 9000 volumes that had belonged to Baron Bülow."

35. May 20, 1816. Boston Pub. Lib. Printed in part by Thomas Wentworth Higginson, "Göttingen and Harvard Eighty Years Ago," *Harvard Graduates Magazine*, VI, 6 f.

36. November 6, 1815. *Life*, I, 80.

37. Journal, April 6, 1816. Some months later, when the second semester had closed, his journal for September 10 reads: "I am gratified to Heaven that another period of my imprisonment has passed, for five so miserable months as the last have been have never before darkened my life." And shortly afterward, November 30, he wrote to Stephen Higginson: "As to relaxation, in the sense of the word in which I used to employ it at home. . . of this sort of relaxation I know nothing here." Boston Pub. Lib.

38. Schultze's admirable acquirements led Ticknor to declare to his father that in the United States "we do not yet know what a Greek scholar is; we do not even know the process by which a man is to be made one." November 10, 1815. *Life*, I, 73.

39. Journal, March 27, 1816.

40. June 5, 1816. *Life*, I, 95.

41. Dr. G. von Selle, of the Göttingen University Library, has kindly given me a copy of Ticknor's manuscript letter, February 17, 1816, to Blumenbach, enclosing some materials on American Negroes and Indians. There is an account of Prince Sanders, a Negro interested in the education of his race, who conducted for a time a free school in Boston for Negro children, and later went to England on the same vessel with Ticknor in April, 1816. Another account is of Paul Cuffy, a Negro native of Nantucket, Mass., who devoted his efforts to the education of Africans, and a third account relates to an "Indian Charity School" at Hanover, N. H., which existed for the purpose of Christianizing northern Indians.

42. August 10, 1815. *Life*, I, 76.

43. November 5, 1816. *Life*, I, 79.

44. November 10, 1815. *Life*, I, 81.

45. June 5, 1816. *Life*, I, 95. His journal for April 6, 1815, and September 10, 1816, refers to lessons in French with d'Artaud and in Italian with Ballhorn.

46. November 9, 1816. *Life*, II, 503.

47. Ticknor's journal for September, 1816, includes a sketch and personal impressions of Wolf, "the Corypheus of German philologists," who was spending a few days in Göttingen. "But the more I admire him as a scholar, the more I dislike him as a man," says Ticknor. "He has openly quarrelled with most of his friends; he disgraced himself by his political conduct when the French were in Halle; and he has sunk from all respect by his vices in old age."

48. *Life*, I, 87–89.

49. November 16, 1816. *Life*, I, 118 f.

50. April 19, June 20, July 6, 1816. *Life*, I, 89–103.

51. June 16. *Life*, I, 98.

52. January 26, 1816. L. C.

53. February 9. Mass. Hist. Soc.; also Boston Pub. Lib.

54. October 14, 1815. L. C.

55. November 25. L. C.
56. January 14, 1816. L. C.
57. February 8. L. C.
58. March 15. L. C.; also Mass. Hist. Soc.
59. April 23. L. C.
60. August 15, October 22. Mass. Hist. Soc.
61. July 10. Mass. Hist. Soc.
62. The invoice enclosed in Elisha Ticknor's letter of November 16 to Jefferson
    lists twenty-one volumes, which, including the costs of freight and duties,
    totals $45.25. Stating in his acknowledgment to Elisha Ticknor his inten-
    tion to defer writing to his son until the latter's arrival in Paris, Jefferson
    said: "And I believe were I 20 years younger, instead of writing, I should
    meet him there and take with him his classical voyage to Rome, Naples
    and Athens. I wish him all the happiness and information, and they will
    be very great, which he will derive from it, and to yourself the sublime one
    of seeing your youth renewed and honored in him." December 12. Mass.
    Hist. Soc.
63. June 6, 1817. L. C. In this letter Jefferson states that the other part of his
    catalogue was committed by his friend Mr. Warden to the Paris booksellers,
    De Bure frères, who, under Warden's direction, filled the order to his satis-
    faction. He is now remitting a further sum to the De Bure frères for addi-
    tional volumes, directing them to accept Ticknor's advice implicitly. A
    duplicate list is enclosed to Ticknor with the request for information con-
    cerning German editions of Livy, Herodotus, Euripides, and Lucian. In a
    letter of the same date, addressed to the De Bure frères, Jefferson calls
    Ticknor "the best bibliograph of my acquaintance" and adds: "He is so
    perfectly acquainted with the best editions of the classics, and especially
    those lately of the German savants, that I pray you to consult him, and
    consider his advices as absolutely my own choice, and giving me the benefit
    of his knolege, so much more recent and extensive than mine." Mass. Hist.
    Soc. On August 14 Ticknor acknowledges Jefferson's request and states
    that, in the order, he has made two substitutions, Schweighäuser's edition
    of Herodotus for that by Reitz and Schaeffer, and the translation of Livy
    by Durat de la Malle for that by Guerin. L. C.
64. Harvard College Records, 1815; Josiah Quincy, History of Harvard Uni-
    versity, II, 323.
65. Letter to President Kirkland, November 1, 1816. Harvard Library.
66. January 4, 1817.
67. February 8.
68. The appointment was dated as of June 1, 1816, and the vote of the Corpora-
    tion, June 30, 1817, was approved by the Overseers on July 17. Cf. Harv.
    Coll. Recs., 1816–17.
69. Journal, September 14, 1816.
70. Journal, September 17, October 16–17.
71. Journal, October 20.
72. On November 30, 1816, Ticknor wrote to Setphen Higginson: "The jour-
    ney we have lately taken was for the express purpose of seeing all the uni-
    versities or schools of any considerable name in the country. This in a
    couple of months we easily accomplished, and of course saw professors,
    directors, and schoolmasters — men of great learning and men of little
    learning, and men of no learning at all — in shoals." Ticknor mss., Boston
    Pub. Lib.

73. Cf. L. L. Mackall, "Briefwechsel zwischen Goethe und Amerikanern," *Goethe-Jahrbuch*, xxv, 4.
74. Cf. H. S. White, "Goethe in Amerika," *Goethe-Jahrbuch*, v, 219–256, and L. L. Mackall, *ibid.*, xxv, 3–37.
75. Journal, October 25, 1816. Published, with slight omissions, in *Life*, I, 113–114, and by L. L. Mackall in Biedermann, *Goethes Gespräche*, II, 370–372. Everett, whose account of this interview with Goethe will be given later, states that "the day after our call on G., George sent him Byron's Siege of Corinth, which had not been mentioned in the interview, of which he did not even acknowledge the receipt." Everett mss., Mass. Hist. Soc.
76. Journal, October 28. Cf. *Life*, I, 115–116, and Biedermann, *Goethes Gespräche*, v, 108–109. On meeting Riemer first, October 26, Ticknor's journal records: "He was formerly very intimate with Goethe and even lived in his house, but Goethe, like many other men of genius, is one with whom very few can be intimate long, and he has within the last two years lost this friend as he had before many others."
77. The journal for Oct. 30 reads: "On the whole, the Weimar theatre has disappointed me."
78. Cf. *Edinburgh Review*, xxvi, 304–37.
79. Journal, October 26–31.
80. Journal, November 1.
81. "I need not mention to you how my time was occupied after G. and E. returned; until the 11th, when we entered our regular lodgings and began the studies of the Semester, they were continually with me," writes Cogswell to his friend, Charles S. Daveis. Cf. *Life of Joseph Greene Cogswell*, by Anna Eliot Ticknor, Cambridge, 1874, pp. 50–51.
82. In addition to his regular studies, Ticknor contributed to the *North American Review* (iv, 166–175) in January, 1817, an article on Michael Stiefel (1496–1567), the reformer, prophet, and mathematician, who, educated in the Catholic Church, became a Protestant and espoused the cause of the Reformation.
83. Journal, March 22, 1817.
84. Journal, March 26–27. Ticknor adds a note: "I translated the whole of Werther as an exercise in learning German before I left home."
85. Journal, March 29. Among the public officials whom Ticknor mentions meeting in Frankfort was Von Berg, president of the Diet, who showed his knowledge of American history by jocosely telling his wife to give Ticknor "a very poor cup of tea," if any at all, for he came from Boston, which had once rebelliously wasted and destroyed several cargoes of it.
86. Journal, March 31.
87. Journal, April 2.
88. Journal, April 14.
89. Journal, April 26, May 16.
90. Journal, May 18. It is impossible here, as elsewhere, to mention all the persons whom Ticknor met in the course of his wanderings. Among others, however, whom he knew in Paris he refers especially to Oehlenschläger, Madame de Staël, Benjamin Constant, Villemain, Chateaubriand, Madame Récamier, Talleyrand, and Lafayette, whom he visited three days at La Grange.
91. August 14. L. C. In his reply on November 25 Jefferson said: "I had before heard of the military ingredients which Bonaparte had infused into all the

schools of Europe, but have never so well understood them as from your letter."

92. Journal, October 20; cf. also *Life*, I, 165.

93. June 6, 1817. L. C. This letter is published in the Federal edition of Jefferson's *Works*, by Paul Leicester Ford (xii, 58–60). Writing to John Adams on September 8 of plans for his educational institution, Jefferson stated: "We shall be ready for a professor of languages in April next; for two others the following year, and a 4th a year after. How happy should we be if we could have a Ticknor for our first."

94. November 25. L. C. Cf. *Life*, I, 300–302, also Federal edition of Jefferson's *Works*, xii, 76–79.

95. An interesting observation during his visit at Nîmes is found in Ticknor's journal for April 26: "I cannot, however, look at the Maison Carrée without being filled with indignation, that the Virginians, professing to take this graceful, light Greek Temple for their model, should have yet made such a clumsy, disproportioned, absurd thing as their Capitol at Richmond. It is a grosser and more cruel caricature of what it professes to imitate than our State House is of St. Peters, because the likeness is more preserved."

96. February 14, 1818. L. C. On February 28 Elisha Ticknor replied, expressing his gratitude to Jefferson for his generosity, which in his opinion had contributed more than any other factor to the success of his son's education in Europe: "Whatever improvements he may make beyond the narrow limits of his father's influence and circumstances, please to set down to your own credit. For without your provident care and kind remembrance, which you have so often shown in his absence, he would never have enjoyed the opportunities which have fallen to him, unless directed as they have been by your experience, wisdom, and forethought."

97. February 14. Published in Library edition of Jefferson's *Works*, xix, 257. For the peculiar history of this letter, which apparently never reached Ticknor, cf. *Life*, I, 302.

98. November 25, 1817. L. C.

99. For an interesting account of Ticknor's residence in Spain supplementing that included in his published letters and journals, cf. George T. Northup, "George Ticknor's Travels in Spain," *University of Toronto Studies in Philology*, Series No. 2, 1913.

100. August 10, 1818. L. C.

101. October 25. L. C. Cf. *Life*, I, 302–303.

102. February 13, 1819. Mass. Hist. Soc.

103. May 27. L. C. Ticknor states that he knows little of Blaettermann personally, having seen him but three times, but that he accepts the recommendations of those in England who know him well and vouch for his training. Later Blaettermann received the appointment and served as professor at the University of Virginia from 1825 to 1840. I am indebted to the Henry E. Huntington Library and Art Gallery for a copy of the manuscript letter, London, June 26, 1824, to Jefferson from Blaettermann in which the latter accepts the appointment.

104. Journal, January 18–31, 1819.

105. Journal, March 16, 1819. Writing to Southey on April 4, Scott calls Ticknor "a wonderful fellow for romantic lore and antiquarian research, considering his country."

106. Journal, March 18.

107. Journal, March 21.

108. Journal, April (n. d.).
109. Cf. Charles H. Handschin, "The Teaching of Modern Languages in the United States," *United States Bureau of Education*, Bulletin No. 3, Washington, 1913.
110. Letter from President Kirkland, September 16, 1819.
111. Letter to President Kirkland, September 21, 1819.
112. Complete records of Ticknor's relation to Harvard, including the manuscript of his lectures, are contained in the Harvard Library.
113. With the appointment in 1735 of a Frenchman by the name of Langloisserie, who was soon discharged because of his religious views, instruction in French was provided at Harvard from time to time. In 1780 Simon Poulin was appointed instructor, and in 1782 Albert Gallatin. In October, 1816, Francis Sales became instructor in French and Spanish, which position he held until his death in 1854. Pietro Bachi was made instructor in Italian in 1826, and in 1829 Francis Maria Joseph Surault received an appointment in French. Cf. *Harv. Coll. Recs.* and Josiah Quincy, *History of Harvard University.*
114. *Harvard Reminiscences*, Boston, 1888, p. 82. Cf. also Emerson's *Journal*, October 6, 1820.
115. On December 30, 1825, Ticknor wrote to George Bancroft, then connected with the Round Hill School at Northampton, Mass., of plans for his department, which was not fully organized, and of the difficulty in securing books for German instruction. "I propose to discourse on German literary history at large. Now, on the whole of this plan, I wish to have your opinion, particularly to any part of it. I propose by it simply to teach a few young men every year to *read* German and to know what German books they may afterwards read by themselves or with their brothers to the best advantage and purpose. If it will effect this, it will effect all that a college life may propose." Bancroft mss., Mass. Hist. Soc.
116. Cf. E. L. Follen, *Life of Charles Follen*, Boston, 1844, and George W. Spindler, *The Life of Karl Follen, A Study in German-American Cultural Relations*, Chicago, 1917.
117. On October 14, 1816, the Harvard Corporation voted to give one Meno Poehls, a native of Hamburg, "permission to give private lessons in German to such students, graduates, and undergraduates, as may choose to attend him." *Harv. Coll. Recs.* The Harvard catalogue for 1820 lists one Frederick S. Gustorf as "Private Teacher of German." James Russell Lowell, referring in his address before the Modern Language Association in 1890 to the early struggle of German in this country, states: "By hook or crook some enthusiasts managed to learn German, but there was no official teacher before Dr. Follen about sixty years ago." *PMLA*, v, 5.
118. *Harvard Reminiscences*, pp. 117 f. For the facilities at Harvard during this period for the study of German, cf. Spindler, *Life of Follen*, p. 105 f. Follen prepared and published a German Grammar and a German Reader for use in his classes. Writing of his Reader to a friend, on February 20, 1826, Follen says: "The first two sheets of my Reader, with a Preface, are already printed; and my pupils, thirty in number, translate valiantly. I have taken the extracts, with the aid of Professor Ticknor and his library, from the principal authors since Lessing." *Life of Follen*, p. 105. The records of the department on file at Harvard show that each year Follen assigned for reading Schiller's *Maria Stuart* and *Thirty Years' War*, and Goethe's *Egmont* and *Tasso*, and for translation into German, from time

to time, "one of Miss Edgeworth's Tales, if the teacher finds it expedient," or portions of the *Spectator*.

119. *Life*, I, 352.

120. Cf. *Life of Follen*, p. 200 f.

121. For the official history of Follen's professorship cf. *Harv. Coll. Recs.*, September 22, 1830 and March 25, 1835. On Follen's resignation, Ticknor recommended G. H. Bode of Göttingen, a former teacher of Greek at the Round Hill School, as instructor in German. But Bode declined the offer, and on Ticknor's recommendation Hermann Bokum was appointed on April 10, 1835.

122. December 24, 1819. L. C. On October 26, 1818, Jefferson had written to Nathaniel Bowditch of Salem, Mass., offering him the position mentioned in this letter.

123. February 10, 1820. L. C.

124. September 1. L. C. On September 28 Jefferson replied, offering to enlist the support of his Board of Visitors and of several Southern institutions in an effort "to remove this barbarism."

125. December 8. Mass. Hist. Soc.

126. June 16. L. C.

127. As early as August 15, 1820, Jefferson wrote to John Adams: "Our University, 4 miles distant, gives me frequent exercise, and, the oftener as I direct its architecture, Its plan is unique, and it is becoming an object of curiosity for the traveller."

128. July 16. L. C. Published in Library edition of Jefferson's *Works*, xv, 454–457.

129. December 25. L. C.

130. March 27, 1824. L. C.

131. August 15. L. C.

132. August 15. L. C.

133. November 8. L. C.

134. December 16. Cf. *Life*, I, 348, and George Ticknor Curtis, *Life of Daniel Webster*, New York, 1870, I, 222–226.

135. In an interesting letter of July 21, 1825, to Edward Everett, Jefferson defends his procedure.

136. January 22, 1825. L. C.

137. George Long, ancient languages, Thomas Hewett Key, mathematics, Charles Bonnycastle, natural philosophy, Robley Dunglinson, medicine, and George Blaettermann, modern languages. For the history of these appointments, as well as for that of three professors of American training who were members of the first faculty, cf. Philip A. Bruce, *History of the University of Virginia, 1819–1919*, New York, 1920, I, 357 f.

138. On January 14, 1825, Jefferson wrote to the Boston publishers, Cummings and Hilliard, concerning textbooks: "We had hoped to have opened our University on the 1st of Feb., but as yet only two of our Professors are in place, those of ancient and modern languages. Three, who were engaged abroad, have for some time been hourly expected, and, on their arrival, those engaged at home will repair to their stations also and the institution be opened. The exact day depends therefore on the arrival of the three." Boston Pub. Lib.

139. xx, 147–180.

140. March 28, 1825. L. C.

141. April 7. L. C.

142. In the same letter Ticknor asks for information concerning the adoption of the motto of our national arms, which he had hitherto supposed to have been "made up for the occasion and intended only to express the union of our states," but which he has observed in the seventeenth chapter of the First Book of Cicero's *De Officiis*. He wishes to know who is responsible for the quotation.

143. Cf. George Ticknor, *Remarks on Changes Lately Proposed or Adopted in Harvard University*, Boston, Cummings, Hilliard and Co., 1825.

144. May 6. *Harv. Coll. Recs.*, 1834–1835.

145. May 13. *Ibid.*

146. Cf. H. B. Adams, "The University of Virginia and Harvard College," in *Thomas Jefferson and the University of Virginia*, United States Bureau of Education, Circular of Information No. 1, 1888, pp. 122–134; John S. Patton, *Jefferson, Cabell, and the University of Virginia*, New York and Washington, 1906; Philip A. Bruce, *History of the University of Virginia, 1819–1919*; and Roy J. Honeywell, *The Educational Work of Thomas Jefferson*, Harvard University Press, 1931, chaps. VII–VIII.

147. In addition to Ticknor's journal in nine volumes covering this second journey to Europe, his wife, the former Miss Anna Eliot, whom he had married in 1821, left a journal, an extract from which was published under the title "Polite Travels in the Thirties," in the *Atlantic Monthly*, July, 1927.

148. Among others, he visited Miss Edgeworth in her home near Dublin, and before leaving England spent a few days with Wordsworth and Southey in the Lake region.

149. Journal, November 17, 1835.

150. In his journal for April 22, 1836, Ticknor records: "Retzsch's conversation is as general as his sketches would seem to intimate and his opinions as decided. He holds Luther to be altogether the greatest man that ever lived." Ticknor was rather critical of Retzsch's paintings, which, he says, "produce less effect than his sketches" (Journal, January 28, 1836); but he enjoyed Retzsch as a man, and before leaving Dresden calls him "one of the most genial, original, and interesting persons I have ever known."

151. Cf. E. H. Zeydel, "George Ticknor and Ludwig Tieck," *PMLA*, XLIV, 879–891.

152. Journal, November 29.

153. January 20, February 2, 1836.

154. Journal, March 9.

155. The journal mentions especially the reading of *Henry IV*, *Midsummer Night's Dream*, *As You Like It*, *Taming of the Shrew*, and *Twelfth Night*.

156. Letter to Dr. N. H. Julius of Hamburg, the translator of Ticknor's *History*, January 25, 1846, in which Ticknor made an effort to secure Tieck's Spanish collection. *Life*, II, 250–251.

157. Letter of July 28, 1850. *Life*, II, 260–61.

158. Journal, May 8. The friendship with Prince John resulted in a correspondence which continued many years. Cf. *Briefwechsel König Johannes von Sachsen mit George Ticknor*, herausg. von Johann u. E. Daenell, Leipzig, 1920. On a brief visit again to Dresden in 1856 Ticknor saw King John, then King of Saxony since 1854, who in 1867 sent Ticknor a copy of his translation of Dante's *Divine Comedy*. About the same time Ticknor forwarded to him a copy of Longfellow's version. Cf. letter, September 6, 1867, *Life*, II, 478–481. When John Lothrop Motley visited Dresden in the spring of 1852 he was cordially received by Prince John. "He spoke," says

Motley, "with much affection and respect of Mr. Ticknor, and alluded in terms of highest praise to his History." Cf. *The Correspondence of John Lothrop Motley*, ed. by George William Curtis, New York, 1889, I, 144.

159. December 6, 1835, he mentions seeing *Wilhelm Tell*, which he was glad " to find could be played so well here," and January 7: "I saw Lessing's *Minna von Barnhelm* very well acted tonight. It is a great pleasure to see the principal German tragedies and comedies, which I did not see at all when I was in Germany before, as a theatre was not allowed at Göttingen and I lived regularly nowhere else."

160. Journal, December 13.

161. Journal, January 14, 1836.

162. Journal, April 7.

163. December 25, 1835, Longfellow mss., Craigie House. Writing from Heidelberg, March 25, 1836, to his friend George W. Greene in Florence of Sam Ward's visit in Heidelberg, Longfellow says: "He has been passing the winter in Berlin and Dresden, and was intimate at Ticknor's, whom he represents as living at ease, in good odor at the Saxon Court, and enjoying himself very highly."

164. The journal furnishes long accounts of Prussia, especially of Potsdam and Berlin, including the art collections and the University.

165. Writing on June 29, 1860, to James Russell Lowell of Ticknor, Charles Eliot Norton says: "He has seen as much and so many of the most interesting people of this century, and has so strong a memory, that his talk is often of the most agreeable, gossipy, anecdotal sort. Yesterday afternoon for instance he was giving me his reminiscences for two or three hours of Madame Récamier, of Béranger, of Saint-Beuve, of Varnhagen von Ense, of Humboldt, of Ancillon, and other celebrities. He did not like Varnhagen, thought him superficial, conceited, a hunter after petty distinctions, a hanger-on of noted men, and he said he was not much liked by those who knew him in Berlin." Cf. *Letters of Charles Eliot Norton*, I, 209.

166. Journal, May 26, 1836.

167. Journal, June 19.

168. Journal, August 7.

169. Journal, August 1.

170. August 31.

171. Journal, February 15, 17, 1837.

172. Journal, August 25.

173. Writing from Paris, September 3, 1844, to William H. Prescott, Count Adolphe de Circourt says of Ticknor: "Indeed, no American since Franklin and Livingston has left among the highest intellectual circles of the old world a stronger conviction of the sound and brilliant development of intellect in the new one." *The Correspondence of William H. Prescott*, ed. by Roger Wolcott, Cambridge, Massachusetts, 1925, p. 498.

174. Edwin P. Whipple, *Recollections of Eminent Men*, Boston, 1887, p. 250.

175. It appeared in three volumes in 1849, and was afterward translated into French, Spanish, and German. The German translation by Dr. N. H. Julius of Hamburg appeared at Leipzig in 1852.

176. His biography of Prescott, published years later, in 1864, is less known.

177. Cf. Horace G. Wadlin, *The Public Library of the City of Boston*, Boston, 1911; "Public Libraries in the United States of America," *United States Bureau of Education*, Washington, 1876, Part I, pp. 863–864; Sidney

B. Fay, "George Ticknor and the College Library," *Dartmouth Alumni Magazine*, I, 1908, pp. 80–90.
178. September 24, 1856. *Life*, II, 334.
179. Cf. Tribute to Ticknor by George S. Hillard, Jacob Bigelow, and George B. Emerson, *Proc. Mass. Hist. Soc.*, February, 1871.
180. *American Note-Books*, Boston, 1850, pp. 371–72; *Letters of Charles Eliot Norton*, II, 315–316. For the history of this interesting house, cf. Lindsay Swift, *Literary Landmarks of Boston*, Boston, 1903; M. A. DeWolfe Howe, *Boston, the Place and the People*, Boston, 1903, p. 232; and Robert M. Lawrence, *Old Park Street and its Vicinity*, Boston, 1922, pp. 81–97.

EDWARD EVERETT

1. December 13, 1813. Everett mss., Mass. Hist. Soc. Unless otherwise noted, the references cited in this study are to materials gathered from the Everett manuscripts at the Society.
2. "Edward Everett's College Life," *Old and New*, IV, 18–27.
3. August 12.
4. March 16, 1813.
5. June 24.
6. In 1813–14 Everett received several letters from Stuart concerning the latter's collection of German theological works. On July 9, 1813, he writes of having met recently in New York a German clergyman, the Rev. John H. Dreyer, who was educated at Göttingen, and from whom he had purchased a number of volumes. When Everett was preparing to go south in the autumn of 1814, Stuart, anxious to increase his collection, wrote on September 12 requesting his assistance. "I hope you will leave no spot unexplored," he says. A copy of Kant's philosophy he thinks would be "a great curiosity." On August 29, 1829, Follen wrote to his friend Charles Beck: "I have this morning returned from a journey to Andover. I saw Professor Stuart and the institution. The arrangements, as far as they meet the eye, are good. More German books in the library than anywhere in the country." Cf. E. L. Follen, *Life of Follen*, p. 188.
7. October 28, 1814.
8. *Harv. Coll. Recs.*, April, 1814, and February 20, 1815, and Josiah Quincy's *History of Harvard University*, II, 312–315.
9. Everett and Ticknor had formed a close friendship as early as 1809. For some years afterward Everett was one of a small group that frequented Ticknor's home every Saturday evening for the purpose of reading and writing Latin. Cf. *Life of Ticknor*, I, 12. While Ticknor was in the South in the winter of 1814–15, Everett wrote that he intended to go to Europe with him. He also had read the pamphlet by Charles de Villers, for a letter from Moses Stuart, October 14, 1813, mentions borrowing a copy from him.
10. On November 28, 1815, the Harvard Corporation voted to extend Everett's period of study in Europe and also granted him the sum of $500 with which to purchase books for the college library.
11. Since Everett's journal does not begin until March 14, 1818, when he was leaving Paris, I have been dependent on his manuscripts at the Massachusetts Historical Society, containing letters addressed chiefly to his brother, also miscellaneous notes, including an "Autobiographical Sketch," which he wrote in May, 1833. The "Mount Vernon Papers," a series of

articles which Everett contributed to the *New York Ledger* in 1858–59, contain much information concerning his travels in England, France, Switzerland, and Italy, but nothing relating to Germany. The biography by Paul Revere Frothingham (Boston, 1925) is an excellent treatment of Everett's career, but does not cover in detail his travels and studies, particularly in Germany.

12. Although Ticknor does not refer at any time to a Harz journey, Everett informs his brother Alexander on March 31, 1816, of a pedestrian tour which they propose to take through that region with a young German student. It is more than likely that they made the trip. Everett and Cogswell visited the Harz together for a week, setting out June 28, 1817. Cf. *Life of Cogswell*, pp. 63–64.

13. *Proc. Mass. Hist. Soc.*, VIII, 137–140. For the high esteem in which Everett was held in Göttingen cf. M. A. DeWolfe Howe, *The Life and Letters of George Bancroft*, I, 39, 43, 56.

14. "I sometimes think it not unlike the dispute of the two Irishmen in the stage, whom we heard quarrel which spoke the best Gaelic. The German has excellent points, but is very raw in many respects," writes Everett to his brother, October 2, 1815.

15. "The degree to which they carry it is extreme," he informs his brother on October 22. "Herr Gott, Herr Jesus, O du lieber Gott, are words for every other sentence." He was especially shocked on hearing one of the young professors use "Gott im Himmel."

16. March 1, 1816, to Theodore Lyman.

17. September 15, 1815.

18. October 2.

19. October 2, 1815, he says of Schiller: "He was a high Kantianer, as they call it. We are going to take Kant by the horns."

20. Letter, October 22.

21. June 16, 1816, Everett writes: "Schiller's History of Holland, to judge from the first chapters, is very good; what a gloomy account he gives of the greatness of Antwerp!"

22. March 31, 1816.

23. May 19.

24. July 15.

25. October 22.

26. William Tudor, then editor of the *North American Review*.

27. June 16.

28. July 15.

29. November 16. On February 23, 1817, Everett informs his brother: "I lately got the Edinburgh Review and read the Life of Goethe more leisurely than I did before."

30. IV, 217–262.

31. November 16, 1816.

32. Cf. Mackall, *Goethe-Jahrbuch*, xxv, 5–6. Everett had already begun to purchase books for the Harvard Library. Writing to his brother October 25, 1817, he states: "I have received a letter from the College ordering 20 German Grammars, 20 German Dictionaries, 5 of Schneider's German Greek Lexicon, 20 Schleussner's etc. So that German seems to look up." Later, through Everett and Cogswell, the large library of the German geographer, C. D. Ebeling of Hamburg, was purchased by Israel Thorndike of Boston and presented to the Harvard Library. Cf. Everett's letter from

Paris to his brother, January 13, 1818, *North American Review*, VII, 288, VIII, 208; also the "Book of Donations to the Library 1812–21," Harv. Lib.

33. July 13, 1817. Cogswell mss. N. Y. Pub. Lib.

34. April 27.

35. A review in the September 1 number of Daniel Drake's *Picture of Cincinnati*, which had appeared in 1815. In a speech delivered at Yellow Springs, Ohio, June 29, 1829, Everett refers to his review in the German journal. Cf. *Orations and Speeches*, I, 207.

36. September 17, 1817, *Harv. Grad. Mag.*, VI, 14. In the same letter Everett expresses his gratitude to the Harvard authorities for "the opportunity of resorting to the famous fountain of European wisdom," and emphasizes the importance of improving American colleges and secondary schools. Writing from Rome, December 22, 1818, to Bancroft, then at Göttingen, Everett states: "With respect to a degree, if they are willing to give it to you without examination, as they did me mine, and you have nothing better to do with 60 or 70 Thalers, you can take it." Bancroft mss., Mass. Hist. Soc.

37. "Autobiographical Sketch," May, 1833.

38. For Everett's further experiences in Europe cf. Frothingham, *Edward Everett*, pp. 41–60.

39. Some years later, January, 1823, Everett published in the *North Amer. Rev.* a review of Humboldt's travels in South America. Cf. also *Proc. Mass. Hist. Soc.*, IV, 314–371, and Everett's *Orations and Speeches*, IV, 170–177, for his further tributes to Humboldt.

40. Everett's journal for London mentions calling on Dr. Nohden, "whom I had seen once in Göttingen, and whose German Grammar I have diligently studied," and also William von Humboldt, who "was quite pleased to find I had read his own German translation of the Agamemnon of Aeschylus." Journal, May, 1818.

41. June 6, 1818. *Harv. Grad. Mag.*, IV, 10. Cf. Everett's article on "English Universities," *North Amer. Rev.*, XII, 1–16.

42. The Harvard catalogue lists as tutors during Everett's professorship: Samuel B. Walcott, 1821–22, and George Bancroft, 1822–23. In 1823–24 the position was vacant, but in 1825 George B. Noyes received the appointment.

43. In 1822 he published a translation of Phillip Buttmann's Greek Grammar, and the following year a Greek Reader based upon that by Friedrich Jacob. Cf. reviews by George Bancroft, *North Amer. Rev.*, XVIII, 99–106, 280–284.

44. Journal, September, 1842.

45. Journal, May, 1851. Cf. also Emerson's journal, April 4, 1820, and *Lectures and Biographical Sketches*, X, 312–313. For further tribute to Everett as a teacher and scholar cf. Andrew P. Peabody, *Harv. Reminisc.*, 93, and *Proc. Mass. Hist. Soc.*, VIII, 101–170.

46. March (n. d.), 1821. Bancroft mss., Mass. Hist. Soc.

47. Cf. S. H. Goodnight, *German Literature in American Magazines Prior to 1846*.

48. Among other things, he sent Jefferson a copy of his version of Buttmann's Greek Grammar, which Jefferson acknowledged, discoursing at length on the use of the ablative in the Greek language. February 24, 1823. Jefferson mss., L. C.

49. *North Amer. Rev.*, X, 115–137. Cf. H. B. Adams, *United States Bureau of Education*, Circular of Information, No. 1, p. 131 f., and Jefferson's letter to John Adams, August 15, 1820. Jefferson mss., L. C.

50. October 15, 1824.

51. July 6, 1825. Jefferson mss., L. C.
52. July 21.
53. April 13, 1821.
54. Journal, September, 1842.
55. November 9, 1835, copy from manuscript kindly loaned me by the library of the Univ. of Göttingen. H. S. White, *Goethe-Jahrbuch*, v, 256, states that, with the exception of Edward Everett, Frederic Henry Hedge was the only person in Boston who could converse in German with Prince Karl Bernhard von Sachsen-Weimar during his visit to that city in 1825.
56. Cf. Edward Everett Hale, *Memories of a Hundred Years*, New York, 1902, II, 14–15. Everett addressed the Williams Adelphic Union Society, August 16, 1837, on the subject of "Superior and Popular Education." Reviewed in *North Amer. Rev.*, XLVII, 261–262.
57. Journal, May 1, 1846.
58. Longfellow mss., Craigie House. For a full treatment of Everett as president of Harvard cf. Frothingham, *Edward Everett*, pp. 265–301.
59. Cf. an address by William W. Goodwin on Cornelius C. Felton, before the Cambridge Historical Society, October 22, 1907.

JOSEPH GREEN COGSWELL

1. While I am especially indebted to members of the Cogswell family for their friendly interest in this study and for their kindness in placing at my disposal all available manuscripts, including Cogswell's autobiographical sketch, his brief journal of his first visit to Europe, 1816–20, and various miscellaneous materials, I have been compelled to make free use of the *Life of Joseph Green Cogswell as Sketched in His Letters*, by Anna Eliot Ticknor, Cambridge, Massachusetts, 1874. This work was printed by subscription for private distribution. An interesting sketch of Cogswell is found in Thomas Franklin Waters, "Augustine Heard and his Friends," *Proc. Ipswich Hist. Soc.*, XXI, 53–78. Cf. also James Grant Wilson, "Joseph Green Cogswell," *Appleton's Journal*, VII, 19–20.
2. February 16, 1817. *Life of Cogswell*, p. 51.
3. July 17. Cogswell mss., N. Y. Pub. Lib.
4. March 8. Cogswell mss., N. Y. Pub. Lib.
5. To Professor J. Farrar, March 9. *Life*, pp. 53–54. On March 30 Everett writes to his brother: "Cogswell has engaged to attend a bushel of lectures the next half year, and is completely in his element." Everett mss., Mass. Hist. Soc.
6. Cf. Kuno Francke, "Goethe and Cogswell," *Harvard Monthly*, x, 132–137, and Mackall, *Goethe-Jahrbuch*, XXV, 6–18.
7. Letter to C. S. Daveis, March 16. *Life*, pp. 54–56.
8. Cogswell presented a letter of introduction from Eichhorn of Göttingen to Eichstädt, director of the Museum. Cf. Mackall, *Goethe-Jahrbuch*, XXV, 6–7.
9. Letter to Mrs. C. S. Daveis, April 17. *Life*, p. 57 f. Cf. Biedermann, *Goethes Gespräche*, II, 376–377.
10. Observing in the library of the Duke of Weimar a portrait of Goethe by Jagemann, Cogswell ordered a replica, which he forwarded to his home. "I prize it highly," he said, "not because I like every part of Goethe's character or writing, but he is unquestionably the greatest poet and genius

that Germany has produced, and has one or two features that one would like to study." *Life*, pp. 64-65.

11. *Life*, p. 59.
12. May 23. *Life*, pp. 60-61. Bancroft, in writing from Göttingen, October 10, 1818, to Andrews Norton of the reputation his countrymen had created there, says: "Mr. Cogswell behaved like an absolute mad man. He studied, and became sick, and studied and became almost dead, and yet studied. Mr. Everett behaved more like a Christian." Bancroft mss., Mass. Hist. Soc.
13. September 2. *Life*, p. 64.
14. July 13. Cogswell mss., N. Y. Pub. Lib.
15. On August 3 Cogswell had written to George Bancroft advising him concerning his study in German universities. He calls some of the Göttingen professors, especially Sartorius, "insufferable," but states that he formed a strong local attachment to Göttingen. "I love it without knowing why," he says, "but it has never been home to me, and a bird of passage like myself never forgets where he has once built his nest." Bancroft mss., Mass. Hist. Soc.
16. November 15. *Life*, p. 73.
17. December 23. *Life*, p. 77. Yet, a few days before this, December 12, Cogswell stated: "I was contented at Göttingen, but all the society I had there afforded me no food for my affections, it was my mind only that feasted." *Life*, p. 76.
18. September 1. *Life*, p. 88. Cf. Everett's account of the Fellenberg school in No. 46 of "The Mount Vernon Papers," *N. Y. Ledger*, 1858-59.
19. May 28.
20. November 21, 1818. *Life*, p. 89.
21. February 19, 1819. *Life*, p. 95. While in Edinburgh Cogswell contributed to *Blackwood's Magazine* for February and March (IV, 546-553, 641-649) an article on "The Means of Education, and the State of Learning in the United States of America." He deplores the utilitarian purpose of education and the lack of educational facilities in America, but resents the European charge of intellectual inferiority in his country. The article was reviewed in the September number that year of the *North Amer. Rev.* by Sidney Willard, who did not know that Cogswell was the author. The article was published by Göschen in Germany during the summer without Cogswell's permission. *Life*, pp. 99-100.
22. Cf. Bancroft's letters to Andrews Norton, May 1, and to President Kirkland, May 19, 1819. Bancroft mss., Mass. Hist. Soc.
23. May 3. *Life*, p. 97.
24. Cogswell mss., N. Y. Pub. Lib.
25. August 28, October 13. *Life*, pp. 107, 113.
26. August 4. *Life*, p. 103.
27. September 25, Bancroft mss., Mass. Hist. Soc. Cf. also Bancroft's letter to President Kirkland, September 18. A printed copy of the original diploma, dated August 23, 1819, has been kindly presented to me by members of the Cogswell family.
28. Letter to Prescott, August 28. *Life*, p. 107.
29. July 10, 1820. Bancroft mss., Mass. Hist. Soc.
30. Mackall has published in the *Goethe-Jahrbuch*, xxv, 8 f., the entire correspondence, with valuable notes appended. In June, 1818, Cogswell sent Goethe a copy of Parker Cleaveland's *Elementary Treatise on Mineralogy and Geology*, which was published at Boston in 1816. The following Novem-

ber he forwarded to him a copy of William Maclure's *Observations on the Geology of the United States of America*, published at Philadelphia in 1817, and a recent issue of the *Journal of the Academy of Natural Sciences of Philadelphia*, containing Maclure's "Observations on the Geology of the West Indies."

31. May 18. *Life*, pp. 97–98. Biedermann, *Goethes Gespräche*, II, 438–439. L. L. Mackall, "Goethe's Letter to Joseph Green Cogswell," *Essays Offered to Herbert Putnam*, New Haven, 1929, p. 321, states that Cogswell presented to Goethe at this time a copy of David B. Warden's *Statistical, Political, and Historical Account of the United States of North America*, 3 vols., Edinburgh, 1819, which Cogswell had reviewed in the *North Amer. Rev.* for July, 1821. Mackall further states that at the end of vol. 1 of Warden's work Cogswell had enclosed a reprint of the second part of his article "On the State of Learning in the United States of America," which had appeared in *Blackwood's Edinburgh Mag.*, March, 1819.

32. May 22. Bancroft mss., Mass. Hist. Soc. Biedermann, *Goethes Gespräche*, V, 116–117. Chancellor Friedrich von Müller, the Weimar court official, who was also one of Goethe's guests the same evening, reports (*Goethes Unterhaltungen mit dem Kanzler Fr. v. Müller*, Stuttgart, 1870, p. 30) meeting "an interesting young American from Boston, of the name of Boxwell," and quotes Goethe as saying: "If I were twenty years younger, I should sail for North America." The name "Boxwell" was, of course, Cogswell, as H. S. White, *Goethe-Jahrbuch*, V, 219, has pointed out.

33. August 28. *Life*, pp. 104–105. Biedermann, *Goethes Gespräche*, II, 443.

34. September 11, *Life*, p. 105. Biedermann, *Goethes Gespräche*, pp. 443–444. When Bancroft visited Goethe on October 12 the poet referred to Cogswell as "ein lieber Mann" and spoke with pleasure of the visits paid him. During another visit of Bancroft on March 12, 1821, Goethe stated that he had often "sent things to Mr. Cogswell" by way of Hamburg. Bancroft's Journal, Mass. Hist. Soc.

35. Bancroft writes, May 9, 1819, from Göttingen to President Kirkland: "Goethe, I hear, talks of sending a copy of his complete works to Harvard, but I suppose the time for his executing his resolution will not come very soon." Bancroft mss., Mass. Hist. Soc.

36. *Life*, p. 106.

37. Cf. *Harv. Coll. Recs.*, IX, 14, and *The Nation*, New York, May 22, 1890. The original letter, though it had been printed, from varying drafts, by Mackall in the *Goethe-Jahrbuch*, XXV, 12–13, was purchased by Mackall in 1924, and in June, 1928, was presented to the Harvard Library. For its interesting history cf. Mackall, "Goethe's Letter to Joseph Green Cogswell," *Essays Offered to Herbert Putnam*, pp. 315–326. "This manuscript," Mackall explains to Mr. Lane, the librarian of Harvard, June 13, 1928, "is apparently the best possible substitute for the most unfortunately lost manuscript of Goethe's letter to Harvard, August 11, 1819, in connection with Goethe's gift of a set of his works to the Harvard Library."

38. Cf. "Book of Donations," Harv. Lib.

39. *Harv. Coll. Recs.*, IX, 15, and *Goethe-Jahrbuch*, XXV, 18.

40. June 12, 1840. Longfellow mss., Craigie House.

41. *Life*, p. 102.

42. October 1. *Life*, p. 108.

43. Cogswell was critical of the Pestalozzi system. "It would exclude memory altogether as a medium of instructing," he notes, "and make use of reason

alone, which is absurd. Reason must be furnished with ideas for the materials of its ratiocinations, and many of these must be laid up in and recalled by memory." Journal, October 28. *Life*, p. 115.

44. *Life of Ticknor*, I, 318.

45. November 21. *Life*, pp. 118–119. As early as February, 1816, before Cogswell had received any training abroad or had had opportunities of observing European educational systems, he wrote to Ticknor, then at Göttingen, that it was time for Harvard "to take a rank above a mere preparatory school," and that scholars and good lecturers were needed; "lecturers, too, who can keep an audience awake." *Life*, pp. 44–45.

46. This was true, according to Cogswell, only of the newly established chair of mineralogy. The combined salaries amounted to $1960 and fees. Cogswell includes chemistry among his honors, but the Harvard catalogue for 1821–23 lists him as "Professor of Mineralogy and Geology, and Librarian." Cf. *Harv. Coll. Recs.*, January 18, 1821.

47. On September 11, 1822, the Harvard Corporation "voted to accept Mr. Cogswell's offer to sell to the College a model of the Observatory at Munich for seventy-five dollars." At the same meeting Bancroft was appointed tutor in Greek. *Harv. Coll. Recs.*, 1822.

48. Cf. Alfred A. Potter and Charles K. Bolton, *The Librarians of Harvard College, 1667–1877*, Cambridge, Massachusetts, 1897, pp. 36–37.

49. His article in *Blackwood's Edinburgh Mag.*, IV, 552, contains a criticism of American libraries.

50. Cf. *Life*, pp. 133–135. On March 4, 1823, the Harvard Corporation voted to approve Cogswell's plan "for a catalogue of the College Library to be printed." Again, on September 8, the Corporation voted thanks to Cogswell for "his extra services in the Library, and that the Corporation understand that he perform such services for completing the publication of the catalogue as the Committee on that subject may desire and need."

51. Bancroft mss., Mass. Hist. Soc.

52. November 20, 1819. Bancroft mss., Mass. Hist. Soc.

53. Many years later, November 21, 1833, Stephen Higginson wrote of Cogswell to a friend: "He could not manage things under control of others, and so left College, and set up Round Hill School." Cf. *Harv. Grad. Mag.*, VI, 18. On a picturesque hill overlooking the Connecticut River, Cogswell and Bancroft found two houses which they at first rented and later, in 1824, purchased for the sum of $12,000, the purchase being made possible by a loan of $8,000 from Harvard authorities. This mortgage was later paid off.

54. *Prospectus of a School to be Established at Round Hill, Northampton, Mass.*, Cambridge, June 20, 1823.

55. N. M. Hentz, who had studied in Paris, was instructor in French. For a thorough treatment of the school cf. John Spencer Bassett, "The Round Hill School," *Proc. Amer. Antiq. Soc.*, XXVII, 18–62. Cf. also *Early Northampton* (published by the Betty Allen Chapter, D. A. R.), Northampton, Mass., 1914, pp. 51–69, 215–229.

56. *Life*, p. 141.

57. *Life*, p. 143.

58. *Life*, p. 145.

59. Susan Hale, *Life and Letters of Thomas Gold Appleton*, New York, 1885, p. 42.

60. *Some Account of the School for the Liberal Education of Boys Established on Round Hill, Northampton*, 1826.

61. The list of instructors in June, 1826, is as follows: Charles Beck, Latin and gymnastics; G. H. Bode, Greek and German; C. C. Felton, mathematics; Donato Gherardi, Latin and Italian; Francis Grund, mathematics; N. M. Hentz, French; William Hutchens, writing; W. D. King, elocution; A. X. San Martin, Spanish; A. G. Villeneuve, French. "In the two German classes there are twelve," it is stated. "The Thirty Years' War of Schiller is used with each." Cf. "Round Hill School, Northampton, June, 1826," N. Y. Pub. Lib.

62. Charles Beck, a native of Heidelberg, was educated at Berlin, Heidelberg, Tübingen, and Basel; he had arrived in this country with Charles Follen in 1824. He taught Latin, as well as gymnastics, at Round Hill, and from 1832 to 1850 was professor of Latin at Harvard.

63. An institution known as "Crony Village," which was provided by the generosity of Cogswell, seems to have been unique. Here the youngsters were given lessons and practice in infant farming, building, and cooking.

64. "Some Souvenirs of Round Hill School," Old and New, VI, 28. Reprinted later in the author's A Sheaf of Papers, Boston, 1875, pp. 9–47.

65. Letters and Recollections of John Murray Forbes, Boston, 1849, I, 44. For further recollections of Round Hill, including tributes to Cogswell, cf. George E. Ellis, "Recollections of Round Hill," Educational Rev., I, 337–344; George E. Shattuck, Jr., "The Century of the Round Hill School," Proc. Mass. Hist. Soc., LVII, 205–209; and Donald G. Mitchell, American Lands and Letters, New York, 1904, pp. 33–46.

66. Cf. The United States Literary Gazette, New York, February 15, 1825.

67. A list compiled in 1831 shows that the school had drawn, at that time, 293 boys from nineteen states, ranging from Maine to Louisiana and as far west as Michigan, and from five foreign countries.

68. Comment on the "President's Report to the Board of Overseers on the State of Harvard University for the year 1825–26." Harv. Coll. Recs., 1827.

69. August 15, 1824. Jefferson mss., L. C.

70. Travels through North America, during the Year 1825 and 1826. By His Highness, Bernhard, Duke of Saxe-Weimar, Philadelphia, 1828, I, 55.

71. March 23. Life, p. 160.

72. March 13, 1830. Life, p. 167. The Round Hill Corporation was chartered February 18, 1829, but it was not organized until January 6, 1830. In November of that year Cogswell leased the property from the stockholders for a period of five years, and continued as superintendent of the school.

73. Outline of the System of Education at the Round Hill School, Boston, 1831.

74. Surveying, statistics, chemistry, natural philosophy, bookkeeping, theology, ethics, botany, mineralogy, and horticulture. Drawing, dancing, music, and other accomplishments were also gradually introduced.

75. The instructors listed are: Charles D. Appleton, George S. Bourne, Stiles French, William Hutchens, Benjamin Pierce, J. M. de Ribero, H. Schroeder, and Solomon Stoddard, Jr.

76. The annual expense has now been reduced from $300 to $275.

77. Life, p. 174. On June 10 he had written Ticknor: "I have made my nine years' labor worse than useless to me, by a loss of at least $20,000 on my investments in real estate." In the summer of 1832, when Cogswell announced that he intended to give up the school as soon as possible, the stockholders of the Corporation released their shares to Cogswell, who, as the sole owner, was encouraged to continue the school another year. The property,

however, remained a burden, and finally, in 1848, he sold it to the Round Hill Cure Retreat Company.

78. November 21, 1833. *Life*, p. 183.
79. January 15, 1834. Longfellow mss., Craigie House.
80. February 14. Longfellow mss., Craigie House.
81. March 3. Longfellow mss., Craigie House.
82. Cf. B. A. Hinsdale, "Notes on the History of Foreign Influence upon Education in the United States," *Report of the Commissioner of Education*, 1 (1897–98), 591 f.
83. August 10, 1834. *Life*, p. 189.
84. March 1, 1835. *Life*, p. 197.
85. Cogswell's services seem to have been in great demand. In 1835 he was offered the presidency of South Carolina College, at Columbia, and later a professorship in the classical languages in the same institution. In January, 1836, he declined an invitation to become president of Jefferson College in Louisiana. "I should have found it hard to connect myself with an institution bearing the name of Jefferson," he wrote afterward. Cf. *Life*, p.204.
86. August 23, 1837. *Life*, p. 210.
87. November 12. On November 6 the younger Samuel Ward wrote to Longfellow: "Mr. Cogswell has always a difficulty in selecting from the numerous opportunities offered daily of directing his true talents and acquirements in channels of advantage to himself and others. I think that he will accede to the universal desire that he should become for a while identified with the periodical literature of the day." Longfellow mss., Craigie House.
88. *N. Y. Rev.*, III, 149–194.
89. VII (1840), 109–136.
90. On June 20 Samuel Ward wrote to Longfellow: "I am delighted that you will write for Cogswell. He has a hard task of it, and it is almost our duty to make some sacrifice in order to help him." Longfellow mss., Craigie House.
91. June 12, 1840. Longfellow mss., Craigie House. On June 18 Cogswell informed Longfellow that, after all, he had found his review too long for the available space and that he had passed it on to Park Benjamin for publication in *The New World*. It appeared in *The New World*, I, 33 f., and later, in abbreviated form, in the *N. Y. Rev.* VII, 522–524.
92. July 20. *Life*, p. 216. On July 30 Longfellow wrote to his friend Samuel Ward: "I fear that this library of Mr. Astor will so occupy Mr. Cogswell as entirely to remove him from journalizing." Longfellow mss., Craigie House.
93. May 27, 1840. *Life*, p. 223 f.
94. *Life*, p. 229.
95. On April 1, 1841, Samuel Ward wrote to Longfellow: "You will be glad to hear that Cogswell has been induced to resign his secretaryship to Irving by Mr. Astor's promise to immediately commence the Great Library to which he will be permanently attached under the most favorable auspices — increase of stipend, etc. This is most pleasant to all of us and, by the improvement of his spirits will infallibly benefit his health — almost as much as the Spanish tour."
96. Cf. H. M. Lydenberg, *History of the New York Public Library*, New York, 1923, pp. 1–56; by the same author, "A Forgotten Trail Blazer," *Essays Offered to Herbert Putnam*, pp. 302–314; and Frederic Saunders, *Historical Sketch of the Astor Library*, New York, 1895.
97. April, 26. 1865. *Life*, p.302 f.

GEORGE BANCROFT

1. *Harv. Coll. Recs.*, June, 1818.
2. Cf. George Bancroft, "An Incident in the Life of John Adams," *Cent. Mag.*, XXXIV, 434–440.
3. August 6. In preparing this essay on Bancroft I have followed entirely the original manuscripts. The *Life and Letters of George Bancroft*, published by M. A. DeWolfe Howe, 2 vols., New York and London, 1908, is of course a valuable study, though it does not contain so full a treatment of Bancroft's European experiences and cultural interests as has been my purpose in this discussion. An interesting sketch of Bancroft is that by William M. Sloane, "George Bancroft, in Society, in Politics, in Letters," *Cent. Mag.*, XI, 473–487. Cf. also Andrew McFarland Davis, "George Bancroft," reprinted from *Proc. Amer. Acad. Arts and Sci.*, vol. XXVI.
4. August 15.
5. Bancroft resided, as had Ticknor and Everett, in the home of Bouterwek, 8 Weenderstrasse, where, as he later, August 18, informed his sister, his rooms were in "a fine wide street, the first in the city, upon the second story, and very clean and commodious."
6. October 3.
7. James Russell Lowell, referring in his address before the Modern Language Association in 1890 to the early struggle of German in this country, adds: "Mr. George Bancroft told me that he learned German of Professor Sidney Willard, who, himself self-taught, had no notion of its pronunciation." Cf. *PMLA*, v, 51. The Harvard Library contains records of books, including a preponderance of German works, which Bancroft borrowed during his senior and graduate years, 1816–18.
8. August 15.
9. On September 5 he writes to Norton: "I have not seen a pedant since I have been in Europe, excepting my present patron, who pretends to teach me correct English, when I wish him to learn me German."
10. Journal, August 30.
11. September 5.
12. October 17. However, Bancroft proceeds to enclose to Norton the following specimens: "*Ach, Gott,* — used chiefly by very young girls, and very old women; *ach, der Herr Gott; ach, allmächtiger Gott; ach, du lieber Gott; Gott im Himmel; Jesus — ach, der Herr Jesus,* or by contraction, *ach, du Herr Je-Gott, Gott, Gott, Gott.* These are some of the forms of speech under which the good kind pious ladies of Göttingen express their feelings. The last, however, I never heard but once and then from a Professor; the rest are on the tongue of every maiden or wife in Göttingen."
13. June 27.
14. August 4.
15. August 13.
16. October 26.
17. December 31.
18. January 9, 1819.
19. Bancroft's friend, Samuel A. Eliot, informed him during the winter that he had been taking private lessons in German, and on June 21, 1819, requesting him to purchase for him German books, including some of the best

plays of Goethe and Schiller, he adds: "As to your learning to waltz, I wish you would teach me on your return."

20. February 22.
21. March 11.
22. April 14.
23. A long letter, April 11, to Norton gives the details of the Kotzebue affair and the attacks of the Russians and Germans on each other.
24. January 17. On December 31 Bancroft had written to Norton of his intention to study Oriental languages and requested him to use his influence as librarian in persuading Harvard to purchase books in this field.
25. May 26.
26. July 6.
27. July 10.
28. August 1.
29. August 23.
30. May 4. Cogswell mss., N. Y. Pub. Lib.
31. September 18.
32. March 28. A curious entry appears in Bancroft's journal for January (n. d.), 1819: "I hear that Goethe married about seven years ago, and I believe a mistress, by whom he had a son. The woman was very disgusting in her manners, and after being married a short time, died of intemperance, i. e., of drinking gin." A similar story was included in Bancroft's letter to Andrews Norton, June 21.
33. Journal, October 12. Biedermann, *Goethes Gespräche*, II, 448–449.
34. November 20.
35. May (n. d.), 1820.
36. Cf. Bancroft's letter in German to Goethe, November 10, 1819, *Goethe-Jahrbuch*, xxv, 19. The particular work, as Mackall points out in "Goethe's Letters to Cogswell," *Essays Offered to Herbert Putnam*, p. 325, was a volume of *Transactions of the Historical and Literary Committee of the American Philosophical Society* (Philadelphia, 1819), containing "An Account of the History, Manners, and Customs, of the Indian Nation, who once Inhabited Pennsylvania and the Neighbouring States," by the Rev. John Heckewelder, a German translation of which appeared at Göttingen in 1821.
37. Journal, October 13.
38. On February 3 Samuel A. Eliot, who had become quite interested in German, wrote to Bancroft requesting him to purchase books for him. He said: "Some German literature, giving the preference always to Schiller's works, as the author who has done most for the language and literature of the country; after him, I should desire some of the best, or rather some of the least offensive, writings of Goethe, as the author whom the Germans seem most to idolize, and of whom I recollect you were particularly fond."
39. January 15, 1820.
40. February 7.
41. March 9.
42. April 2.
43. For Bancroft's amusing description of his Harz journey, as well as his experiences in riding lessons, cf. letters of June 1 and July 6 to Norton in Howe's *Life of Bancroft*, I, 70–75.
44. Patton had arrived in Göttingen in August of the previous year to study Hebrew and Arabic. Cf. Bancroft's letters, August 13 and November 4, 1819, to Kirkland, and July 6, 1820, to Norton.

45. July 6.
46. August 19.
47. September 16.
48. September 17.
49. Journal, December 3.
50. Bancroft had at first thought of going to Halle to study. Writing on February 7 to Norton of plans, he states that he would not go to Halle, "for all the Hebrew Gesenius has in his scull or his library. . . . If Göttingen is a little hell, Halle is a place the devil would blush to show his face in."
51. October 28, 1820.
52. Journal, January 1, 1821.
53. Journal, September 28. Writing to Everett on December 28 Bancroft says: "I took a philosophical course with Hegel. But I thought it lost time to listen to his display of unintelligible words."
54. February 1, 1821.
55. Journal, December 19, 1820. An entry in the journal the following day reads: "*Louise*, a poem by J. H. Voss, is, I find, very uninteresting. There is a pleasant simplicity about it; but it has none of the charm which makes the *Hermann und Dorothea* of Goethe so delightful."
56. Journal, December 19.
57. September 30, October 2.
58. November 5.
59. November 13.
60. November 5.
61. Journal, December 24.
62. November 5.
63. December 28.
64. December 3.
65. March 24.
66. Journal, March 2.
67. Hedge had at first studied in a private school at Göttingen, and later at Ilfeld in the Harz, before being transferred to Schulpforta. Writing from Berlin, December 28, 1820, to Everett, Bancroft states that he is in despair about Hedge, and "as a last hope" has just had him brought to Schulpforta, where he hopes "he will do something," for "thus far he has only proved a perpetual torment to me." From Heidelberg, April 2, Bancroft writes to Everett that Hedge has given more promise at Schulpforta, after being withdrawn from Ilfeld for "impertinence and unbeschreibliche Faulheit."
68. After a visit to the "excellent library" on March 5, Bancroft enters in his journal: "I looked at some books; at Tieck's translation of Don Quixote, which is praised as eminently good. Tieck certainly has a lively imagination, though in his original pieces he is often tedious by the length of his descriptions."
69. Journal, March 7. Biedermann, *Goethes Gespräche*, II, 500–501.
70. Journal, March 12. According to Goethe's diary it was "Herr Beresford aus der Gegend von Boston" who called on him. Cf. *Goethe-Jahrbuch*, xxv, 19. This was of course Bancroft, as Mackall points out, *Essays Offered to Herbert Putnam*, p. 324.
71. July 18, 1821.
72. Cf. Howe, II, 177.
73. Journal, May 7.
74. His journal for August 10 in London states: "This is the most singular place

for puffing and extolling one's own verses on earth, I believe. . . . This eagerness of puffing or telling lies, or telling big stories pervades all classes, politicians, publishers, tailors, merchants, and booksellers."

75. October 13.

76. February 23, 1822.

77. This, it will be recalled, is the same information which Byron had furnished Ticknor in Venice five years previous.

78. May 22.

79. Letter to John B. Hill, January 3, 1823. Bancroft mss., N. Y. Pub. Lib.

80. September 18.

81. Cf. John Spencer Bassett, *The Middle Group of American Historians*, New York, 1917, p. 141.

82. January 7.

83. "It was the only time in my life," he wrote to President Eliot in July, 1871, "that I applied for an office for myself, and this time it was not so much an office as a permission that I desired. My request was declined by our alma mater, so that I had not the opportunity of manifesting my affection for her by personal services."

84. Cf. an address by William W. Goodwin on Cornelius C. Felton, meeting of the Cambridge Historical Society, October 22, 1907.

85. A letter years later, January 8, 1835, to Everett in appreciation of his review in the *North Amer. Rev.* of the first volume of Bancroft's *History of the United States* says: "It was your advice to our excellent Kirkland, which carried me to Germany; it was your letters which made me friends there, taught me how to keep in the ruts, and how to profit by my opportunities. I saw, then, at Göttingen, the impossibility of reconciling the acquisitions of a German university with the notions of Boston; I remember telling you so."

86. December 3.

87. *Life of Cogswell*, p. 135.

88. Stephen Higginson, in a letter to a friend years later, November 21, 1833, passed severe judgment on Bancroft, stating that he returned to Harvard from Europe unfit for anything: "His manners, style of writing, Theology, etc., bad, and as a Tutor only the laughing butt of all College. Such an one was easily marked as unfit for a School." Cf. *Harv. Grad. Mag.*, p. 17.

89. May 26, 1819.

90. July 6.

91. August 1.

92. August 23.

93. October 3.

94. December 3, 1822.

95. April 1, 1823.

96. November 5.

97. "Recollections of Round Hill School," *Educational Review*, I, 341. Cf. also George C. Shattuck, "The Century of the Round Hill School," *Proc. Mass. Hist. Soc.*, 57, p. 207.

98. It is reported that in later years Bancroft did all he could to withdraw this volume from circulation. Cf. Samuel S. Green, *Proc. Amer. Antiq. Soc.* April 29, 1891, p. 7.

99. Cf. *North. Amer. Rev.*, XVIII, 280 f.

100. Reviewed by Everett in *North Amer. Rev.*, XVIII, 390 f. Ticknor sent Jefferson a copy of Bancroft's translation, stating, "I think it among the very

best works on Ancient History and Character." Cf. his letter to Jefferson, December 25, 1823, L. C.

101. In addition to works mentioned in this discussion, the *North Amer. Rev.* contains the following contributions by Bancroft: "Value of Classical Learning," xix, 125; "Classical Learning," xxiii, 142; "Von Dohm's Memoirs," xxvi, 285; "Duke Bernhard of Saxe-Weimar's Travels in America," xxviii, 226; and "Letters of Joseph II of Austria," xxxi, 1.

102. xvii, 268 f.

103. "The Ideals," "Hope," "The Complaint of Ceres," "Fridolin, or the Journey to the Forge," and "The Dignity of Women." The first two and the fourth of these, with three additional, "The Division of the Earth," "Columbus," and "The Words of Faith," are included in Bancroft's *Literary and Historical Miscellanies*, p. 206 f. On December 15, 1824, Mrs. Hemans wrote to Bancroft: "I have heard your translation of Schiller's beautiful 'Ideale' spoken of in high terms, and should highly prize a copy of it, if you would be kind enough to favor me with one."

104. February 9, March 26, and June (n. d.), 1824, Sparks mss., Harv. Lib. On September 13 Bancroft wrote to Sparks: "Am I a lady's man? If my *Goethe Review* does not settle that point, I may as well go hang myself, or put on the weeds of a hermit," and Sparks replied three days later: "You have got some foolish notions in your head about a 'lady's man.' Keep it well in mind, that the true way to be a lady's man is to be a man's man."

105. *North Amer. Rev.*, xix, 303 f. A separate reprint, Boston, 1824.

106. The poems "My Goddess," "Mignon," "The Violet," "The Angler," "Song of the Captive Count," "The Salutation of a Spirit," "Joy," and "The Eagle and the Dove," with two additional, "The Mournful History of the Noble Wife of Asan Aga" and "The Divine," are reprinted in *Literary and Historical Miscellanies*, p. 231 f. "The Salutation of a Spirit" is included in Longfellow's *Poets and Poetry of Europe* (Philadelphia, 1845), p. 294. Mrs. Hemans wrote Bancroft, April 11, 1825, "I never saw the 'Angler' nor the 'Violet' so lightly and buoyantly rendered before, and I have to thank you not only for your translation of, but your observations upon that striking little piece, 'The Salutation of a Spirit,' which have thrown a light over its purpose, and developed a beauty I had not till now been aware of."

107. H. S. White, *Goethe-Jahrbuch*, v, 224–226, gives an analysis of Bancroft's essay on Goethe.

108. Cf. Bassett, *The Middle Group of American Historians*, p. 156.

109. July 10, 1824. Sparks mss., Harv. Lib.

110. November 17. Sparks mss., Harv. Lib.

111. "Weimar in 1825," *Putnam's Mag.*, viii, 259, and *First Years in Europe*, Boston, 1886, p. 165 f.

112. Cf. Mackall, *Goethe-Jahrbuch*, xxv, 20, 36. Mackall states that Varnhagen von Ense presented Goethe with a copy of the essay. The translation of Goethe's letter is given in Howe's *Life of Bancroft*, i, 182.

113. "I send you the article on Herder as you desired. It cannot be far from the desired length. As I have written it purely at your request, take it and do with it as you will. It will please me best in the form, in which it pleases you," wrote Bancroft. The letter was without date, but was received by Sparks November 13, 1824.

114. *North Amer. Rev.*, xx, 138 f.

115. Bancroft appends two of the folksongs from Herder's collection, "To a

Flower" by Rist, and "A Sicilian Song" by Meli. Both are reprinted in *Literary and Historical Miscellanies*, p. 226 f.

116. Cf. Goodnight, *German Literature in American Magazines prior to 1846*.
117. *American Quarterly Review*, II, 171–186, "German Literature," a review of *Die Poesie und Beredsamkeit der Deutschen von Luthers Zeit bis zur Gegenwart*. Dargestellt von Franz Horn, Berlin, 3 Bde., 1824.
118. *American Quarterly Review*, III, 150–173, "German Literature," a review of *C. M. Wieland's Sämmtliche Werke*, Leipzig, 1827, and *Gotthold Ephraim, Lessings Sämmtliche Werke*, Berlin.
119. On April 26, 1828, C. C. Felton wrote to Bancroft: "I have just read the last Quarterly. I am glad you are engaged in setting forth to the American public the merits of German learning and scholarship. Your two articles have interested me very much, and I sincerely hope that the next number will be enriched with a third."
120. *American Quarterly Review*, IV, 157–190, "German Literature," a review of *Gesch. der deutschen Poesie u. Beredsamkeit*, Friedrich Bouterwek, 3 Bde., 1819; *Andenken an deutschen Historiker aus dem letzten 50 Jahren*, A. H. L. Heeren, 1823; and Franz Horns *Umrisse*, etc., 2te. Auflage, 1821.
121. *American Quarterly Review*, VI, 189–216.
122. *American Quarterly Review*, VII, 436–449.
123. *American Quarterly Review*, X, 194–210. On September 9, 1831, Robert Walsh, the editor, wrote to Bancroft: "Your small article on German poetry has been inserted in the Review and found acceptance with the literati."
124. Contributed to Ripley's *Specimens of Foreign Standard Literature*, III.
125. XXVI, 360–378. This review by Bancroft is erroneously assigned by Goodnight, *German Literature in American Magazines*, 83 f., to the Rev. William Ware. Dwight's publication was also reviewed by George S. Hillard, *North Amer. Rev.*, XLVIII, 505–514. Another review appeared in the *N. Y. Rev.*, IV, 393 f., but I have been unable to identify the author.
126. July 23, 1839. Longfellow mss., Craigie House.
127. Cf. Howe, *Life of Bancroft*, I, 185 f., II, p. 1 f.
128. Bancroft's sketch of Bismarck, sixty-five pages in length, is contained in the Division of Manuscripts, N. Y. Pub. Lib.
129. Cf. Lawrence M. Crosbie, *The Phillips Exeter Academy, A History*, pp. 283–284.
130. July 4, 1872.
131. July 26, 1872. I am indebted to the William A. Speck Collection of Goetheana, Yale University, for the privilege of copying this manuscript letter.
132. Besides Bancroft, it enrolled among its members the names of Taylor, Bryant, Parke Godwin, Longfellow, Holmes, Whittier, Calvert, John Jacob Astor, John Pierpont Morgan, Andrew D. White, and many others.
133. Cf. Bassett, *The Middle Group of Historians*, pp. 198–199.

HENRY WADSWORTH LONGFELLOW

1. Letters, December 5, 31, 1824. In quoting from Longfellow's letters and journal I have consistently followed the original manuscripts in Craigie House, rather than Samuel Longfellow's *Life of Henry Wadsworth Longfellow*, published in two volumes, Boston, 1886, and later in three volumes, 1891, which contains some of the materials, though often in abbreviated form. A part of the present essay was included in "Goethe and Longfellow,"

in the *Germanic Review*, April, 1932. Since that time James Taft Hatfield has published his *New Light on Longfellow*, which is an exhaustive study of Longfellow's relations to Germany.

2. January 24, 1825.
3. October 2, 1826.
4. October 19.
5. December 23.
6. December 3.
7. February 28, 1827.
8. August 25.
9. September 10.
10. While at Göttingen Longfellow resided at Rothestrasse 25. After placing memorial tablets on the houses in which he and several of his countrymen had lived, the American students at Göttingen held a celebration on July 4, 1890, to honor Everett, Bancroft, Longfellow, and Motley. The program consisted of several brief addresses and the reading of an interesting letter from Bismarck, intimate friend of Motley and Bancroft. In the course of his remarks Professor Brandl referred to the influences which led to Longfellow's coming to Göttingen, to his studies at the University, and listed the books which Longfellow drew from the library. These were about twenty volumes, dealing chiefly with the literature of France, Spain, and Italy. However, Brandl emphasized Longfellow's enthusiasm for Germany and German literature as being greater than that of Coleridge or Carlyle. Cf. *Fest-Reden bei der Erinnerungs-Feier an Edward Everett, George Bancroft, Henry W. Longfellow und John Motley*, Göttingen, 1890, Harv. Lib.
11. March 10.
12. Cf. *The Life of Longfellow*, I, 166, for a facsimile of Longfellow's pen drawing of Preble and himself, made at Göttingen, 1829.
13. Act. II, sc. 2, ll. 803-807.
14. The William A. Speck Collection of Goetheana, Yale University, contains an interesting sketch, dated Göttingen, April 3, 1829, which Longfellow drew of himself seated at a table, reading a volume of Goethe.
15. June 18.
16. Cf. F. L. Pattee, "Longfellow and German Romance," *Poet-Lore*, XVII, 61.
17. October 15, 1829.
18. Letter to President Quincy, June 18.
19. Letter from President Quincy, December 1, and *Harv. Coll. Recs.*, December 31, 1834.
20. December 14.
21. Journal, May 23, 1835.
22. Journal, May 21.
23. Journal, May 31, June 1.
24. Journal, June 3. Writing a few days later, June 11, of his visit, Longfellow states: "Mrs. Carlyle has a pin with Goethe's head upon it, which that great author sent her himself. She is very proud of it I assure you." Cf. Thomas W. Higginson, *Henry Wadsworth Longfellow*, Boston and New York, 1902, p. 92.
25. September 20.
26. An entry in his journal for Amsterdam, October 17, reads: "I have got to-night a book which keeps me late from my bed. It is a copy of *Reynke de Vos* in the old Low German tongue. How very beautifully the old poem commences. Verily, these old German poets were like the birds themselves.

They sing in sunshine among leaves and flowers." Again, on November 1 he was giving his attention to one of his favorite German authors: "Looked over the Poems of Uhland. His little ballad of 'Der schwarze Ritter' is beautiful. His imagination seems to be steeped in the poetry of the past — the songs of the Minnesingers."

27. Journal, December 7.

28. Journal, December 12, 1835, and letters to his father, January 24, May 7, 1836.

29. After a brief visit, Bryant left on January 25. His family remained in Heidelberg, and returned home with Longfellow the following summer. In writing to Parke Godwin, October 26, 1880, of this association with Bryant, Longfellow states: "I can remember only that I once dined with him, and that we took two long walks together. And this is all. It was only after his departure that I became intimate with his family, who remained behind." Bryant-Godwin mss., N. Y. Pub. Lib.

30. In recalling in later years his association with Longfellow at this time, Ward writes: "We had discussed German poetry and philosophy, Goethe, Schiller, and Heine, and I remember how his eyes sparkled when I narrated my halt at Weimar to see the tombs of the two poets who lie side by side there, and to pay a visit to Mrs. Anna Jameson, who was then the guest at Goethe's residence, of the great poet's daughter-in-law, Frau von Goethe." Cf. Samuel Ward, "Days with Longfellow," *North Amer. Rev.*, vol. cxxxiv, p. 458.

31. Journal, February 18.

32. February 11.

33. January 5 and January 9.

34. The journal for January 4 reads: "'The High Song of the Only One' is a masterpiece of harmony."

35. The stories particularly mentioned are Tieck's "Elves," "Rotkäppchen," "Runenberg," "Peter of Provence," "The Friar of Magelone," Jean Paul's "The Death of an Angel," Chamisso's "Peter Schlemihl" and "Das verlorene Spiegelbild," and Hoffmann's "Serapionsbrüder." The journal for January 19 reads: "I am getting out of patience with Hoffmann. These tales of horror are entirely repugnant to my way of thinking."

36. Salis' "Song of the Silent Land," which he translated on February 6, particularly appealed to him.

37. Journal, February 24, 29, March 2.

38. Journal, March 8.

39. Journal, May 27. On May 28 Longfellow attended in Mannheim a performance of *Nathan der Weise*.

40. Journal, March 24. Cf. also *Hyperion*, Book II, chap. 8.

41. Journal, April 7, June 7.

42. Journal, April 4, 18. Cf. *Hyperion*, Book I, chap. 5.

43. Journal, December 20.

44. Journal, December 29.

45. Journal, December 30.

46. *Hyperion*, Book II, chap. 3.

47. Journal, March 8.

48. There is merely a brief mention of the visit. On June 18, while returning from a sojourn to Ems, he was again in Frankfort, but does not refer to Goethe's house. It will be recalled that he visited Frankfort twice in 1829

without referring to Goethe. Nor does the journal for any period mention a visit to Weimar.

49. Book II, chap. 8.
50. Journal, May 2.
51. May 30.
52. June 8. Cf. *Hyperion*, Book II, chap. 8.
53. Journal, June 4. "Goethe I do not like," Longfellow quotes him as saying. "He desecrates everything he touches. It is as if you should take a beautiful rose, and trample it in the dirt and then say, 'There's your rose — your beautiful rose.'"
54. Journal, June 4.
55. March 29.
56. The journal for Thursday, May 26, comments at length upon the uncleanliness of Heidelberg, and nocturnal conduct on the streets.
57. Journal, May 14.
58. Journal, June 20.
59. Journal, June 25.
60. Journal, June 30. The same day Longfellow mentions seeing in a suburb across the Isar a performance of *Dr. Faustus' Mantle and Wishing-Cap*, "a low farce with some humor."
61. Journal, July 1.
62. August 9.
63. The reference is clearly to Werther's letter of May 10.
64. December 7.
65. February 1, 1837.
66. February 26.
67. *Memoirs of a Hundred Years Ago*, New York, 1903, II, 243–244.
68. Appointed on Ticknor's recommendation by a vote of the Harvard Corporation, April 10, 1835. In 1838 Bokum was replaced by Bernard Rölker, a Westphalian, who had studied at Bonn, and who became one of Longfellow's most intimate friends.
69. Cf. *The Life and Letters of Edward Everett Hale*, Boston, 1917, I, 23.
70. May 12.
71. May 18.
72. May 25.
73. August 23.
74. *Life and Letters of Edward Everett Hale*, I, 26.
75. *Life and Letters*, I, 31.
76. December 10. The friend addressed as "Mein liebes Fräulein" was Mary Appleton.
77. *Life of Longfellow*, I, 281.
78. It appeared in the *Knickerbocker Mag.*, October, 1838.
79. Cf. W. A. Chamberlin, "Longfellow's Attitude toward Goethe," *Modern Philology*, vol. XVI (1918), pp, 1–20.
80. Cf. *Hyperion*, Book II, chap. 8.
81. As indicated in his notes, Longfellow quotes frequently from the reviews in the *Foreign Quart. Rev.*, vols. XVI and XVIII, of Menzel's *History of German Literature* and Eckermann's *Conversations with Goethe*.
82. He quotes the translation by John S. Dwight which he later included in his *Poets and Poetry of Europe*, I, 295.
83. Ll. 3432–3458 are quoted.
84. He quotes from Mrs. Austin's *Characteristics*, I, 100–103.

85. "The young author rose at once into European fame," says Longfellow, "and even long pathetic scenes from the *Sorrows of Werther* came from China, painted on tea-cups. What sentimental tea-parties there must have been in those days!"
86. In a footnote Longfellow refers to Werther's letters of June 21, July 18 and 26, and September 6 as "specimens of sickly sentimentality."
87. XLII, 409–449.
88. He refers to Mrs. Austin's *Characteristics*, II, 266; III, 76, and to *Dich. u. Wahr.*, Books VII and XVI.
89. In his notebook Longfellow writes: "Marlowe's *Faustus* is a very meagre thing. The scenes are taken from the old tale, and wrought up with little art and, if possible, less poetry." Still, he admits there are passages of "rare beauty."
90. Published by Cotta in 1831.
91. For 1838 we note seventeen separate assignments.
92. He refers to Scheible, *Das Kloster*, II and V.
93. Besides Marlowe, he mentions Lessing, Müller, Lenau, and Klingemann. Of the translations, he lists Gower, Hayward, Blackie, Syme, Anster, Birch, Talbot, Anonymous of 1838, and Bernays.
94. Cf. Eckermann, January 27, 1824.
95. Book IV, ll. 130–145, 513–539.
96. Reference to l. 3569.
97. Longfellow refers to the records of the Maine Hist. Soc., I, 272.
98. Many years later, June 2, 1877, we note this entry in his journal: "Reading the Frogs of Aristophanes, I was struck with the thought that it was a good introduction for the Second Part of *Faust*."
99. An entry in the journal for June 3, 1851, reads: "Lecture on the Second Part of *Faust*, with extracts, — the first and the whole of the last act."
100. V, 1–48.
101. March 29, 1850.
102. James K. Hosmer, *The Last Leaf*, New York, 1913, p. 218.
103. *North Amer. Rev.*, L, 145 f. Among many other reviews cf. one by Samuel Ward, *N.Y. Rev.*, V, 438–457. Ward calls *Hyperion* "an event in the annals of scholarship and literary taste."
104. January 2, 1840.
105. Cf. Book II, chap. 8; also a letter to Ward, April 21, 1839.
106. Book I, chap. 6.
107. Book II, chaps. 2, 5, 6, 10.
108. Book II, chap. 8.
109. Letter to Greene, July 23, 1839. In the same letter Longfellow writes: "A Miss Fuller has published a translation of 'flunky' Eckermann's Conversations with Goethe."
110. Cf. *N.Y. Rev.*, VII, 522–524, and *The New World*, I, 33 f. On May 28, 1840, Longfellow wrote to Greene, then in Rome: "Felton's translation of Menzel will be very à propos just now, when everybody talks about German literature and German philosophy, as if they knew something of them."
111. January 15, 1840.
112. The "Catalogue of the Members and Library," which Longfellow presented to the Harvard Library, gives the history of this society. It was founded on June 19, 1835, by a group of ten students of the High School and Theological Seminary of the German Reformed Church. Some months later the High School was moved to Mercersburg, and led to the establish-

ment of Marshall College, which afterward became merged with Franklin College at Lancaster. Cf. Joseph Henry Dubbs, *History of Franklin and Marshall College*, Lancaster, Pennsylvania, 1903. This society, which is still quite active at Franklin and Marshall College, listed among its honorary members, including Longfellow, the names of John Jacob Astor, William Cullen Bryant, James Buchanan, John C. Calhoun, Henry Clay, James Fenimore Cooper, Richard Henry Dana, Alexander H. Everett, Charles Follen, Washington Irving, Andrew Jackson, Francis Scott Key, James Gates Percival, Jared Sparks, Roger B. Taney, Martin Van Buren, Daniel Webster, and Friedrich Wilhelm III of Prussia.

113. Passages translated from Jean Paul were published in the *Boston Notion*, March 13, 1841 (reviewed in *Arcturus*, New York, 1, 316 f.), and in the *Knickerbocker Mag.*, XXII, 87 f. An entry in Longfellow's journal for April 2, 1844, says: "Translated a hymn from Simon Dach, — 'Blessed are the Dead.' Very quaint and pious." Various other German poems which Longfellow translated appeared in magazines — Uhland's "The Luck of Edenhall," *Boston Notion*, March, 1841; Wilhelm Müller's "The Bird and the Ship," *Southern Quart. Rev.*; 1, 502; O. L. B. Wolf's "The Good George Campbell," "Poems from the German of Julius Mosen," and Simon Dach's "Annie of Tharow," *Graham's Mag.*, XXII, 102, 240; XXV, 53.

114. March 5, 1840.

115. XX, 134–137.

116. Journal, June 4.

117. Cf. Marie Applemann, *Longfellow's Beziehungen zu Ferdinand Freiligrath*, Münster, 1916, and James Taft Hatfield, "The Longfellow-Freiligrath Correspondence," *PMLA*, vol. XLVIII.

118. June 20, 1842.

119. The journal for Coblenz for Sunday, July 10, says: "Bought an elegant copy of the Nibelungen Lied while wandering through the streets alone."

120. Letter from Felton to Longfellow, October 1.

121. The journal for Nuremberg, Saturday, September 24, reads: "Glorious old place! and yet not so antique as I anticipated." Longfellow visited the scenes of Hans Sachs and says: "Read to my companion the poetic tale of "Der Geist mit den klappernden Ketten."

122. Higginson, p. 190, states: "It can be said fairly that it is intrinsically one of the most attractive of a very unattractive class."

123. "Annie of Tharaw" and "Blessed are the Dead" by Dach; "The Wave of Life" by Tiedge; "Song of the Silent Land" by Salis; "The Luck of Edenhall," "The Castle by the Sea," and "The Black Knight" by Uhland; "The Bird and the Ship" and "Whither" by Müller; "The Sea hath its Pearls" by Heine; "Statue over the Cathedral Door" and "Legend of the Cross-Bill" by Mosen; and "The Two Locks of Hair" by Pfitzer.

124. Included beside Longfellow's sketch of Goethe's life are the "Dedication of Faust" by Fitz-Greene Halleck; the cathedral scene in *Faust* by Hayward; "May Day Night" by Shelley; "Salutation of a Spirit" by Bancroft; and the following by Dwight: "Loved One Ever Near," "Solace in Tears," "To the Moon," "Vanitas," "Mahomet's Song," "Prometheus," and "Song of the Spirits over the Waters."

125. The New York Public Library contains a manuscript letter from Longfellow to his publishers, Carey and Hart, June 28, 1845, in which he states: "I like the portrait of Schiller very much, and yet I do not think it should have been put in without some other head, as there is no particular reason

for Schiller being chosen as the representative of the whole fraternity of poets."

126. I am indebted to the Henry E. Huntington Library and Art Gallery for the privilege of examining letters exchanged between Longfellow and Taylor. In a letter of April 28, 1870, Longfellow wrote to Taylor: "I have in press a new edition of the Poets and Poetry of Europe, and in a Supplement which is to be appended, I wish very much to insert the Death Scene of Faust from your translation. Is it far enough advanced to enable me to do so, and are you willing?"

127. Cf. *Hyperion*, Book II, chap. 5, and *Life of Longfellow*, I, 399. These later versions, with Longfellow's translation of Platen's "Remorse," were reprinted in "A Handful of Translations," *Atlantic Monthly*, September, 1870, and two years later in *Three Books of Song*.

128. An exceptionally interesting discussion of the relation of these poems to German sources is found in the eighth chapter of Hatfield's book. Cf. also brief treatment by J. P. Worden, *Über Longfellow's Beziehungen zur deutschen Literatur*, Halle, 1900, and by T. M. Campbell, *Longfellow's Wechselbeziehungen zu der deutschen Literatur*, Leipzig, 1907.

129. February 9.

130. Journal, June 8, 12.

131. July 17, 1850.

132. February 26, 1852. "Mr. Keneally," he writes, "must be the author of 'The Awakening of Endymion,' which has so baffled us."

133. Journal, February 7, 1852.

134. Letter from President Walker, September 11, 1854. *Harv. Coll. Recs.*, vol. xx.

135. February 19, 1855.

136. February 15, 1859.

137. January 3, 14, 1863.

138. February 9, September 29, 1871.

139. February 27, 1872.

140. June 28, 1876.

141. February 26, 1872.

142. January 14, 1856.

143. Letter to Greene, October 24, 1872.

144. This drawing, which is dated January 17, 1871, Longfellow has inserted in his interleaved copy of *Faust*.

145. *Old Cambridge*, pp. 133, 140.

146. Journal, January, n. d., 1871.

JOHN LOTHROP MOTLEY

1. *John Lothrop Motley, A Memoir*, Boston, 1879, p. 7. In gathering materials for this study of Motley I have used original manuscripts available, but many references are to George William Curtis, *The Correspondence of John Lothrop Motley*, 2 vols., New York and London, 1889. This work was supplemented by *John Lothrop Motley and His Family*, containing further letters and records, published by Motley's daughter and Herbert St. John Mildmay, London, 1910. Motley seems to have kept no journal, and unfortunately no biography of him has been written. Interesting sketches of Motley are included in Edwin P. Whipple's *Recollections of Eminent Men*,

Boston, 1887, pp. 155–203, and in John S. Bassett's *The Middle Group of American Historians*, pp. 223–232.

2. Holmes, *Memoir of Motley*, p. 11. After examining in the Harvard Library a copy of the *Collegian*, of which only six numbers were published, I have been unable to identify any Goethe translations by Motley.

3. Cf. Holmes, *Memoir*, p. 15, and H. S. White, *Goethe-Jahrbuch*, v, 231. Holmes quotes as his authority for this statement a letter from Thomas G. Appleton, Motley's early friend and classmate in school and in college. Confirmation of the authenticity is lacking, however. Nowhere in his journal or letters does Cogswell refer to it. In 1842 Motley gave Ottilie a copy of his article on Goethe in the *N. Y. Rev.* for July, 1839. "This is the only article by my father on Goethe of which I have any knowledge," writes E. C. Harcourt to L. L. Mackall, January 6, 1906. Cf. William A. Speck Collection of Goetheana.

4. May 24. *Correspondence*, I, 11.

5. He engaged rooms immediately in the Buchenstrasse, now known as Prinzenstrasse 12.

6. *Corresp.*, I, 14–15.

7. *Morton's Hope*, Book II, chap. 3, p. 148.

8. *Morton's Hope*, Book II, chap. 6, p. 169.

9. July 1. *Corresp.*, I, 19 f. In his journal for Octover 30, 1851, Longfellow reports: "Read at Lecture today Motley's account of Göttingen and its students, to the great edification of my own." Longfellow mss., Craigie House.

10. August 12. *Corresp.*, I, 25.

11. Cf. "Göttinger Studentenleben zu Bismarckszeiten," *Sonntagsblatt der New Yorker Staatszeitung*, January 12, 19; October 5, 12, 19, 26; November 2, 9, 16, 23, 30; December 7, 1902; Erich Ebstein, "John Lothrop Motley und Otto von Bismarck als Göttinger Studenten," *Die Gegenwart*, June 18, 1904, vol. XLV., no. 25, pp. 392–396; J. P. Grund, "Bismarck and Motley," *North Amer. Rev.*, vol. CXLVII, pp. 360–376, 481–496, 569–572; Gustav Wolf, *Bismarcks Lehrjahre*, Leipzig, 1907; and Erich Marcks, *Bismarck. Eine Biographie*, Stuttgart and Berlin, 1909, I, 83–130, for Bismarck's student days in Göttingen and Berlin, and Louis Leo Snyder, "Bismarck und Motley, eine Studentenfreundschaft," *Hochschule und Ausland*, March, 1930, pp. 11–16, and *N. Y. Times Mag.*, July 20, 1830. Cf. also Sidney Whitman, *Personal Reminiscences of Prince Bismarck*, London, 1902, p. 18.

12. Holmes, *Memoir*, p. 18.

13. Book II, chap. 1, p. 125. Further passages in the novel contain Motley's account of Rabenmark's experiences in Auerbachs Keller in Leipzig, his appearances and conduct in Göttingen, including a description of his rooms, his duels, his comment on student life, and his ambitions for the future. Cf. Book II and Louis L. Snyder, "Morton's Hope, or the Memoirs of a Provincial," *Hochschule u. Ausland*, April, 1931, pp. 10–22.

14. August 12. *Corresp.*, I, 24.

15. August 12. *Corresp.*, I, 25.

16. In the house of an elderly gentleman named Logier, Friedrichstrasse 161.

17. Edwin P. Whipple, *Recollections of Eminent Men*, p. 161.

18. Holmes, *Memoir*, p. 18.

19. January 17, 1834. *Corresp.* I, 33.

20. November 4, 1833. *Corresp.*, I, 31.

21. June 2. *Corresp.*, I, 35.

22. *Morton's Hope, or The Memoirs of a Provincial*, 2 vols., New York, Harper and Bros., 1839. It was published in London by Colburn the same year in three volumes. The book is now very rare. The New York Public Library has a copy; the only copy which I have been able to find abroad is in the British Museum.
23. Book II, chap. 5.
24. It is said that Motley in later years regretted the publication.
25. May 30, 1839. Longfellow mss., Craigie House.
26. v, 518.
27. I, 449–452; 478–483.
28. Book II, chap. 1.
29. III, 397–442. Review of *Aus mein Leben. Dichtung u. Wahrheit*, Stuttgart and Tübingen, 1833. *Memoirs of Goethe; written by Himself*, New York, 1824, and Sarah Austin, *Characteristics of Goethe, from the German of Falk, von Müller*, etc., London, 1837.
30. v, 1–48. Review of *Goethes Werke und nachgelassene Werke*. In 55 Bänden. Stutt. u. Tübingen, 1834. The Speck Collection of Goetheana at Yale contains Motley's "Commonplace Book," which has notes used by Motley for this review.
31. Longfellow mss., Craigie House.
32. *Corresp.*, I, 70.
33. February 17, 1842. *Corresp.*, I, 103.
34. LXV, 85–108. In 1845 Motley had published an article entitled "Peter the Great."
35. LXIX, 470–498. This is nominally a review of Talvi's *Geschichte der Colonisation von New England*, Leipzig, 1847. In the same year (1849) Motley published his second effort at novel-writing, *Merry Mount*, the scene of which is laid in Colonial times. It was practically a failure, too, though it received more recognition than had *Morton's Hope*.
36. September 13, 1852. *Corresp.*, I, 140.
37. July 30. *Corresp.*, I, 177.
38. Letter to Dr. J. Franklin Jameson, April 13, 1895, from Alexander W. Thayer, who was connected with the legation at Vienna at the time of Motley's appointment. The same information is contained in a letter from Motley to Holmes, November 14, 1861.
39. August 31. Holmes, *Memoirs*, p. 120.
40. Correspondence, II, 127. In his speech before the Reichstag, February 6, 1888, Bismarck quoted this song, which, he stated, he had learned from his "dear deceased friend, John Motley."
41. May 23, 1864. *Corresp.*, II, 159–160.
42. May 28, 1864. Mildmay, *Motley and his Family*, p. 199.
43. October 10. *Corresp.*, II, 315.
44. July 25. *Corresp.*, II, 340.
45. August 2. *Corresp.*, II, 349.

INDEX

INDEX